MAVERICKS IN THE WORKPLACE

Mavericks in the Workplace

Harnessing the Genius of American Workers

WILLIAM G. LEE

New York   Oxford
Oxford University Press
1998

Oxford University Press

HD
53
.L44
/ 1998

Oxford   New York
Athens   Auckland   Bangkok   Bogotá   Buenos Aires
Calcutta   Cape Town   Chennai   Dar es Salaam
Delhi   Florence   Hong Kong   Istanbul   Karachi
Kuala Lumpur   Madrid   Melbourne   Mexico City
Mumbai   Nairobi   Paris   São Paulo   Singapore
Taipei   Tokyo   Toronto   Warsaw

and associated companies in
Berlin   Ibadan

Published by Oxford University Press, Inc.,
198 Madison Avenue, New York, New York 10016

Oxford is a registered trademark of Oxford University Press, Inc.

Library of Congress Cataloging-in-Publication Data
Lee, William G.
Mavericks in the workplace : harnessing the genius
of American workers / William G. Lee.
p. cm.   Includes bibliographical references and index.
ISBN 0-19-511656-9
1. Creative ability in business–United States.
2. Diversity in the workplace–United States.   I. Title.
HD53.L44   1998   658.3–dc21   98-23710

1 3 5 7 9 8 6 4 2

Printed in the United States of America
on acid-free paper

Contents

Preface vii

Acknowledgments ix

1. Introduction: Recapturing American Ingenuity 3

2. A City on a Hill: How Americans Bond 15

3. Town Halls and Covenants: How Americans
    Organize Naturally 31

4. Revolution, American Style 49

5. Give Me Liberty: Governance That Unleashes
    American Ingenuity 59

6. The Federalist: Building Global Enterprises on
    Individual Initiative 77

7. A Philosophy of the Unexpected: How Americans
    Find Opportunity 96

8. We Hold These Truths to Be Self-Evident: How
    Americans Exploit Opportunity 110

9.   The Entrepreneurial Employee: Unleashing
a Classic American Type   128

10.   Only Americans?   147

11.   The Myth of the Transformational Leader   158

Notes   171

Selected Readings   185

Index   189

Preface

A book about American workers? Written (primarily) for American executives and managers?

What might have seemed like an odd topic just a few years ago has become vitally important now. Companies are finding it increasingly hard to attract quality American workers, and increasingly hard to hold on to them. And a recent, year-long study by McKinsey & Company concludes that this problem will get much worse in the coming years. (Significantly, the McKinsey study is called "The War for Talent.")

Further, American companies have grown too accustomed to looking "out there" for performance improvement–to alliances or acquisitions, for example, or technology and information systems, experts and broad-based management programs, and so forth. Commenting recently on the present surge in mergers and acquisitions, investor Warren Buffett expressed a strong desire to see companies grow organically. He observed that the success of outstanding companies such as Wal-Mart, Microsoft, and Intel has been overwhelmingly from internal growth–developing the resources and people they have.

There's an even more basic reason for focusing on American employees. It is tragic whenever an organization overlooks so powerful, and proven, a wealth creating force. American ingenuity–the resourcefulness and inventiveness of everyday, ordinary people–settled a vast wilderness, built a great nation, and developed the richest economy in history in a remarkably short time. Yet today we see American companies focusing instead on high strategy, visionary leadership, experts and sophisticated theories, all of which, as we'll see, are out of touch with the cultural and political forces that have shaped American society, and thus shape American workers.

What does it take to attract and hold on to the best American workers, and tap their potential to improve corporate performance? These are not easy tasks. The solution requires more than Human Resources programs, signing bonuses, better perks, or even rich compensation schemes. Executives and managers must be given genuine insight into what makes Americans tick–our social, cultural and political makeup–a subject almost entirely ignored by management writers.

If you manage, lead, or otherwise are responsible for American workers, *Mavericks in the Workplace* provides you with the knowledge you'd need if you took over a workforce of Germans, Brazilians, or Malaysians. Before leading them in an important project or installing a promising new management technique, you'd want to become very clear on: How do these people *naturally* form into groups and bond with each other? To what kind of leadership do they best respond? How do they normally make things happen and get things done *before* being inundated with management theories and buzzwords? These are the questions we'll answer here–about *American* workers.

Most important, and most difficult to answer when it comes to Americans in particular, is this question: What unleashes the tremendous economic potential of so resourceful, yet so diverse and often so contentious a group as a workforce of Americans–the most talented of whom are often the most iconoclastic? With all our differences and diversity, what do we have in *common*?

I've sought answers that go well beyond contemporary surveys and polls of Americans workers. I've drawn on intensive research performed by social historians since World War II into our social, cultural, and political makeup as they have pieced together this puzzle: How have ordinary Americans naturally associated throughout our history to meet the challenges and exploit the opportunities presented by a shifting, rapidly changing environment? Continuing themes and patterns have emerged again and again throughout history as Americans formed communities, organized associations, and created wealth to an extraordinary extent. This knowledge, suitably boiled down and clarified, is now available here to anyone who manages and leads American workers today.

Acknowledgments

I have many people to thank for their help with this book—particularly those who read through previous manuscripts and provided insightful feedback: John Trani and Mark Onetto at GE Medical Systems, Dan Young at GTE, Bob Frey at Cin-Made, Paul Doyle at Donnelly, Jerry White at SMU's Caruth Institute, Zenas Block, and sharp-eyed Bethell Anne Osborne. Special thanks to Whitworth "Skip" Ferguson, formerly of *The Economist Intelligence Unit* and now at Princeton Theological Seminary, whose editorial skills were almost as helpful as his considerable business knowledge. Thanks also to Herb Kelleher at Southwest Airlines and Gordon Forward at Chaparral Steel for very stimulating discussions on these ideas. Very special thanks go to that amazing brother-sister team, Dr. Susan Fischer and Mr. Greg.

Particular thanks to my friend, historian Tom Fleming, who has read through several drafts of this manuscript, always with perceptive and encouraging feedback. Also many thanks to Professor Edward Countryman, with whom I spent many enjoyable and fascinating hours discussing the development of American society as I wrote this book. Much appreciation also to Stanley Elkins for his review of this manuscript.

My gratitude as well to the editorial staff at Oxford, and in particular to Herb Addison, who was a pleasure to work with and whose input during the drafting of the book was just right, and to Kim Torre-Tasso for making the book as good as it could be.

MAVERICKS IN THE WORKPLACE

1

Introduction

Recapturing American Ingenuity

Look, there's this thing called "American ingenuity." We know it exists—
hell, it built the country. It tamed a wilderness, settled a huge frontier,
developed the richest economy in the world—you could go on and on—
it took us literally to the moon! Yet too much of what we do seems to
stifle and suppress this very trait in our own people, as well as turn off
new people we'd like to hire.

When you get right down to it, when you get past the management
theories and latest buzzwords, we've got to find and tap this trait in
our own employees. The sooner the better!

A growing number of executives and managers are saying just that,
in one way or another, to their employees, their bosses, their customers—and to people like me. Forget for the moment grand strategy, the future of technology, the changing shape of markets, and all
the other things visionary leaders are supposed to think about. This
book focuses on creating organizations that appeal in a fundamental
way to American workers, and that can tap their considerable
wealth-creating potential.[1]

Let me emphasize, this book is not about a generic workforce. It
focuses on *American* workers in particular, with all their strengths as

well as their considerable difficulties. Neither does it dwell on the myriad and confusing differences encountered in a diverse workforce, or address how to handle these. Instead we'll get answers to a question much too infrequently asked in the Age of Diversity:

> *How can you find common ground on which to attract, organize, and get the most from so resourceful, yet so individualistic, so diverse, and often so contentious a people as a workforce of Americans?*

In one sense the answer is simple. We know what such workplaces look like, whether they're characterized as "high performance," or "high commitment," or "participatory." Increasingly, they look like American society itself.

They become less hierarchical and more egalitarian. Front line people acquire greater power and responsibility, as well as greater job mobility within the organization. Leaders actually respect their opinions, and place less emphasis on bossing them and more on informing them so they can decide for themselves. Rewards are based less on pleasing superiors and more on meeting the actual demands of the market place. Such organizations become increasingly dynamic. Teams and other cooperative groups don't wait for top-down directives—they form voluntarily in order to meet needs and exploit opportunities. Top-down-imposed management programs driven by outside consultants using sophisticated theories increasingly give way to reaping the knowledge and creativity of individuals within the organization.

Study after study, in industry after industry, shows that such practices dramatically improve business performance across a variety of indicators, including productivity, quality, and profitability.[2] But apart from such studies is the most basic common sense: Why expect an organization based on hierarchy, adherence to broad-based management programs, and the primacy of the organization to attract the best people from a society based on equality and freedom, entrepreneurism, and the dignity and worth of the individual? More than four out of five Americans who don't work in organizations with participative practices wish they did; an even greater number of those who do are happy they do so.

Yet despite the studies and the simple sense that such organizations make, they remain the overwhelming exception in American business. Fewer than 10 percent of American workers work in true, systemically participative organizations.

This only means, of course, that such practices not only provide a way to improve business performance dramatically–they can also provide a substantial, and evidently sustainable, competitive advantage. But to achieve it, management must overcome considerable barriers to embracing such practices, barriers that are too infrequently acknowledged. Let's start by taking a moment to look at those roadblocks, and then get down to the business of seeing how to overcome them.

MAVERICKS IN THE WORKPLACE

To gain some perspective, imagine for the moment a foreign national executive who's taking over an American workforce for the first time. Let's say he wants one thing above all: to get the best possible contributions to company performance from his people. Although he's well versed in current management thinking and aware of the conventional wisdom surrounding American management practices in particular, he brings an entirely open mind to the task.

Before installing systems, procedures, and programs, such an "outsider" would likely want first to learn something about America's social, political, and cultural history–just as he'd want to know something about Denmark's or Singapore's if he were taking over firms in those countries. What makes Americans–whom he would find are quite distinctive–uniquely themselves, and not German, Japanese, or British?

He'd want to know how the people who make up his workforce naturally bond, and how they instinctively organize. What do they aspire to? What kind of leadership will they accept best and respond to most easily? What sort of governance fits them most agreeably? How do they ordinarily make things happen and get things done– and in particular, how do they uncover opportunity and exploit it– that is, how *did* they do these things before they were inundated by management fads and buzzwords?

Without a good understanding of such issues, the most creative strategy and cutting-edge management systems in the world will be useless.

In Search of American Ingenuity

Even the most cursory study of American history and culture would quickly reveal one thing to our foreign national executive: The American reputation for ingenuity is no hype. It's been a natural and powerful wealth-creating force from day one, going back to the Massachusetts Bay Company Puritans, who carved the most prosperous living in the New World out of a savage and infertile wilderness; to the Yankee sea traders and New England factory builders who opened rich global markets and created American manufacturing; to the frontiersmen who opened and the pioneers who settled the American West; to the merchants, traders, and entrepreneurs who spearheaded the Industrial Revolution, ushered in the age of the automobile, the airplane, the transistor, the mainframe computer, the personal computer, and cyberspace—and meanwhile helped conquer totalitarianism.

And this same dynamism is very much alive today in America—witness the software, networking, telecommunications, and medical technology industries, as well as the revitalization of traditional industries like steel and heavy machinery. Our executive would figure that this same resourcefulness exists abundantly in any American workforce—particularly his own—and he'd be quite right. Aside from running their own households and volunteering in their communities on a scale unknown to other societies, they are exceptionally venturesome. One in three American workers dreams of starting his or her own business; of those, almost one in five—some 10 million Americans—are in fact in the process of doing so.[3]

Yet companies are tapping perhaps 10 percent of such talents and energy, which only encourages Americans to be more creative *outside* of work. Our foreign national executive would make it his top priority to harness and cultivate that other 90 percent and put it to work *within* his organization.

That said, he'd realize there's more to the story. For all their enterprising virtues, Americans are notoriously hard to organize. They're individualistic, skeptical of authority, touchy about their rights, often self-seeking, and prone to bicker rather than cooperate. And the most creative and entrepreneurial among them are often the most iconoclastic—the mavericks—who can be the most difficult ones of all to organize and lead. Surprisingly, these traits are not addressed very well by American companies. Indeed, our foreign executive would be shocked: Despite the sophistication and technical achievements of modern American management, it is often remarkably out of touch with the most basic traits and sensibilities of American workers.

Where American Management Goes Wrong

A widely accepted and deeply held management ideology in America holds that organizations which face great challenges require strong, take-charge leaders. These are executives who can make sense of the chaos with their exceptional vision and foresight, who have access to sophisticated analytical tools and theories to make their vision a reality, who have the charisma to attract followers and "transform" them from self-interested individuals into a cohesive unit, and the courage and persistence to lead the enterprise to greatness. At its most benevolent, this is the "transformational leader"; at its least, the "SOB executive."

That such a concept of leadership would ever work in a society like America's, whose most dynamic members are often creative iconoclasts and independent-minded individualists, would strike our foreign executive as doubtful. And a growing body of evidence strongly suggesting such leadership doesn't work in actuality would confirm his suspicion. It is *not* what unleashed wealth creation in American society. It's not even what created our greatest business organizations, contrary to much conventional wisdom on the subject (more on this in a moment).

Nevertheless, the take-charge leader is deeply ingrained and institutionalized in American business. American management schools instill it, consulting firms encourage and sell it, management literature trumpets it, and large parts (though not all) of the investment community applaud it. In addition is the simple visceral appeal of such a management ideology. Let's face it, there is something comforting about a hero-leader charging forward in turbulent times to get things done and make things better.

To change such a view—and it will be widely held *within* his organization as well—our foreign executive will have to overcome considerable institutional barriers. But here is his saving grace: In any sizable group of Americans he is quite sure there will be plenty, particularly among the more independent and creative types in his firm, who are ready to reject the take-charge leader view of business. But to get to them and enlist their support in transforming his organization, our foreign executive will need an even more compelling ideology—a set of ideas about how the organization should function together with tangible mechanisms to make it work—that appeal in particular to the people who seem most difficult to organize.

Unfortunately, empowerment and participative management advocates are not providing a very compelling alternative to the take-charge manager. Their ideology—despite its calls for greater employee power and initiative—doesn't really fit Americans much better. Advocates urge managers to treat people with respect, act as unselfish and above-the-fray leaders, and in general, be nice while getting employees to be equally nice by cooperating, emphasizing teamwork, and acting like owners. Such a view would strike our foreign executive as rather naive in a society whose people are robustly competitive, self-reliant, a bit rough around the edges, and just as skeptical of paternalistic authority as they are of any other kind.

Companies that embrace genuine employee participation are unleashing the forces of democracy in their organizations, for good as well as for bad. United Airlines learned this when its employees bought the company and elected their own management group, amidst glowing expectations of greater harmony and cooperation. Within eighteen months the new employee owners were condemning executive bonuses and then got into a nasty public fight with management over their own pay. While democracy does indeed have tremendous wealth-creating potential, it can also spawn factions, release festering resentments, and create social chaos—which shouldn't surprise anyone. Our foreign executive, for example, would learn that this is precisely what happened to the United States when democracy was first unleashed here. Taming such forces required considerable thought and sophisticated political tools—not exhortations to cooperate. Only when such tools were implemented did democracy's tremendous economic potential flourish on a large scale throughout America.

This is the challenge our foreign executive would set for himself: to find and instill a management ideology that will somehow unite American employees who are openly self-interested, stubbornly independent-minded, and frequently combative, and unleash their considerable wealth creating potential. He'll need one that's more powerful than the prevailing strong-manager notion, more sophisticated and realistic than employee participation, and above all, that fits the traits and sensibilities of American workers better than either of these. How would he find such a tool? Where would he look?

THE EXECUTIVE AS SOCIETY BUILDER

He would do well to start by looking more closely at American leadership. Though he found that the strong-manager view of leadership is wrong for Americans, this is not to suggest in the slightest that leadership is unimportant here. To the contrary, great leadership has clearly been vital to building America from the first, starting with early American leaders like Massachusetts Bay's John Winthrop, through the Founding Fathers, and on to the great American industry builders and entrepreneurs of the present day. However, and this is the crucial point, these were most often *not* the kind of leaders described by the transformational leader model.

In America the great enterprises have been built, not by visionary leaders, but by great *organizers*. Rather than conceive and follow some vast, transforming strategic *vision*, successful American leaders create and strengthen dynamic *societies* (and every organization is a small society) that foster the inventiveness of people throughout the community, often leading to results no one could foresee.[4] (We'll return to this idea again throughout the book, and sum it up in Chapter 11. "The Myth of the Transformational Leader.")

David Packard, who helped create one of America's greatest enterprises, was far from a visionary. He had no idea what Hewlett-Packard's main business would be when he and Bill Hewlett started it, and he would later oppose the company's crucial moves into computers and display monitors. Packard's most valuable creation was the Hewlett-Packard organization itself, with its phenomenal ability to reinvent itself again and again—often in ways he initially objected to or even opposed! "The problem is, how do you develop an environment in which individuals can be creative?" as he put it. "I believe that you have to put a good deal of thought to your organizational structure in order to provide this environment."[5]

This insight, which our foreign executive would glean repeatedly from his study of American leaders, would provide him with a major breakthrough. Indeed, the point would be driven home most clearly by the American Founding Fathers themselves: After all, they achieved arguably the greatest leadership challenge ever by organizing Americans into a coherent and lasting nation that successfully unleashed their economic potential. If the experience of the founders has one consistent theme, it would be this: Forget trying to be a great, visionary leader who foresees the future, decides what to do about it, and gets "buy in" from people to follow your vision; *they* never did, as we'll see. Start thinking of yourself instead as a "society builder." Forget for the moment your enterprise's strategy, activities, operational processes and all the things it *does*. Focus instead on its political, social, and cultural aspects—on how it's *organized and governed*. Concentrate on the power that leaders wield, the status people have, the behaviors and moral outlook they adopt, and the values they emphasize.

To the strong manager, such organizational traits must be determined by strategy—by the needs of the organization as perceived by top management. To ensure this, it may resort to directives, even intimidation, or perhaps human resources programs to persuade (or manipulate, depending on your point of view) people throughout the organization to go along. But as sociologist Daniel Bell has pointed out, changes in culture or moral outlook can't be engineered or decreed. To take hold, they must be grounded in "the value and moral traditions of the society, and these cannot be 'designed' by precept."[6] When leaders attempt to do so, they sacrifice authenticity and legitimacy, and their most intelligent followers will be the first to know it.

This insight would provide the key to our foreign executive, as he seeks to unleash his American workforce. In his quest for a more persuasive, and more effective management ideology to instill in his organization, he would draw as accurately as possible from America's own social, cultural, and political heritage. He had started by studying these in order to better understand American management. Now he would realize that this knowledge can give him something much better: a substantial, and sustainable, competitive advantage.

Using such historical knowledge to address hard organizational challenges is nothing new. When FedEx chairman Fred Smith wanted to build a company that treated employees fairly and which employees *believed* was treating them fairly, he turned to seminal documents such as the Constitution, Bill of Rights, and Civil Rights Act, and instilled their precepts into FedEx's organization. These became the primary reason FedEx employees treat its customers so well.

When General Electric chairman Jack Welch wanted to free employees from oppressive middle managers (and after Japanese-style quality circles had failed to do so), he turned to the New England town meeting—"the best school of political liberty the world ever saw," according to Thomas Jefferson—to help them do so. These became the model for GE's now famous Work Out.

Years after Alfred Sloan finished his reorganization of GM's businesses into a massive corporation that was unified and coherent on the one hand, yet acceptable to GM's powerful division heads on the other, he remarked "more than once," recalls Peter Drucker, "how he had gone back again and again to the American Constitution" for this difficult task.[7]

Now the most important challenge facing organizations is to place more power in the hands of front line employees, as companies deal with rapidly changing technologies, unfamiliar and volatile global markets, increasingly demanding customers, and a host of other pressures that can't be solved by headquarters. Companies must find a way to radically change the status of employees from subordinates conforming to the demands of a hierarchy to something like corporate citizens taking initiative and pursuing opportunity.

As it turns out, the best source of insight for achieving this is nothing less than the defining event that created American society itself. Where New England town meetings can free employees from oppressive bosses, and the Bill of Rights can provide grievance procedures employees will embrace as fair–the American Revolution itself can show how to transform a society in a way that will resonate with and energize American workers. Here's why.

What Executives Can Learn from the American Revolution

As an engine of social change, we now know that the American Revolution achieved what empowerment and participative management programs dream of: It transformed a hierarchical society based on control and tradition-bound thinking into a free society based on individual liberty and an unencumbered outlook. It destroyed monarchical rule and established republics–many centers of power–throughout America, replaced subordination with equality and paternalistic dependence with self reliance. It opened institutions of power to widespread participation, conferred a new respectability on ordinary people who'd always occupied the lower rungs of society, and gave a new sense of dignity and worth to all work no matter how menial.

The results speak for themselves. Far from flying apart after the Revolution as Europe's autocrats had predicted, America took off like a rocket, releasing tremendous economic energies that astonished even the men who led it. In just the fifty years or so between 1763 and 1812 (about the age of Wal-Mart), it converted an economic backwater of fewer than 2 million mostly tradition-bound, hierarchy-ridden subjects huddled along the Atlantic coast into a half continent-wide republic of 10 million bustling, initiative-taking individuals who became more liberal-minded, more entrepreneurial, more democratic, and more modern than any people in the world.

And for executives who, like Jack Welch, recognize the ongoing need to "keep pulling the dandelions of bureaucracy" as he puts it, the Founding Fathers built in an even more important trait: the capacity for society to *continue* reinventing itself. In a word, they *institutionalized* revolution and made it ordinary rather than traumatic. Power in America would transfer in an orderly way; it could shift back and forth as needed between local and central organs, it would freely admit new participants and new ideas, its checks and balances would prevent concentration and abuse.

The genius of American society is that it was built on this precept:

America would reach its greatest economic potential not by depending on a great, visionary leader at the top to take charge, but rather by

devising governance mechanisms that would maximize the freedom of
individuals throughout society—and thus unleash initiative and creativ-
ity in ways no leader could ever imagine.

But the importance of this knowledge to executives doesn't stop
here; it provides much more than just another example for transforming an organization. The Revolution provides *the* ideology for
such a transformation. This is the source of our shared understanding, with its deep emotional appeal, of how a society should work.
This ideology can confer a legitimacy on change that textbook organizational theories can never provide no matter how logical or cutting-edge they may be. In the search for what Americans have in
common, for what appeals to them on a deep level and will bring
them together, our foreign executive might well feel he has struck
gold.

Finding Common Ground

Unlike people in other countries, Americans don't share one race, or
ethnicity, or frozen cultural traditions. What we do have in common
is a set of *ideas*, articulated with greatest clarity and force in the years
up to and following the American Revolution about the kind of
society we want to live in: How should it be formed? What status
should it give people? How can it maintain coherence while ensur-
ing individual freedom? To what kind of leadership will its people
respond?

The answers all flow from the one thing Americans have realized
they shared down through the centuries, despite all our differences:
namely, a common desire for *liberty*. And the American concept of
liberty—based on Thomas Jefferson's single, still-radical statement
that "all men are created equal"—is particularly robust. Americans
will form into coherent groups, accept leadership, cooperate, and
even bond with one another, but getting them to do so requires coming to terms with this still-radical concept.

Here is where our foreign executive would find a wealth of information from recent intensive research by a generation of talented
American and European historians. Aided by the computer and
sophisticated analytical tools, they have focused their attention much
less on grand events, high-profile leaders, and transcendent ideas,
and much more on what ordinary people thought and did to build
the nation. And it was ordinary people, hundreds of thousands of
them, including farmers, artisans, shopkeepers, small merchants, and
nascent businessmen, as well as the tough-minded and intelligent

leaders who emerged from their ranks, who were the major players in the transformation of American society and the principal agents of change. They more than any other influence inspired the sophisticated ideas articulated by leaders like Jefferson; and they were the ones who instilled them in the towns and communities of America, with a passion that more aristocratic American leaders never mustered.[8]

Those Americans refined and clarified hard concepts that every truly participative organization must deal with, like it or not, such as accountability, rights, and power. Out of their dialogue and debate emerged the social mechanisms that best deal with these concepts in our society, like citizen, community, and republic—far richer and more dynamic, as well as more compelling emotionally, than empowerment, delayering, and horizontal organizations.

For those wondering what a diverse American workforce can possibly have in common, there is only one answer: the ideas and ideals flowing from the American Revolution. It freed lower-class white men—or more precisely, gave them tools to free themselves—from a centuries-old tradition of economic and political subordination to their "betters," while unleashing their considerable capacity for wealth creation. The governance it established would then go on to liberate other traditionally oppressed groups, including blacks and women, and establish their equality. And it would prove immensely appealing to disenfranchised and oppressed people from around the world, and still very much does. In the hundred years after the Napoleonic wars, for instance, fifty million Europeans left that continent. Of those, fully 70 percent—thirty five million—came to America for the freedom and opportunity it offered.

This isn't to say building such a society is easy and without problems of its own. But the subsequent sustained explosion of economic energy, which would propel the United States in a remarkably short period of time into the richest, most powerful nation in history, justified the founders' still-radical concept. For our foreign executive who's seeking lasting, healthy, and profitable transformation of an American organization, here is what the doctor ordered.

How to Use This Book

Of course, this book is for *American* executives and managers who want their organizations to get much better at attracting employees and putting their talents to use.

It is not intended to stimulate a comprehensive, organization-wide program. Rather I would urge leaders to take its ideas to wherever a substantial, tangible need or opportunity exists—a unit, an office, or a division that needs to increase its productivity, for example, or improve its product innovation, or serve its customers better, or generate more new business. Go to where you're sure that a top-down, consultant-led, broad-based leadership initiative won't work—where the change must be made by the people down in the ranks who must live with the result. Indeed, go to where you suspect the *real*, underlying need isn't just to change "what we do," but rather to change "how this place works"—that is, where the real need is to change how decisions are made, how opportunity is uncovered, how people are rewarded, or perhaps even to give people a better reason for wanting to work there in the first place.

I would urge you then to distribute this book, or whatever parts of it are relevant to the particular need, widely. Send them not just to a few leaders but to people throughout the targeted unit, especially the ones who must live with the result—it is written for them too. Use the ideas it contains to spark a bottom-up dialogue and debate directed toward meeting the challenge. The result will not only improve the present situation but also improve the *organization* by giving employees tools they can use in the future to take initiative and use their own resourcefulness.

I can assure you, the ideas this generates will be surprising and creative—they may also be tedious at times and troubling—but they can ultimately change your organization dramatically for the better. And the new organization that gradually takes shape will strike people as fair, give them a heightened sense of purpose and mission, and fit with how they naturally think about the world. In what other way can an organization expect to unleash American ingenuity?

We'll proceed then, by asking, How do you attract Americans naturally and bond them to a group?

2

A City on a Hill

How Americans Bond

Imagine a company that sends out a hundred people or so to set up a business in an entirely new region. In fact, the region it wants to develop is literally a wilderness. The conditions are so rugged that over half the group fall seriously ill the first year; at one point only seven have the strength to carry on. Yet carry on they do, overcoming sickness, hostile and even violent locals, and a host of tough, unanticipated problems to establish a beachhead. Asked later where they found the strength and resolve to carry on, one of the original members said, "We're not like other people who get discouraged by small things." That's motivation!

That's also a true story (except that over half the original members *died* that first year). They were the American Pilgrims who came to Plymouth Bay in 1620, followed a decade later by the Massachusetts Bay Company Puritans, who added organizing talent to the same spirit and pluck. And Massachusetts Bay is the very prototype of American community. For organizations looking to tap the idealism and passion of an American workforce, and skeptical of New Age techniques for doing so, here is the source to turn to.

THE PROVEN POWER OF AMERICAN COMMUNITY

What accounts for such devotion from a group of Americans—and how can organizations recapture this? Clearly Massachusetts Bay offered people the chance to prosper, but there was much more; there had to be. After all, it attracted tens of thousands of Europeans from largely comfortable, middle-class lives to hazard a dangerous ocean crossing and live in a hostile wilderness. For those seeking riches only, other places such as the Netherlands offered better prospects.

Massachusetts Bay beckoned with the chance to find meaning in the world. Indeed it offered people a way of life as inspiring as any in history: the opportunity to live according to their highest ideals—in their case, the New Testament life—not just on Sunday but every day of the week. *This* became the source of their remarkable cohesion and sacrifice, working its way into everyday life; this was the reason they would turn out en masse to raise the frames for their meeting houses as well as each other's homes and barns.

Furthering their community was more than a mission in self-improvement; central to the strength of their devotion was their belief that they were making the world a better place.

"We shall be as a city on a hill," prophesied their great leader John Winthrop, as they sailed to America, "the eyes of all people are upon us." They would provide a beacon of hope to those they left behind, including Europe's oppressed and suffering millions, by remaining true to their God. They would show that people could actually live the New Testament life while pursuing prosperity. No one has ever expressed Americans' self-image or sense of destiny better; Ronald Reagan would use the same "city on a hill" image more than three and a half centuries later, to revive American morale after a decade of military and diplomatic humiliations, government scandal, oil shortages, and inflation.

This sense of destiny fueled a cutting edge of extraordinary power, carving the most successful economy in the New World out of a harsh wilderness—an experience rich with lessons for organizations today. The Massachusetts Bay settlers cleared away Old World restraints on enterprise—like guilds, permanent monopolies, and wage and price controls—with abandon. They replaced them with innovative practices such as protection of private property, a budding market economy fueled by venture capital, and, above all, reliance on the initiative and entrepreneurism of individuals.

Their remarkable industry was grounded in superb values we now call the Protestant work ethic: from the simple "An hour's idleness is as bad as an hour's drunkenness" and "never waste precious time," to their belief in the dignity of all work no matter how menial, to Cotton Mather's exacting ethics in business dealings. Mather held that strict honesty which nevertheless deceives is not acceptable; members of the community should be "transparent" in all dealings with each other. Those who might dismiss such ideals as naive are wrong: There was nothing naive about a people who subdued a wilderness.

They were particularly vigilant against greed by any of their members, especially leaders, and relied heavily on religious and moral values to restrain it. Their great insight contradicted the conventional wisdom then, and now, that morality and business don't mix. The Puritans believed they did mix—indeed, that moral values would enhance the prosperity of the community—and proved it.[1] It appears that the elaborate set of shared moral and religious values they decided to pursue so vigorously, which to them was getting back to basics of the most fundamental kind, freed them to innovate with great energy and creativity in all other areas of their lives including business. Here is a lesson in social dynamics that we need to relearn.

The subsequent continuing impact of early New England on American society is hard to overestimate; its principles, noted Alexis de Tocqueville while observing from an approximate midpoint in America's history, would "extend their influence beyond its limits, over the whole American world."[2] They would deeply influence both the Founding Fathers who built the nation and the entrepreneurs and industry builders who created its economy. They are the prime source of American values—"the great influential fact in the history of the American mind," as Daniel Bell put it—and therefore are essential for us to understand because, as Bell points out, such values "are not amenable to 'social engineering' or political control."[3]

An Antidote to American Individualism

Contrary to how we sometimes appear, Americans are not *just* self-interested individualists. From day one of our history, we've eagerly sought one another out and formed communities when there were needs to be met and work to be done. These communities arose in America not by fiat from some higher power—there was no way some remote authority could have adapted as brilliantly as the Massachusetts Bay settlers did to such harsh and unanticipated circumstances—but rather were self-selected. Communities came first, from the earliest American settlements and towns to farmers' societies and cooperatives, business associations, overland companies that settled the West, service groups and volunteer organizations, churches, and labor unions, down to Internet chat groups today, *then* government. They have pervaded every aspect of American growth and economic development.

And not just in the lives of white Americans, but of all Americans, including black Americans and native Americans, as historian Edward Countryman has shown. Why? Because each faced the same problem: the need to find ways to associate in a rapidly changing world–whether to advance themselves or to face common dangers, or both.[4]

And what a powerful engine for making things happen and getting things done! The Massachusetts Bay settlers fostered a thriving society in a hostile and infertile wilderness. The descendants of these resourceful builders became the "Yankees," one of the great exemplars of American ingenuity, who transformed themselves from fishermen into maritime traders and merchants, and then transformed themselves again into factory builders. Even on the frontier–the great theater of rugged individualists like Daniel Boone and Zebulon Pike–it was "moving communities" such as the Ohio Associates and the Green and Jersey Company that Americans formed themselves into, to cross vast spaces and settle new regions.

The sheer vitality of this social building block is striking. European visitors to America couldn't believe the speed with which major metropolises such as Philadelphia sprang up in the wilderness in only a few decades, instead of the centuries it would have taken in Europe. The energy, creativity, and cohesiveness such cities and towns displayed didn't come from any central authority, but from self-selected associations within them, from "communities within communities." The most famous example was Benjamin Franklin's "Junto," a group of young nobodies in Philadelphia who had no formal authority when they started out, and no social or political connections. Yet they helped transform that city–creating a volunteer fire department, organizing for military defense, influencing legislation, establishing a public library (the first subscription library in America), and serving important roles in establishing the first hospital for the poor (the Pennsylvania Hospital, which is still thriving) and the Philadelphia Academy (now the University of Pennsylvania).

Most important, these communities provide a model for organizing Americans in a way much more natural than that found in many organizations, with Massachusetts Bay serving as a superb prototype. American communities followed a recurring pattern with distinctive dynamics, different from teams, or patriarchal "families," or military-style hierarchies, that companies can draw on for establishing cultures that fit their employees better.

WHAT MAKES A COMMUNITY?

There are, of course, a lot of opinions about this, many of which are utopian versions of how communities "ought" to work or "had better" work in our troubled times. But our interest here is in how they've worked in *fact;* in which ways has history shown that communities function best and appeal most to Americans in the grit and sunshine of real world experience? There are two essential traits:

First, communities provide an opportunity to find meaning in the world, as we saw with the early New Englanders. We'll see in the rest of this chapter how companies are recapturing this motivator today.

Second, they embrace democratic values. Where Europe was hobbled by tradition and dogmatism, the New Englanders devised cutting-edge social and political innovations—including liberty, individual rights, participative governance, humanitarianism, and universal education. These came from no theory, but were worked out by practical people in the process of subduing a wilderness, which resulted in a remarkably dynamic and innovative society. We'll examine these innovations more closely in the next chapter.

How to Get People to Bond

A few years ago managers at GE Plastics needed to create greater cohesion among employees. A recent acquisition of longtime competitor Borg-Warner Chemicals had made this particularly important. Some way had to be found to bond GE's 9,000 young, aggressive, highly competitive employees, accustomed to a somewhat Darwinian culture, to Borg-Warner's 5,000 older, more collegial employees—who were highly skeptical about working for GE.

GE Plastics had been organizing team-building events for years at its annual retreat in San Diego, with golf tournaments and picnics so people could get to know each other, a ropes course and wilderness adventures to engender trust, and deliberately silly events like tricycle races and water-balloon tosses to lower inhibitions. But the camaraderie didn't last long or extend into everyday working relationships.

Joel Hutt, manager of marketing communications, then tried to create a project that would be more "relevant": an intense day of erecting several houses in a nearby desert using GE materials, so that people would understand their product line better as they bonded with each other. The desert "town" project was successful; teams responded enthusiastically and were proud of what they accomplished at the end of the day.

But when the demolition crews came to tear down their work, Hutt realized that something was still missing. "I remembered thinking it was a shame to waste all that effort." What could really animate these events, he realized, was a sense of genuine meaning. "Instead of playing golf or going fishing or sailing, why not take the tremendous energy and creativity of four or five hundred people and do something constructive, with enduring value—something to help other people?" From that insight, GE Plastics made the leap from short-term bonding exercises to community building.[5]

At the marketing department's next annual meeting, Hutt presented a video of previous years' golf tournaments and other events. When it was over, he made a surprising and bold announcement to the 470 attendees: Those days of nothing but fun and games were over, which was promptly greeted by a chorus of disappointed groans. Then Hutt said, "What if we took this group . . . took all the energy in this room, and did something constructive, something that has enduring value? I'd like to show you a different video." He then ran one of a badly run-down local YMCA, the Copely Family Y.[6]

Once a haven for kids in a low-income neighborhood rife with gangs and drug abuse, the Copely Family Y was now a shell with broken windows, graffiti on the walls, a yard overgrown with weeds, and an interior that looked even worse. Interviewed on the video, the Y's executive director estimated it would take half a million dollars and several years to fix the place up properly, if it could be done at all.

"Well," said Hutt when the lights were turned back on, "I'm here to tell you it's not going to take years. . . . We're going to do it in eight hours, and we're going to do it tomorrow!" Unknown to the marketing employees, Hutt and his team had spent months assessing their skill levels, figuring out the logistics for such a project, and locating technical support. The response from the audience was immediate and electric: People cheered from their seats, and 99 percent of those present volunteered to participate.

They were then divided up into thirty preselected teams, designed in part to mingle nonspecialists with specialists, and in particular to mix former Borg-Warner employees with old GE employees. Hutt asked them to choose team names, mottos, and logos, and then elect project leaders and officers for the various tasks such as logistics, materials procurement, and safety—with only one restriction, that no GE executive or manager could play any leadership role. Their enthusiasm was palpable as the teams plunged into serious, detailed planning for the next day or met with contractors for short, intense training sessions. The next morning, work teams arrived at the Copely Y fully prepared and went straight to their first tasks: pulling up stained carpet, removing battered lockers, knocking out broken windows, and scraping old paint off walls. With top-40 and reggae music blaring from loudspeakers, GE employees painted, laid tile, set windows, built a new retaining wall, fixed basketball backstops, replaced the irrigation system, rebuilt a soccer field, and landscaped the yard.

From Competition to Community Building

The intense competitiveness of the GE employees was evident at the start of the Copely Family Y project; one team had even rented cars to get to the site first. But that gave way over the course of the day to greater cooperation, different from that experienced in earlier team competitions. Now employees wanted all the teams to win. When one team finished its tasks early, its members didn't gloat; instead they pitched in to help another team finish. "People worked incredibly intensely," observed one manager. This was not a party . . . yet spirits and humor were exceptionally high."[7]

After just twelve hours, the Y looked like a different place. The teams had finished more than 99 percent, not of a plan, but of what the facility actually needed. The results: 11,000 square feet of tile laid; 230 square yards of carpeting laid; 550 gallons of paint applied; 1,000 flowers, trees, bushes, and shrubs planted; a yard full of grass seed planted; 21 cubic yards of concrete poured. (GE brought in private contractors to finish the rest.)

Hutt repeated the process at annual retreats for other GE Plastics departments: tackling renovation projects for a homeless shelter, a safe haven for kids in a dangerous San Diego neighborhood, another YMCA, and an overnight Y camp. The effect on the nearly 2,000 employees who participated was profound. Many likened them to old-fashioned barn-raisings, a manufacturing employee recalling, "We pulled off something no one thought possible at 8 A.M. And we were leaving something behind. It was just a great feeling, better than we felt a couple of years ago after eight hours of golf." Two years later another employee could still "remember that I felt I had done something for a community, and that makes you feel good. Of all the meetings I've been through, the Copely Y project stays with me. . . . I'll never forget it."[8]

What about the original concern—getting Borg-Warner employees to accept their former competitor, with its intense culture, as their new employer? A mergers and acquisitions specialist who'd advised

GE on previous acquisitions, concluded that the San Diego projects were, in fact, the turning point. The reason: After a day of driving nails, digging holes, planting shrubs, and painting walls together, the rivalry dissolved in their effort to contribute to a worthy purpose. After the renovations, many Borg-Warner employees went home and told their families their minds were made up–they were going to work for GE. As one put it, "any questions I had about if this is the kind of company I want to work for ... those questions were gone ... absolutely. For us to be able to pull this off and to want to do this really make all the difference."[9]

WHY IDEALS ARE GOOD BUSINESS

As energizing as the GE restoration projects were, why not put as much energy *meaning into the business itself*? What if the GE employees were as passionate about their own company's mission as they'd been about making an impact on San Diego's underprivileged? Why not pursue community in its more inspiring form: a place where people come not just to perform tasks and earn a paycheck, but to realize their better selves even in their everyday business–a place where they can live their ideals?

For those who think such an aspiration is unrealistic and not "good business" in a tough and competitive world, keep in mind: Central to the Massachusetts Bay Colony's mission was to live and conduct business according to the highest ethics, as well as to make the world a better place, and no enterprise has ever faced more daunting circumstances or succeeded more superbly.

The argument against that proposition goes like this: Business has one legitimate purpose: to make money for its shareholders. Morale-building or other "off-to-the-side" activities like the GE restoration projects are fine if they improve morale and cohesiveness and don't take too much time away from business; but such motives have no place in the operations and strategy of the business itself. Business is not about pursuing ideals; it's about creating wealth. In a famous *New York Times* article, Nobel Prize–winning economist Milton Friedman made a strong argument that there is only one "social responsibility of business"–namely, to increase its profits lawfully. Any business that takes seriously the notion of any other social responsibility on its part is "preaching pure and unadulterated socialism." After all, said Friedman, what right does management have to spend shareholders' money on "socially responsible" projects that taxpayers refuse to fund?[10]

But Friedman, though a formidable (if somewhat mechanistic) logician, is wrong because his contention is outside the mainstream of American social and cultural experience. It would be astonishing if his concept of corporate purpose would prevail in a society so clearly shaped by the quest for meaning. From a simple, human standpoint, what employee was ever motivated to get out of bed in the morning and go to work to enrich a shareholder?

Consider what it takes to get Americans to commit to the most daunting human enterprise—war. Time and again American leaders have turned to our distinct need to find a larger meaning in the world. If we're convinced that our actions and our sacrifice have significance beyond personal or narrow national interests, then we'll even go to war. All three of the great conflicts in which our immediate security was not clearly at stake, where there was no Pearl Harbor—the Revolution, the Civil War, and World War I—were fought for much more than "protection of our homes," say, or to strengthen and secure the "Fatherland." Equally essential to getting Americans to sacrifice was a higher moral principle, such as establishing liberty and the just rights of man in the Revolution, or abolishing slavery in the Civil War.

The professorial Woodrow Wilson came into his own as a leader when, after groping for a way to convince Americans to fight in a European conflict, he recalled his own Presbyterian roots. "Holding aloft the torch of idealism," as one respected historian put it, Wilson "mobilized public emotion into an almost frenzied outburst" with his idealistic call "to end war" and "to make the world safe for democracy." Conversely, an important reason for our failure in Vietnam was the lack of a compelling moral purpose.[11]

Engaging People Emotionally

How hungry are people to find meaning in their lives? When Jack Stack (now CEO of Springfield Remanufacturing Company) was a young supervisor for International Harvester, he was struck by how much people wanted to feel their work was important. And the reason they didn't was not because of any deep, existential mystery.

Engine assembly-line workers, for example, who were bogged down in their narrowly defined jobs, had no idea what happened to the engines they built. So Stack got all the sales brochures and promotional literature he could find, with their glowing accounts of the company's engines and all the good things they did for people, and showered them on his line workers. He showed his employees that they were building engines that powered tractors which worked farms and put food on people's tables, or powered trucks that carried goods throughout the United States.

The result was a swelling increase in pride and sense of purpose. One assembly worker told Stack he'd been out driving with his son and saw a truck containing one of the engines he had worked on. "I said to my son, 'your Daddy built that engine.'" "Probably the highlight of my life at that time," recalled Stack. "And I said to myself, 'This is the job I want for the rest of my life.'"[12]

A Purpose Beyond Profits?

Why not put a larger sense of purpose in the company's mission itself?

Would such a purpose distract an enterprise from its responsibility to create wealth, or would it somehow *enhance* wealth creation, as Tocqueville realized it had in New England? There are too many highly successful companies today who insist on pursuing a purpose beyond making profits—such as Levi's (socially responsible global expansion) or Southwest Airlines (a fun and loving place to work)—to just dismiss the possibility.

The impressive study by Stanford's James Collins and Jerry Porras provides strong evidence that such "purpose-pursuing" not only satisfies deep aspirations in Americans—but is also compatible with the highest level of business success and may enhance it. Collins and Porras carefully selected the eighteen greatest companies they could find for their study—"the best of the best"—determined by surveying hundreds of CEOs from around the country and in every type of industry. Then they limited the final group to companies that had proven themselves over the long run, for at least fifty years. The final group was superb, including Merck, 3M, Hewlett-Packard, Motorola, Nordstrom, General Electric, Johnson & Johnson, and Boeing.

Rather than study each in isolation (a frequent mistake), Collins and Porras compared the practices of these companies with their "also-ran" competitors such as Pfizer, Norton, Texas Instruments, Zenith, Melville, Westinghouse, Bristol-Meyers Squibb, and McDonnell Douglas. Note that the "also-rans" are quite good; their stocks outperformed the stock market by more than 100 percent from 1926 to 1990. But the best companies picked for the Collins and Porras study were far better, outperforming the market by more than *1500 percent* during the same period.

Collins and Porras found that of the eighteen best performers, each one regards pursuit of high ideals as important as turning a profit. And seven of the eighteen go much further: They regard "profitability or shareholder wealth as being only a part of the company's objectives, and not the primary driving objective." Further, when discussing the level of returns they desired, they used words like "reasonable," "adequate," or "fair," or spoke of "profitability as a necessary condition to pursue other aims."[13]

And it is these other aims that give employees passion, commitment to their company, and a sense of common cause with each other: in Boeing's case, pushing the envelope in aerospace technology; in GE's, improving the quality of life through technology and innovation. These companies expressed no interest in seeking "maximal" or "highest" returns.

What was particularly fascinating was the outlook of the eighteen comparison companies, the also-rans: They adopted the Friedman view of business purpose. *None* thought there was any objective more important than profitability or shareholder wealth, and seven of the eighteen went further: "Any idealistic concerns these companies might have," write Collins and Porras, appear to be "deeply subordinated to making money." They regard maximizing wealth "as the reason for existence and number one goal far ahead of any other."

Most telling was the head-to-head comparison of the eighteen best performers with their eighteen also-ran counterparts, the companies they had far outperformed for decades. Fully seventeen out of the eighteen best were *more* ideals-driven and *less* profit-driven than their competitors (and the eighteenth was tied with its competitor).

A Purpose Beyond Profits–Especially *When Times Are Tough*

It might be contended that it's easy for a Merck or Hewlett-Packard to declare and practice high ideals, with all the success they've enjoyed, but such an approach to business is clearly foolish for most struggling companies, particularly in a tough environment. Wrong again. Collins and Porras found that the most successful companies often turned to their core ideals not just when things were going well, but when they were struggling to survive.

Take Ford, which is interesting here because its own record for idealism is hardly perfect, from its nasty labor battles in the 1930s to the exploding Pinto in the 1970s. Still, in a time of dire circumstances during the early 1980s when Japanese competition had left Ford reeling with a $3.3 billion net loss in three years (43 percent of its net worth), it reconnected with its idealistic roots. Amid the frenzy of activity to keep the company alive, Ford did something remarkable; it paused to clarify its guiding principles.

Ford's management took a fresh look at its "three P's"–people, products, and profits—and decided that people should "absolutely come first," with product and profits second and third respectively. This was the first step in the company's effort to battle back, which culminated with the Ford Taurus becoming the best-selling car in the United States. And Collins and Porras found evidence that in pausing to reorient its business, Ford was reaching back to draw on the ideals of founder Henry Ford.[14]

Henry Ford? Idealist?! Despite a deservedly cantankerous reputation, he believed passionately that his company could be an instrument to better society. He wrote that he had no interest in an "awful profit"; he would rather build many cars at a "reasonably small profit" so that as many people as possible could use and enjoy them, and so that he could employ as many workers as possible—"the two aims I have in life." These were more than sentiments. When demand for the Model T soared, Ford continued to *lower* prices (58 percent between 1908 and 1916), even in the face of a shareholder lawsuit to stop him. When he roughly doubled the wages of Ford autoworkers to five dollars a day, he was bitterly attacked by no less than *The Wall Street Journal* for "economic blunders if not crimes." Naively, suggested the *Journal,* Ford had introduced "spiritual principles in a field where they do not belong."[15]

Virtue and Profits Can Be Combined

Some of the ideals described above, such as pursuing innovation or treating customers well, have a clear connection to strategy. They're obviously good business. What about a commitment to outright virtue as part of a company's larger purpose? A true commitment to virtue would require specifying ethical conduct, unrelated to any strategic considerations, that would be expected of the company and its employees no matter what the effect on profits.

Whether or not *this* is good business is a closer question. After all, it could be argued, this is still a business. We may well need a purpose beyond just making money—something with greater emotional and human appeal. But why not find one that is directly linked to our ability to make money? This doesn't mean we should engage in unlawful activities. We should obey the law, of course, set up compliance procedures, and make sure our people consult with lawyers on close legal questions in order to cover the company and ourselves. But beyond that, we do have to make a profit.

Collins and Porras state their support for this virtue-neutral view, concluding that it doesn't matter *what* a company's core ideology is—

so long as it *has* one beyond making profits. Their favorite example: hugely successful cigarette-maker Philip Morris, with its defiant smoking culture that flies in the face of a mountain of evidence that cigarettes kill.

Nevertheless, it appears we *can* say to those who'd *like* to build a corporate community committed to virtuous conduct, who'd find that a more appealing environment to work in but may be a bit squeamish about saying so: There is strong evidence that this too is fully compatible with business success and may enhance it. At least in America.

The best study of the impact corporate culture has on long-term performance, by Harvard's John Kotter and James Heskett, squarely addressed this issue.[16] It was particularly insightful because (like Collins and Porras) Kotter and Heskett didn't merely ask what successful companies (like Albertson's, ConAgra, Bankers Trust, and several others) do; they compared their practices with those of less successful competitors (such as Winn-Dixie, Archer Daniels Midland, and Citicorp). They concluded that one important factor leading to long-term success was the inclusion, in effect, of virtue in the company's culture.

In particular, companies that place more value on treating fairly all key constituents—stockholders, customers, and employees—that actually care deeply about them as opposed to seeing them as a means to making money, outperformed their less virtuous competitors in every case studied. One reason is not hard to see. "In general," noted Kotter and Heskett, "the pattern seems to be this. When managers care deeply about their main constituencies, they pay close attention to those constituencies. When something in the firm's context changes—such as the level of competition—managers are quick to spot this trend."[17]

The compatibility of virtue and profits has strong roots in America. A deeply impressed Alexis de Tocqueville pointed out the compatibility of the New Englanders' idealism with their profit-seeking impulses. They pursued, he said, "with almost equal eagerness material wealth and moral satisfaction. . . . These two tendencies, apparently so discrepant, are far from conflicting; they advance together and support each other."[18] This profound insight is affirmed by Kotter and Heskett.

Further, despite Collins and Porras' contention that "it doesn't matter" *what* a company's core ideology is, there are indications it does—from their own findings. Of the eighteen best performers, thirteen (and arguably fourteen) specify virtuous behavior as part of their core ideology—either as part of their overarching purpose or as a core value that is never to be compromised for the sake of financial gain. Fully seven (3M, Boeing, Ford, GE, Merck, Motorola, and Procter & Gamble) include some combination of honesty, integrity, and/or ethics as core values. Several have virtuous corporate purposes: Johnson & Johnson (the company exists "to alleviate pain and disease"); Merck ("We are in the business of preserving and improving human life. All of our actions must be measured by our success in achieving this goal."); Marriott (to "make people away from home feel that they're among friends and really wanted").[19]

But beyond statistics is the simple, distinctly American attraction to virtue. This is not to say Americans are any more virtuous than other people, or to ignore the decidedly unvirtuous conduct we see all around us. But as the perceptive Tocqueville saw when commentators of his time were wringing their hands over rampant American selfishness, Americans may well be world class self-seekers, but their self-seeking is remarkably enlightened because they recognize the value of helping each other and their community. They "maintain," he observed, "that virtue is useful and prove it every day."[20]

Look at the multitude of voluntary associations Americans form to take on a myriad of tasks left to the government in other societies. Tocqueville was struck by this same tendency over a century and a half ago, astonished at the hospitals, prisons, schools, and libraries formed and run by volunteering Americans, as well as churches and seminaries, missionary programs, and so on. People in a truly free society recognize the need, and the benefit to themselves, of being public spirited. "They therefore do not deny that every man may follow his own interest, but they endeavor to prove that it is the interest of every man to be virtuous."[21]

Isn't this still true? When Merck took streptomycin to war-ravaged Japan after World War II to fight a catastrophic tuberculosis epidemic, for example, there were no profits or any other foreseeable economic benefit such as goodwill to be gained. But Merck pursued that effort, as it has pursued similar efforts in China and elsewhere in the third world, in part because its highly dedicated scientists believe deeply in the company's mission of "preserving and improving human life." Equally true, its executives traditionally believe that such actions are vital to Merck's extraordinary economic success. Merck is now, for instance, the largest American pharmaceutical maker in Japan. More important is the superb and dedicated workforce such a dynamic corporate community attracts. "The long-term consequences," says ex-CEO P. Roy Vagelos of such actions, "are not always clear, but somehow I think they always pay off."[22]

Which Values?

Which values should your company pursue? It would seem absurd to impose some list of ideals and aspirations on people, and expect it to create passion and commitment. How incongruous, when employees are being urged at the same time to exercise more judgment and assume more responsibility in their organization.

Massachusetts Bay's values, which were called "The New England Way" and spelled out in the *Cambridge Platform*, were created not by top leaders who handed them down to the towns and churches. They were created by a synod of representatives from the church congregations; and the congregations voted again on the finished document. Their values and beliefs were therefore unique to their community, and widely shared. And they took them quite seriously, including a system of fines and other punishments for violating them. Those who didn't share them had "free liberty" to do so, declared Nathaniel Ward in 1647, as well as "free liberty to keep away from us, and . . . the sooner the better."

Even huge General Electric, with hundreds of thousands of employees, undertook a similar participative effort when it created its current values statement. Chairman Jack Welch wanted one that all employees would "own," would actually follow, and that would be vigorously measured and enforced. He therefore sought the widest possible employee input, dismissing objections from some executives about the impracticality of doing so. The process, which took more than two years, required drafters to submit versions of the new values statement for vigorous debate by managers at GE's training center in Crotonville. Their inputs, which numbered in the thousands, were then incorporated. Discussion of the values was then introduced—and is ongoing—among frontline employees during the company's famous town hall Work Out meetings. The process was time-consuming and difficult, but worth it because it created a clear and energizing sense of commitment and shared purpose on the part of GE employees, following the deep cuts and intense dislocations of the 1980s.[23]

A similar process was used by Johnson & Johnson to simply re-examine its existing credo, when Chairman James Burke thought it had grown stale. Burke ordered group meetings held throughout the organization to decide if people still believed in it. "If we're not going to live by it, let's tear it off the wall," he told his executives. Johnson & Johnson managers spent months in worldwide meetings discussing and challenging the J&J credo, clarifying what it meant in the current context of their business, and in the end wound up keeping it. But now they felt rededicated to it, and put it back on the walls with a fresh look.

The American Puritans have taken a great deal of heat, of course, for their intolerance of dissenting religious views, but their reason for doing so, and the reason that policy ultimately failed, was not because of some sort of reactionary defect in their character. Their reputation as repressive spoilsports wearing black clothes and steeple-shaped hats has been exaggerated; to the contrary, they liked beer, horse racing, colorful clothes and furnishings, and the charms of the opposite sex. They furnished their homes with taste and beauty. Theirs is not only a legacy to be proud of, as historian Samuel Eliot Morison observed, but to build on.

They'd made and kept an impressive commitment to live their religious ideals together as a community. They simply didn't want to get bogged down arguing endlessly over what those ideals and beliefs were—as their more effete brethren in Europe tended to do. They were ultimately unable to preserve that commitment because Massachusetts Bay became a civil society, and therefore couldn't keep outsiders with different values and beliefs from moving in—an influx that eventually corrupted their original vision.

But companies that have discretion over whom they choose to hire, can screen out people who don't share their values when they hire and when they promote. And as both the Collins and Porras, and the Kotter and Heskett studies suggest, it certainly appears to be in their best interests to do so. General Electric's Larry Bossidy (later CEO of AlliedSignal) put it to management trainees this way, "Get clear on what your values are and whether they fit with GE. If they don't fit, make the decision to get out."[24]

3

Town Halls and Covenants

How Americans Organize Naturally

We've seen how our sense of community gets Americans to stick together and persevere. We'll take a good look here at how it *thrives*—how it opens the way to wealth creation by individuals, particularly in novel situations.

Imagine for the moment an enterprise that achieved this level of performance. Starting from scratch in what was, literally, a wilderness, it grew from nothing to over twenty thousand people in just a dozen years. And they were extraordinarily dynamic by any standard. Thriving smiths, wheelwrights, carpenters, and weavers emerged, and industries like fishing, shipbuilding, and trade were organized by people who'd expected to farm until they encountered a rocky and infertile country—the first in a series of superb adaptations they made in a string of daunting, unanticipated circumstances. A land recently covered with "hideous thickets" where "wolves and bears nursed up their young," as one settler described it, blossomed into a center of international commerce, its streets bustling with French, Portuguese, and Dutch traders. Despite intense hardships, they tamed a cold, forbidding, sometimes savage region, carving out a more prosperous, healthy, and stable way of life than anywhere else in America at the time.[1]

Who were they? The same pious, devoted, persistent, values-driven Puritans of Massachusetts Bay. Not only had these early Americans learned how to lead meaningful lives together, they'd also figured out how to create wealth in a big way.

How did they, and the most dynamic American communities ever since, do it, and what can organizations learn from their experience?

Leading People Who Don't Like to Be Told

It might be thought that such success in mastering unforeseeable contingencies requires domineering, take-charge, visionary leadership, atop a patriarchal organization in which people were willing to do what they were told. But nothing could be further from the truth. Commonwealth leadership, which was often superb (as we'll see below), was far from visionary; its attempts to direct commercial development in Massachusetts Bay almost uniformly came to grief.[2] Further, hardy souls who'd crossed the Atlantic to face a wilderness grew less and less willing to toe the line for any would-be domineering leader. Even the great John Winthrop–a model of modern, liberal, flexible leadership who had coined the Bay Colony's "city on a hill" mission–occasionally got tossed out of office when people objected to his policies (prompting his European friends to wonder why the Bay colonists "toss and tumble about" their leaders so disrespectfully). Incomprehensible though it was to the Europeans, this was a sign not of weakness, but of strength.

The Bay Colony's rapid development depended, in fact, on experiment, adaptation, even trial and error at times, by people throughout the community–a pattern repeated again and again in the growth of American enterprise ever since. Its superb foreign trade, which would become the life blood of New England's prosperity for more than a century, was established in fits and starts. The first trading ventures were designed to make money in local New England markets but found these were too limited. Then they tried exporting Bay Company goods, but found the cost of delivery to foreign markets too high to make them competitive. The ultimate solution? Combining their exports with those of other American colonies, and consolidating them for overseas shipment to reduce unit costs–one of history's great wealth-creating formulas.

The key to the Bay Colony's extraordinary dynamism–its ability to adjust to the unforeseen, adapt to it, and exploit it as an opportunity–was a distinct set of democratic values that worked their way into its governance. These values not only appealed to the hardy, independent-minded souls who'd come there, they were also much more suited to developing enterprises in complex situations. When these values were added to the Bay Colony's strong religious and ethical code, the result was an economic powerhouse.

And note: The governance processes and mechanisms they and American communities since then have devised arose not out of social theory texts of the day (which would have disparaged such methods anyway), but naturally, from the need of a spirited people to find ways of working together in a risky world. They were grounded on this concept: Rather than assure people "We'll protect you if you'll do as you're told," they were based on the premise that "We're all in this together." There was no imprimatur from some patriarchal authority, but rather an agreement between people who stood on an equal footing while recognizing their need to associate in an unpredictable world, whether to advance themselves or protect themselves or both.

That's precisely the foundation on which the most dynamic American communities since then have been based, and on which organizations today are trying to build. In particular, they want to pass on to employees—rather than shield them from—the opportunities as well as risks of the marketplace. The American community achieved this important formula that often eludes patriarchal organizations: Its members recognized that their interests were intimately linked with the success of the enterprise as a whole.

TOOLS FOR UNLEASHING
AMERICAN INGENUITY

Starting Point: A Covenant

The defining moment for the Massachusetts Bay Company—indeed a defining moment for American society as we now know it—occurred at the beginning when its leaders surreptitiously took their charter with them from England. This had the legal effect of moving control of the colony from remote London to Boston. Gradually, inevitably, a democratic and federal approach to governing emerged in the Bay Colony, in which power was pushed to the lowest possible point. Bay Colony leaders increasingly applied that spirit of local control in all their policy making, not always because they were enlightened, but because circumstances often forced them to.[3]

Two requirements proved essential for organizing people in an unpredictable environment:

- Every person must be totally responsible for his or her actions, particularly those touching the welfare of other people; and
- All authority must be based on agreement or "covenant" between the members of the community.

That is, governance was placed on a constitutional, as well as a moral basis. And it required something much stronger than our notion of "empowerment," which often only delegates authority to people. The Bay Colony changed the intrinsic status of people, instituting privileges that couldn't be revoked. It wasn't a democracy, but at its healthiest it moved in that direction. Our own society, devised a century and a half later by the American Founding Fathers, as well as the social tools for unleashing employee initiative used by many companies today–have their origin, and arguably still their most dynamic application, in these principles of Puritan community.

Its members enjoyed extraordinary status–many of them were shareholders in the Bay Company–and participated actively in the life of the community. They elected officials annually, established a body of laws and a bill of individual rights. They met regularly in their famous New England town meetings–the ones that so impressed the Virginian Thomas Jefferson over a century later–to discuss, challenge, and vote on important community issues. In time, the humblest citizen in town would feel perfectly free to stand up and challenge the richest, an idea Jack Welch turned to in his effort to break up General Electric's stubborn bureaucracy and free up employee creativity (see page 40). Whenever new settlements were started in the region, their members would invariably draw up and agree on their own covenant containing the principles by which they agreed to live and work.

They were intensely preoccupied with "liberty" because of their intense distrust of power. "It is necessary," as one member put it, "that all power that is on earth be limited." The Bay Company's first compilation of laws was called, significantly, "The Body of Liberties." It began by paraphrasing Magna Carta, then it described limitations on judicial power and proceeded to state all laws in terms of the "liberties" of the members of the community. Their governance was a remarkable and tangible recognition that a community's success is best achieved by maximizing the freedom of its members.

Leadership That Fits a Democratic Society

What sort of leader did emerge in a community of self-determining citizens? Bay Colony leaders focused less on what people did, and more on how well they were organized—and in particular, how judiciously power was wielded. How are leaders being selected? What are the proper limits of their power? What is the proper division of power between local and central organs?

Such an approach to governance seemed to energize everything it touched, even their churches, which themselves were remarkably dynamic. Under a decentralized "congregational" system, individual churches were formed not by administrative edict but by covenant among the members of the prospective congregation. Ministers were chosen by their congregations, often *out* of their congregations, and could be dismissed by them if they failed to meet the spiritual and moral needs of the members. Each church had wide latitude to set its own policies. There were no bishops, no elaborate hierarchy. The result: remarkably vibrant churches that vigorously communicated the community's values and kept them fresh. Ritual and vestments were abolished from worship, just as fancy but obscure literary reference were removed from sermons. Instead, Bay Colony ministers became famous for their "plain style" of speaking, and the clarity and practical usefulness of their sermons.

Consider the reams of instructions flowing from headquarters at some companies on, say, how to set up a field office. Contrast that with the Bay Colony's guidelines for setting up a local congregational church: How large should any particular congregation be? Small enough, said the *Cambridge Platform*, so that people could "meet together conveniently in one place," and large enough to "conveniently carry on church work." How should worship services be conducted? "In such a manner, as all circumstances considered, is most expedient for edification." In other words, "Figure it out yourselves, keeping in mind our shared values."

Such dynamic governance, grounded in democratic values, kept the churches, as it had the Bay Colony's commercial development, from falling into the trap of tradition-bound thinking and irrelevance. Instead they served a vitally important purpose by explaining what people wanted to know: How to apply their shared religious and ethical convictions to real circumstances in everyday life, including business and work—which was vital to the community's cohesiveness.

Why Education Is Fundamental

Governance based on democratic values required not only a distinct kind of leadership, but also a new relationship between the community and its individuals. If people were going to truly participate, to have a genuine say in policy making, they needed to be educated. It is no coincidence that many great educational leaders and reformers in American history—from Benjamin Franklin to Horace Mann, James B. Conant, and John Dewey—have been New Englanders from Puritan stock. The Bay Colony Puritans knew that a vibrant, participative society would require well-educated citizens, and the system of free, popular education they devised may have been their most impressive innovation. It was exceptionally well thought-out.

For example, parents were responsible for teaching their children the "three Rs" by act of the Bay Colony. Settlements of more than fifty people were required to hire a schoolmaster; of one hundred or more, to establish a school—four of which are still operating today! Education had clear purposes: Children learned to write and "speak pieces" so they could communicate accurately, to "cipher" so they could conduct business, and to read so they could study their Bibles and thus grow in the community's shared ideals. Harvard College was established to provide educated public servants for Bay Colony governance and learned ministers for its pulpits. Companies today who embrace theories like total quality or reengineering for their own sake can find a lesson here. Bay Colony education created self-determining citizens and enlightened leaders as opposed to passive subjects indoctrinated in a theory.

This emphasis on education and the excellence of its schools vaulted Massachusetts Bay past other American colonies in commercial and scientific achievement. Even more powerful, the schools meshed with the community and with families "to capture and fill the minds of generations of New England youth with an attachment to the values and hopes of the founders," as one historian put it. "Accordingly, while the surface life of the colonies changed, much of the Puritan tradition would persevere to help shape a new nation."[4]

The importance of education to a participative enterprise is hard to overstate. Today Motorola spends more than $200 million per year educating employees (including costs of employee time and travel). First established about fifteen years ago, "Motorola University" now has a full-time staff of two hundred, complemented by three hundred outside contractors. Every employee receives a mandated forty hours of course work per year from a sizable curriculum that includes engineering, manufacturing, sales, management, and professional development, together with referrals to outside courses offered by colleges or other vendors. Its primary emphasis is on frontline employees; it both screens new hires for basic skills in reading, writing, and math, and provides remedial courses in these subjects for existing employees. In addition employees can take courses ranging from total quality and statistical processes to how to give effective presentations.

The return on this investment is astonishing. Early studies at Motorola, before Motorola University received its current broad charter, had shown that every dollar spent on sales training had returned $29 in increased sales performance. An intensive internal study of Motorola plants, which happened to occur in the midst of a drive to improve product quality, confirmed the magnitude of that figure. Plants that carefully educated their workers in quality-improvement techniques and then reinforced this by allowing them to apply the techniques in their work, in a participative environment supported by management, were realizing a return of $33 for every dollar spent on training.

Apart from the data was simple common sense: An educated work-force can do much more. "The more people learn how a machine works and how to fix it themselves without waiting two hours for someone else to fix it," remarked one manager, "the more productive your plant is."[5] Motorola employees have become increasingly skilled at understanding data generated by the computer-based machines they operate. They can now provide status reports on output, quality, or work-in-process that were formerly done by supervisors, allowing the plants to make faster adjustments in scheduling or materials flow. And they can handle more tasks—such as equipment setup, machine changeovers, and troubleshooting—that require the ability to read manuals, understand machine gauges, identify the causes of problems, do simple calculations, understand and graph data, and so forth.

Motorola: Community Building with Third-World Employees

Are there limits to who can handle such democratic values and responsibilities? Is the dynamism of an American community appropriate to all employees in any circumstance? Two American firms that are aggressively expanding overseas, Motorola and General Electric, don't see why not. For them, the appeal of these values is proving to be universal.

Certainly if any workforce seemed destined for passive subordination, it would be the one at Motorola's walkie-talkie plant in Penang, Malaysia, where factory workers are accustomed to being treated like disposable, unthinking cogs. But Motorola's Penang workers initiate suggestions at a remarkable rate—forty-one thousand in one recent year alone, worth $2 million in savings to the facility. Further, the plant's research and development team of two hundred engineers is all Malaysian. The ethic at Penang is the same as it is at Motorola's

U.S. plants: Employees at all levels are expected to get out of their narrow job descriptions and work together to find and solve problems.

The tool used to achieve such an outlook is the same as it is in the company's U.S. plants–education. New hires at Penang must pass tests in math, English, and basic science, like their American counterparts. Then they spend two full days in classes on quality that include statistical processes and team building, followed by mandatory yearly training, as in the States. All skilled workers at Penang go on to serve as on-the-job mentors to the beginners who follow them. Motorola continues the education of its best production workers so they can become full-fledged technicians, and provides to engineers free outside schooling up to a master's degree.

The result is not just better performance, but a better atmosphere at the Penang facility, with a sense of pride and individual worth obvious among employees. One woman who came to Motorola from a repressive factory elsewhere in Malaysia speaks now of her personal goals. She wants to have a "better career," she says, and hopes to become a manager or quality engineer someday. She wants to do what is best for the company because she feels like "one of the family here." In that, she's not quite right; there is little paternalism at the Penang factory. Employees are well aware they have to hustle to stay ahead of increasing low-wage competition in other parts of Asia, most notably China, and could lose their jobs if they don't. What has energized the Malaysian worker and her peers and nurtured their growth isn't family, but a growing sense of community.

General Electric: Building A Community with Former Communists

General Electric Lighting wanted to instill this same participative atmosphere in the midst of a famously oppressive society–at its Tungsram plant in Hungary. The company's new head, Hungarian-born George Varga, focused on educating not just employees but a new kind of leader as well. Here was a company that had been run by communist management for years. All decision-making had been concentrated in a few people at the top, with everyone else expected to do as they were told. "If anything, new ideas were punished," noted Varga. "Therefore a mass of very talented, very good people had their initiative eaten out."[6]

After substantial rounds of cutting (done as humanely as possible: The first round of 3,300 cuts included only seventy-four involuntary terminations), Varga began working to loosen the grip of the company's autocrats. His very selection–he openly declared "I don't know anything about lighting"—sent the message that micromanagement was out.

Under Varga, GE taught Tungsram managers nonautocratic methods that emphasize setting objectives, delegating, and communication. He brought in American managers with "get up and go," not to take charge of Tungsram, but to provide models that might arouse latent initiative in the Hungarians. He also sent Hungarian managers and workers to the United States both to gain technical knowledge and to "get the U.S. atmosphere." Automatic pay raises were abolished, replaced with a merit pay system. To the surprise of many observers, the Hungarians began responding to these organizational changes with greater assertiveness and initiative.

Company newspapers, bulletin boards, and periodic meetings were instituted to update employees and encourage their input in decisions, thus creating a sense of shared purpose. Workers were asked, "What do you want to know?" in a survey. (Their answer: The unvarnished truth, bad news as well as good.)

These reforms allowed Varga to introduce GE's renowned Work Out meetings, an exercise in western-style democracy. Varga thought the organization was now ready for rank-and-file employees to participate, a wonderful irony: Ordinary Hungarian workers— who'd listened to communist rhetoric about worker participation for generations—were finally experiencing it under an American "capitalist" manager. The response was "amazing," noted Varga. Now the Hungarian employees assemble in meetings, challenge any method or procedure that doesn't make sense to them, identify problems, devise solutions, and take responsibility for implementing them. The results have been so good that three of Tungsram's suppliers now use this technique with their own employees.

Social scientist Ivan Volgyes has been fascinated by the impact of Varga's reforms on people from a hierarchy-ridden society. "What George has done is create a sense of community at Tungsram," he notes. "That's very unusual in Hungary's hierarchical structure. I think it's nothing short of a revolution."[7]

BATTLING HIDDEN BUREAUCRACY

What is striking about the American concept of community is its versatility and power. Americans have kept turning to it, again and again to bring people together and get things done—to settle wildernesses, build cities and towns, tackle common problems and dangers, and pursue opportunity. And they still do.

In 1988, Chairman Jack Welch grew frustrated with General Electric's failure to encourage more employee initiative and creativity, a frustration that would eventually lead to the creation of the famous Work Out meetings. The company had already spent years reviewing its core values and incorporating input from several thousand employees, and was committed in particular to more empowerment and less bureaucracy. This wasn't just a nice or trendy idea; massive layoffs required that fewer GE employees get more done. But people continued complaining to Welch that their bosses weren't letting them work smarter, just harder; they were still required to do all the same old unnecessary tasks and pointless report-filing.

GE executives had tried before to generate greater worker input, with forums like Japanese-style quality circles. But these required deference to authority—employees discuss only "their piece" of instructions handed down from on high—which grates on American employees. "Japanese companies are very hierarchical," said one executive, "we aren't. American workers don't stand up and salute." Welch wanted something more radical, a more open and freewheeling forum for employees that would embolden them to challenge oppressive bosses and hold them accountable, "to force leaders who weren't walking the talk to face up to their people," as he put it. For this, he turned to the New England town meeting—an institution with which the Massachusetts-bred Welch was intimately familiar. Anticipating new two-way dialogues between leaders and those being led, he called the new meetings Work Out.

New England Town Meetings at GE

Welch now places Work Out meetings at the center of his celebrated efforts to revitalize the company; he regards no social innovation as more important. He would later say, after describing the savings achieved by a series of town meetings in a GE turbine plant, it was "embarrassing to reflect that for probably 80 or 90 years, we've been dictating equipment needs and managing people who knew how to do things much better and faster than we did."[8]

Work Out started in a series of meetings in groups of thirty to a hundred hourly and salaried employees and their bosses. They were held off-site initially, for three days, with no coats or ties allowed in order to blur the distinction between bosses and workers. At first bosses left the room during discussions, which were led by outside facilitators to ensure candor. The meetings seemed so unusual to employees who'd never been asked their opinions that one consultant called them "unnatural acts in unnatural places." But unlike the quality circles, they developed into a natural and effective method for vigorous employee involvement.

The early town halls addressed easy problems—ridiculous procedures, clear ways to increase efficiency, and other "low-hanging fruit"—which helped build confidence in the process. In one, a factory worker said he had to shut down his machine for an hour several times a month to fill out forms and get approval for new gloves. Why all the hoops, he asked? Because "in 1973 we lost a box of gloves," said someone in the back. "Put the box of gloves on the floor, close to the people," said the manager.[9] In another, a field service engineer in Power Generation complained about a five-hundred-page report he had to fill out whenever he repaired a customer's turbine. It was well known that no one read the report, but in this case there was a good reason for it. The information could help manufacturing plan future production of turbine replacement parts. Subsequent town halls then helped devise a much shorter report that could be submitted using a laptop computer in the field, which did get read and incorporated into production.

Over time the meetings progressed to more systematic, ongoing efforts to increase productivity. After complaining about the milling machines in one New York plant, employees received authorization to test, approve, and purchase $20 million worth of replacements. The result: Cycle time for milling steel in the plant dropped by 80 percent, lowering inventory costs and increasing customer responsiveness. Later, customers and suppliers were included in the plant's town meetings to figure out better ways to design and produce products. "We demonstrated," said one executive, "that if you talked to the people, asked them what to do about something, and then did what they said, your business normally runs better. It's a simple idea that managers with IQs of 150 can't bring themselves to understand."[10]

Rooting Out Change-Averse Behavior

And as Welch had hoped, the meetings developed customs that quickly exposed change-averse managers who were undermining employee initiative. Everyone at GE came to understand that all issues are fair game in Work Out meetings; problems can be defined and concrete proposals can be recommended by anyone. And managers can't brush recommendations aside; they must respond to suggestions, usually on the spot (that alone distinguishes Work Out from canned quality or empowerment teams). Only if a problem needs further study can they delay a decision, in which case a decision date goes on a calendar (typically thirty to ninety days out).

And to prevent too many "no's" or "maybe's," the manager's boss sometimes sits in the back of the room. In addition, every session results in a list of "actionable items"; a "champion" is also picked beforehand who's responsible to make sure the actionable items are implemented. Work Out is thus much more than a discussion group; it's a governance tool that has increased and institutionalized employee power, and provided a way to hold leaders accountable.

One competitive advantage that has resulted: the ability to spread knowledge rapidly throughout the organization–from an impressive range of sources including customers, competitors, partners, or simply other companies it admires–a traditional strength, by the way, of American democracy (which hierarchical organizations typically manage to stifle). For instance, GE Appliances and Power have cut product introduction times by more than half, using techniques adapted from Caterpillar. GE Appliances and Capital Services have learned "Quick Market Intelligence" techniques from Wal-Mart to make major improvements in asset turnover and customer service. Several GE businesses are using inventory turn methods created by American Standard, resulting in double digit improvement in working capital turnover for at least two consecutive years. The town halls have been vital to spreading such new knowledge around GE's organization in all these efforts.

Another result of the town halls: They help create leaders appropriate to an American organization. For example, in one of the first Work Outs, a shop steward named Jimmy stood up to question why the plant was still getting dangerously weak screws. Management had been promising for months to get ones that wouldn't break; they should have gone to the supplier to let someone know. Jimmy, known as a rebel, was testing his boss. With some hesitation, the manager sent Jimmy himself to the supplier with two other colleagues. They wound up getting the problem fixed, and also turned a maverick into a leader, which sent an important message to other employees. Now there is no supervision in Jimmy's part of the plant, and if he needs help he asks for it.

Most important is the infusion of democratic values into GE's governance. Here is the enduring strength of the town meetings, and why they're vital to GE's future. Once exposed to real self-determination, employees aren't likely ever again to brood in silence under the thumb of some would-be autocrat. One plant worker observed that he used to assiduously avoid his manager, often going a whole year at a time without saying a word. "Now I may raise a problem at our Monday morning meetings or go talk to the manager in his office. A few years ago, I wouldn't even want to be there," he says. Not any more. "I feel comfortable going in to see a manager."[11]

That's the language of citizenship. Eventually, employees started spontaneously calling the town meetings themselves, as the need arose. "A year ago people would call me up and ask permission to hold a Work Out session on some problem," remarked one general manager. "Now I get phone calls from Fairfield congratulating me on this great Work Out that I didn't even know was going on."[12] Further, employees felt free to alter its format as needed: One plant even rejected the term Work Out, which reminded workers of recent and painful layoffs, preferring the term "High Involvement." And they opposed the town meeting arrangement, which they regarded as too "event oriented." They preferred instead to divide the factory into ongoing teams of fifteen to twenty workers, each of which took on the responsibility of running its part of the business while staying as far away from management as possible. Welch had no objection; to the contrary, he saw such tinkering with the concept as evidence of the program's growing strength and acceptance.

A final note. Does Work Out work, say, with GE's French or Chinese employees? GE's culture, says GE Medical Systems former CEO John Trani, "transcends national boundaries. Action Work Outs are, in one way or another, happening at GE all over the world. Even the joint ventures tend to adopt them." Trani has found ways to get even deferential Japanese employees to speak up at the meetings; "We try to get the leaders to do so first," he says. "We also bring Japanese employees to the states in multiyear assignments. They wind up embracing our values, which include speaking up and challenging bureaucracy, by the time they go back."

BONDING PEOPLE TEMPORARILY

The idea of community, with its shared values, covenants, and sense of attachment, may be fine for established and relatively stable companies like General Electric, one might say. But many firms, particularly newer technology companies, are operating in a radically different economy characterized by rapid change and turbulence. This economy, it is thought, requires a sleek "virtual organization" where work will be increasingly temporary, performed by independent contractors who go from job to job, virtual company to virtual company, with no attachments.

But that scenario looks doubtful if for no other reason than Americans' historic inclination to form deeper associations. It seems unlikely that has suddenly disappeared: A random sampling in 1994 of more than two thousand working Americans found, for example, that 60 percent still anticipated long-term relationships with their organizations—despite the waves of downsizing rocking businesses that year. Over 50 percent felt a lot of loyalty to their employers, and over 80 percent felt at least some loyalty.[13]

Further, companies increasingly realize the best way to distinguish themselves from competitors is not by ramping up and down with temporary workers who bring only generic expertise, but by patiently developing people who acquire, over a period of time, firm-specific expertise. Such companies find ways to avoid layoffs— often overlooked by others who embrace downsizing too quickly— with temporary wage or hour reductions, for example, or job rotation, retraining, "insourcing" work previously outsourced, and so forth.

That said however, there are still some companies in some situations who must regard parts of their business as temporary and who need the freedom to eliminate jobs. But this doesn't have to mean that all semblance of community is lost, leaving only an arms-length, purely transactional relationship with workers. To the contrary, the American concept of community has proven versatile enough to bind people together even in these temporary situations.

"Temporary Community" Is Not an Oxymoron

The great American migration westward—achieved by overland companies such as the Ohio Company of Associates from Virginia, or the Green and Jersey County Company of Emigrants to California— shows how to adapt the concept of community to temporary associations and give them strength. These were transient or "traveling" communities, formed not because people knew and liked each other and wanted to live together, but because they needed each other for a risky undertaking. In addition to the risk of outright failure of the enterprise, there was the possibility of disease, starvation, natural disaster, Indian attack, and, of course, death. These transient communities provided a highly flexible way for people to commit to each other and to their shared endeavor: They formed, added and subtracted people, and broke up with equal ease, depending on how well they served both their intended purpose and the interests of their members.

For all their variety, these transient communities had certain key features in common. Given the nature of the enterprise, it might seem one of these would be a take-charge leader who tells people what to do. To the contrary, the framing of a constitution and laws for governing, somewhat reminiscent of the Massachusetts Bay covenants, became a well-established custom.[14] These codes, often modeled consciously on the U.S. Constitution, were typically brief and simple. They described the community's purpose and pledged fealty of each member to that purpose and to each other, based on the obvious recognition that no individual was likely to survive on his own.

Using these pragmatic constitutions, the overland companies formed small highly democratic societies. Issues were decided by majority rule—including who the captain or leader would be. Officers served short tenures, perhaps twenty days or at most a few months. The result was very effective temporary organizations.

The value of their covenants or constitutions lay not in the particular procedures they stipulated, but in the astuteness with which they *aligned the individual interests of members with those of the group.* As Randolph Marcy's widely used guide for forming overland companies advised, such agreements should aim to "make the individual interest of each member the common cause of the whole company." Marcy urged, for example, that the members raise a fund for replacing anyone's animal that broke down or died along the way. They should also include an agreement that if anyone's wagon or team broke down, the company would carry that person's baggage and the captain would see to it that he had transportation equal to any other member. "Thus," noted the astute Marcy, "it will be made the interest of every member of the company to watch over and protect the property of others as well as his own."[15]

In developing these constitutions, members took this question into account: "What advantages did such an association offer its members?" In response, members agreed to rotate herding and guarding animals because they knew it meant they could sleep soundly and have some time off. Help would be available if they needed to ford streams, push their wagons over hills, or make a road passable. These covenants thus acknowledged the obvious fact that without establishing such common interests, their companies would break up fast and people would move on to others that would.

Community in Silicon Valley?

This is the language intelligent companies have hit upon to deal with employment in exceedingly turbulent markets—a particular problem for technology firms. On the one hand, firms in such markets have to be able to eliminate jobs in stagnant businesses. On the other, they must find ways to compete for scarce workers who can take them into rapidly expanding new industries. Often their response to these twin pressures is to offer a "new covenant" between company and employee, based on the now widely embraced notion of "employability," first broadly publicized in a 1994 *Harvard Business Review* article by Robert Waterman, Judith Waterman, and Betsy Collard.[16] Since employees can no longer be sure of maintaining a job, they must maintain their ability to find work in changing markets. Under the new covenant, companies agree to help them do so.

At its best, the agreement works something like this. Frank Aragona, an upper-level customer service employee at Raychem (a specialized industrial products maker) felt dead-ended in his job a few years ago. After approaching a decade of working in the same area of his plant he was considering leaving the company, but first decided to try a lunchtime seminar at the company's career counseling center. His interest piqued, and he began working on self-assessment with a counselor, which confirmed that he did indeed need a change, while providing a needed dose of reality. Aragona dropped his wish to become an historian and found a position within Raychem in international sales—one that appealed to the "explorer" in him while building sensibly on his existing skills. Aragona got both a promotion and a raise, and Raychem converted a discouraged and stagnated employee into a freshly enthusiastic one. Both were winners.

Such new employer-employee covenants can create a more mature relationship, allowing both sides to solve problems that previously festered. Suppose a valuable but somewhat burned out software engineer wants off an operating system development project—perhaps it's her fifth in a row—to get into software development for the Internet. A typical response from her manager: "We have an important release date coming up for our new operating system. How can I let one of my best people go to another part of the company when I need her here?"

But if he doesn't, she'll likely quit anyway and go to work for a start-up Internet company, a scene repeated every day in Silicon Valley. And if she did, her boss would figure something out; why not figure it out now, before a valuable employee is lost, and try to accommodate her wish to change fields in an effort to keep her? A workable mutual covenant might require that both employer and employee take responsibility for developing skills she finds rewarding and satisfying and that the market finds valuable. The Internet software she's interested in may well be a big and important market of the future; the very fact a bright employee wants to pursue it indicates a potential new core competence for the company. She should be allowed to pursue it. At the same time, the company retains a say about *when* she moves so it can also protect the existing project.

Getting Respect

So far so good. But often companies that embrace the new covenant forget the formulation that worked so dependably for the temporary communities that moved the nation westward. That is, they forget Randolph Marcy's observation that such agreements must skillfully align the individual interests of people with those of the group as a whole. Here's how this can happen.

Determined first to make themselves as attractive as possible to sought-after workers, and then overlooking Americans' traditional desire to associate, a company will convey this message to employees: We can't assure you a career, and neither can anyone else, so we won't even try. But we'll give you the tools to make you employable anywhere and go so far as to provide you with services like access to career counselors outside the company. Apple, one of the pioneers of employability, told its employees in effect that it couldn't offer them a career, but it could prepare them for their next job.

The result: Such a company will, like Apple did, lose some of its best people. Instead of helping employees grow within the company, it winds up helping them leave. Stanford's Jeffrey Pfeffer, a prominent organizational behavior expert, expresses astonishment that Silicon Valley companies who create such programs are surprised when this happens. "Having told people that they need to be 'career self-reliant' and having provided them with the necessary resources [to become so], the companies are then surprised when they face the very turnover their programs have helped foster."[17] The situation is ironic. Companies that didn't respect employees they laid off now fail to get respect from employees they want to keep.

Rather than appeal to the mercenary interests of employees, employability agreements should bind the mutual interests of employees and their company.

One Silicon Valley firm, Sun Microsystems, has moved its own "career action" program closer to this principle. The Sun program now focuses on *in*placement; career self-reliance there means finding new challenges within the company, as opposed to gaining new skills to take elsewhere. When outplacement is needed, this is done separately by outside firms, to reinforce this distinction.

Thus when employees go to career seminars at Sun, they take assessment tests, benchmark their skills against the best in the industry, and determine what training and education they need to fill the gaps–just as in a conventional employability program. But now Sun reinforces these with periodic brown bag lunches to discuss growth areas within the company, a company intranet that lists job openings and training opportunities inside the firm, and encouragement by Sun managers to do informational interviewing anywhere that interests employees–within the organization.

Such a more balanced "new covenant" helps create a sense of community in a region not known for its fellow feeling. The very act of reconsidering the employer-employee relationship in this way–by frankly acknowledging the interests of both sides and seeking solutions jointly–is itself an expression of community. In addition, when Sun managers participate in information networks that keep people informed of new job openings elsewhere in the company, they interact with a much wider collection of people than they normally would, creating a sense of an important, company-wide shared purpose. When task forces are formed to look for people to fill vacant slots, that effort strengthens it further.

Community in Silicon Valley? It can happen.

4

Revolution, American Style

How does an enterprise substantially change, particularly when change to products, say, or processes, strategies, or even the organization itself must be radical? How does an organization *revolutionize* itself—in a way that fits the traits and sensibilities of an American workforce?

Constructive Revolution

The usual type of "revolution" practiced by many executives strikes fear into the hearts of people. It means an aggressive, even ruthless Lenin and Mao "kill them all" approach to change:[1] Heads roll, employees suffer abrupt, mass layoffs and other callous treatment, fear reigns. It is frankly astonishing that anyone would think that such oppression would improve the strength and vitality of any organization—especially a sick one. As for a reasonably healthy company that just wants to release its creative and entrepreneurial energy, who would want any part of that?

A second type of revolution—what might be called the French version—is more disconcerting to leaders. The initial goal of freeing the people from oppression degenerates into excessive democracy, creating anarchy rather than constructive transformation. The people's pent-up emotions are unchained, chaos ensues, and this time the heads of kings and aristocrats roll until a dictator like Napoleon takes control and restores order. The ultimate result: If there is any real change at all, it's a change for the worse.

The American Revolution, on the other hand, provides a third model–quite different from these first two–for deep, constructive, and lasting transformation. Among revolutions in history, it was both unique in its temperance as well as extraordinary in the depth of change it fostered. It didn't require dire conditions and crushing oppression; Americans revolted in 1776 even though they were as free and prosperous as any people in the world, and knew it.

Neither was it led by a strong-armed leader who burned manor houses, lopped off aristocrats' heads, and killed lots of people–or incited mobs to do so. By all such measures, the American Revolution was a tame and genteel affair. American leaders yielded "to the torrent" of spontaneous and widespread discontent in order to "better direct its course."[2] Their success in doing so lay in their ability to adapt to human nature and a changing world–rather than exert control over or manipulate them.

The result of this new style of revolution was sweeping and constructive change on a scale most organizations only dream about. America's particular need then was as challenging as any enterprise ever faced: to throw off British rule and find new ways to structure society and its governance. What a burst of creativity and new ways of thinking were released in the effort–what a sense that "anything was possible"! Familiar concepts like sovereignty and liberty were completely overturned. The very purpose of government itself was fundamentally changed from promoting the good of the whole to protecting individual liberty as well. New or radically altered ideas about governance, like representative democracy and the extended republic, were introduced, and new mechanisms like separation of powers were devised to make them work. The American state and national governments that emerged were so new and so different that scholars groped for terms adequate to describe them.

Equally important, of course, this burst of creativity *worked* superbly. The new ideas spawned by the Revolution provided the basis for a radically new society with a new order that would enjoy spectacular, and now after more than two hundred years, long-term success.

Here's how this third type of revolution worked.

THREE KEYS TO
REVOLUTIONIZING AMERICAN SOCIETY

What spurred the transformation of American society—and what can change-minded managers learn from it? Three elements were key:

1. *The Grass Roots*
   The energy and ideas for the American Revolution came largely from the grass roots.
2. *The Threat*
   What moved Americans was not an inspiring leadership calling them to a new utopia, but the realization that continuing under the status quo would threaten their livelihoods and their personal autonomy.
3. *Sophisticated Communication*
   Sophisticated and rapid means of communication were essential to the ability of Americans to act in concert—not only to throw off the status quo, but to devise effective new institutions to replace it.

The most important source of energy for the American Revolution came from the grass roots. It was *not* conceived in the minds of a few senior Founding Fathers who wisely foresaw, before anyone else did, the need to separate from Great Britain, and then went out to get "buy in" from the people. Its energy and ideas came as much, if not more, from down in the ranks of society. The Stamp Act protests, for example, the first serious expression of discontent with the status quo, were spontaneous outbursts up and down the Atlantic coast, which completely surprised every American leader, even the forward-thinking Benjamin Franklin.

Indeed, the ideas of America's revolutionary leaders often lagged behind the revolutionary sentiments of large segments of the population. Thomas Jefferson's brilliant rhetoric in the Declaration of Independence, for example, gave voice to ideas and emotions *already* well established throughout the country.[3] By the time Congress made George Washington commander in chief of the Continental Army, revolution as well as the beginnings of political independence from Great Britain were well under way throughout the country: State governments were up and running, local militia had routed the British at Concord, and twenty thousand farmer-soldiers surrounded bewildered British troops hunkered-down in Boston.

The level of participation by ordinary Americans at all levels of society in the destiny of their country was remarkable—and the critical factor in achieving dramatic change. Artisans in New York City, for example, purchased Mechanics Hall and formed a "general committee" to articulate their own view of America's future. Militia privates in Philadelphia established their own committee that proposed to elect all officers, even at the highest ranks. Even in gentrified Virginia, yeoman farmers began pushing their way into public policy councils and insisting on important roles. This ongoing, bottom-up energy and passion were vital to America's capacity to keep producing excellent new leaders as conditions changed: The superb revolutionaries of 1763–1776 such as Samuel Adams and Patrick Henry, were mostly replaced with even more brilliant nation-builders such as George Washington and James Madison between 1776 and 1787.

What *did* convert them? What unleashed the energy and passion needed to reform the whole of American society? It wasn't patriotic zeal, however inspiring the prospect of fighting to protect one's just liberties and those of one's countrymen might seem; even in the midst of the war with Britain, patriotism quickly gave way to profiteering and political squabbling.

Rather, Americans were moved to throw off the status quo, fight a war against a dangerous and vengeful enemy, and reinvent a society they had always felt a deep attachment to because they understood that continuing under British rule threatened their livelihoods and their freedom. There are important insights here for organizations seeking to energize their workforces.

Harnessing Energy at the Grass Roots

The shrewdest revolutionary leaders, such as Boston's radical Samuel Adams, didn't bother to devise a soaring vision or body of revolutionary dogma. Rather, they worked tirelessly to *communicate* the latest tangible threat to American safety and liberty, and they *fostered* ongoing communication between like-minded revolutionaries throughout America.

Adams wrote forty articles for the *Boston Gazette* after the Boston Massacre, the first deadly encounter between Americans and skittish British troops in the years leading up to the Revolution. In a town meeting held after the skirmish, Adams proposed forming the now-legendary Boston Committee of Correspondence, so that local patriots could meet, formulate ideas, and, above all, communicate with other revolutionaries throughout the colonies. "Let every town assemble," wrote Adams, "Let associations and combinations everywhere be set up to consult. . . ." His plan was ridiculed by traditional leaders as useless and trifling—what *authority* did such people have, what power could they wield? But the brilliant Adams understood the power of bringing together Americans who were facing a common threat.

American boycotts organized by such committees in response to the Stamp Act, for example, forced the mighty British Parliament itself to back down and repeal it, under siege from English merchants and manufacturers and hundreds of unemployed English workers. With the crisis thus averted, the committees disbanded—but Adams saw that the pattern could be easily reprised as subsequent British threats emerged.

Adams's idea quickly took flight and became vital to mobilizing collective action. Patriots in some eighty towns throughout Massachusetts soon created their own committees of correspondence, exchanging and spreading information and propaganda—using newspapers, pamphlets, and an increasingly efficient postal system. These groups, under various names like Boston's Sons of Liberty, were creatures of discipline and order, not anarchy. Often they were created by local town councils, and had their own carefully framed "constitutions." Their purpose was specific: to respond to the latest British threat and exchange vital information with other committees of correspondence, to develop new ideas, and to plan concerted action such as boycotts if needed.

Patriots in Virginia such as Jefferson and Patrick Henry noticed Adams's success and took the next step by creating an intercolonial committee of correspondence. Within a short time, every American colony had a central committee through which it could exchange information and ideas with other colonies.[4]

The importance of this grassroots energy to the success of the American Revolution can't be overstated. This, and not some inspiring vision or hero leader on horseback, was the key to making revolution a reality in America. The committees of correspondence gave order and discipline to widely dispersed sentiments, spawned a new generation of dynamic leaders, and fostered essential ideas about what should replace the status quo. They evolved directly into the legislatures and congresses that would, with remarkable dexterity, take over the operations of government from the ousted British.

FOMENTING A REVOLUTION, AMERICAN STYLE

Doesn't such a model for revolution make more sense in a free society—and in the organizations that operate there? Particularly where a workforce includes a high percentage of independent minded, self-determining, and resourceful employees? The situation in many such companies is strikingly similar to pre-Revolutionary America. Like Americans then, employees are well aware of the threats to their livelihoods—whether from competition or from more exacting customers. And like them, they have increasingly sophisticated methods to communicate and plan concerted action. Why not build on these, encouraging one's own "torrent of energy" for fundamental change? Here's how some companies are doing so.

Tap Ideas at the Grass Roots, Then Gain a Critical Mass of Support

Some executives are finding what America's revolutionary leaders discovered: Insight, creativity, and knowledge essential to fundamentally change an enterprise, even to the extent of changing its strategy, are spread throughout an organization.

Chrysler's dramatic turnaround in the early 1990s, for example, was not spearheaded by a charismatic CEO armed with a vision. Rather, the post-Iacocca regime under Robert Eaton performed brilliantly because it tapped the knowledge already embedded in the organization. It turned out that middle managers down in the ranks had the answers, including the ideas that went into the sleek new LH cars with their clever "cab forward" design. Chrysler's new management was smart enough to gain a critical mass of support for ideas already worked out by people in the organization.

Similarly, jam and jelly maker J. M. Smucker energized its stagnant business a few years ago, in a market regarded as mature, by enlisting a group of 140 employees to rethink strategy. Then these employees acted as ambassadors to solicit input from all two thousand people in the organization. The result was a dozen new strategic initiatives, including formation of alliances to "co-brand" products such as a new line of Smuckers jellybeans, manufactured by Brach & Brock Confections.

And, despite a growth rate of 70 percent a year in the volatile telecommunications business, the Nokia Group decided to expand strategic thinking by involving 250 people in its 1995 strategy review. They came up with a number of new product options, including a "smart car" unit in Germany that applies the company's knowledge of cellular communications to make navigation and road guidance systems for automobiles. Nokia Group executives have found that engaging so many people in strategy creation makes strategy implementation easier. The process wins a "high degree of commitment," observed one executive, and in any case, planners end up with a number of good ideas they haven't considered before.

None of this suggests that leadership should rely on employees to tell them what the company should be doing; employee input can't supplant a top management that is bankrupt of strategic ideas. But employees should participate actively in the strategic decisions they'll ultimately have to implement.

Foster Communication

But, goes one objection, lower-level people lack the perspective to participate in real strategy formulation. Division managers, for instance, caught up in the day-to-day rush of running their own business, have no time for creatively exploiting, or even recognizing, "synergies" with other parts of the company. Hewlett-Packard chairman Lewis Platt directly challenges the rationale for centralizing strategy-making with the CEO as chief strategist. Platt's solution is not to remove lower-level people from strategy creation and lose their knowledge, but rather to find ways to correct their lack of perspective. That is, rather than control strategy at the top, Platt fosters communication among the units so they can influence and shape it.

He states cheerfully that he doesn't create business strategies; rather he brings the general managers of HP's various businesses together to find ways of exploiting opportunities in the gaps or "white spaces" between their individual businesses. These sessions are broadly attended—they include customers and suppliers—and an expansive view is encouraged in the hopes that dramatically new business opportunities will emerge. Participants define and think about the "ecosystem" of their business: the wider environment that includes suppliers, distributors, customers, competitors, and so forth.

One session held for HP's auto industry business included people who make service-bay diagnostic equipment for Ford, others who make work stations for auto manufacturing plants, and others who make electronic components for automobiles—together with various customers and suppliers. The question was posed: What could all these units do together to create new value for the industry? The process spawned genuinely creative ideas that the company would never have generated through a staff-driven strategy process, including "smart" highway systems as well as integrated systems that collect auto service data and feed it immediately back to Detroit.

But note: Division managers just one or two levels down from the top in an organization aren't necessarily in close touch with ideas and sentiments on the front lines. It's these frontline people, after all, who have to implement strategies. One way to tap their knowledge is to involve frontline supervisors, such as shop foremen, in strategy creation. They're often the ones who know best whether strategic plans will work, and since these plans often *won't* work as initially drawn up, they'll know best how to fix them. Unlike staff, who often rely on hard data or "the numbers" to formulate new ideas that can wind up being divorced from realities faced by employees, frontline managers who've been around and have seen a lot rely on experience, "feel," and their own self-evident observations. Such input results in better strategy-making: strategic plans that actually get implemented and achieve results.

This is a major departure for most companies, but a growing number are making it, and not only in the United States. Executives at British Nissan's factory, for example, consult all 230 supervisors while formulating corporate strategy. The company has found that not only does this process create better-informed strategies, it also increases information flow from the shop floor up to senior managers–an ideal many companies talk about but never figure out how to achieve.[5]

Giving floor managers and shop foremen larger roles in strategy-making can strengthen the organization in many ways. It can help keep top management's thinking grounded in the real world. It can also help legitimize, and thus generate support for, strategic decisions among frontline employees. Contrary to conventional wisdom, plant and shop-floor supervisors are *more* likely to embrace new manufacturing methods than higher level managers are. The reason?–anything to make their jobs easier! Ford learned this wisdom almost by accident while developing the fabled Taurus. Executives at its Atlanta factory decided to try something new–asking supervisors how to build a better car–and received surprisingly valuable input. One veteran, for example, devised a simpler body-assembly process that remote managers would never have dreamed up in their offices. It cut production time, improved quality, and saved substantial money.

Communicate the Threat, Let People Figure Out How to Respond

Jack Stack, who would later build the highly admired Springfield Remanufacturing Company, learned the value of communicating the goal to people–particularly a goal that arises from a real threat–when he faced a number of dire circumstances as a young manager at International Harvester.

When he was made superintendent of the worst-performing division in the company, for example, he saw no hope of turning it around using conventional International Harvester systems. Five hundred union workers were building three hundred engines a day, broken down into hundreds of highly segmented tasks. Changing just one engine on the line required reallocating some 275 jobs. An engineering analysis showed that the production line was capable of achieving a ten dollars per person higher output, but that was theory. How could Stack and his engineers achieve such a gain in practice under a union contract that forbade management from adding one minute to one section of the line without changing every other job, to ensure "fairness"?

So Stack decided to go directly to his people and tell them what the real need was: to increase overall productivity of this, the worst-performing division. He issued a competitive challenge: If they could beat their all-time best number, he'd buy them all coffee. If they could beat it again the next week, he'd buy coffee and rolls. If they could beat it again a third time, he'd have them over to his house for pizza and beer. Three weeks later, his wife and he were entertaining the entire first shift, two hundred people.

Impressed by the results, Stack continued to prod the division with interdepartment bets. The eventual result was a productivity increase that more than tripled the engineer's forecast of ten dollars per employee and a division that was now finishing first in productivity comparisons with other International Harvester facilities.

Stack tried the same approach again after he moved to the tractor division and learned that it was eight hundred tractors short on a contract with the former Soviet Union, had only one month (twenty workdays) to go before ship date, and was squeezing only five tractors a day off the assembly line. The company was facing a huge penalty, and plant officials agreed that heads were about to roll, and they should keep this a secret.

But Stack went directly to the assembly line again and laid out the whole situation, letting workers know what was at stake and asking them to find some way to meet the deadline, improbable as it seemed. He posted a sign outside his office: "Our Goal: 800 Tractors." Now the workers, accustomed to performing tightly defined, highly segmented jobs according to standards they regarded as meaningless, were presented with a meaningful challenge. And Stack made clear they had the freedom to figure out how to meet it. By the end of the month, they'd assembled and shipped 808 tractors–having increased their production rate from five to an astonishing fifty-five per day.[6]

Stack became so confident that he could turn under-performing businesses around in this way, he and a group of managers bought one from International Harvester in the early 1980s–which became Springfield Remanufacturing Company (SRC). (Stack was right: Their original investment of $100,000 grew to $25 million in ten years.) A few years ago, a competitor for the company's fuel-injection pump market, a very low-margin business, tried to take a big customer away by cutting prices 6 percent below SRC's. The customer gave SRC three months to cut its costs accordingly, a serious threat to the business since the company's engineers saw no way to do it. So Stack took the problem to the pump-room employees themselves. He explained what they were up against: The pumps sold for about two hundred dollars and they had to find a way to knock twelve dollars off the cost to save the account. "Then I put a picture of the other company's CEO on the wall," says Stack, "along with a copy of its financial statements. I said, 'Here's the guy who's trying to take your jobs away from you, and I'm afraid I don't know how to stop him.'" That stoked their competitive fires.[7]

The pump-room employees formed a task force and put up a thermometer set at two hundred dollars. Then they started talking about where they could save a few cents here or a dime there. They scrutinized their hardware; they went over all material costs with a fine-tooth comb. One member noticed that a vendor charged more for an item than the local Ace Hardware did. After three months they had cut the price not twelve dollars but forty dollars, for a 20 percent reduction in cost that no engineer could have achieved–saving the account as well as their jobs.

5

Give Me Liberty

Governance That Unleashes
American Ingenuity

There is no doubt that increasing the participation of employees in decision-making can substantially improve corporate performance. Study after study in industry after industry, from textiles to integrated steel to semiconductors to retailing, has shown this. Companies that give employees greater knowledge and decision-making power, and make substantial use of participative tools such as information sharing, training for multiple jobs, performance related pay, and suggestion systems are able to substantially improve productivity and quality, and reduce waste and employee turnover. A well-designed, multi-industry analysis by Rutgers' Mark Huselid of the *financial* impact of such tools shows a remarkable influence, when they are integrated into a system of "high performance" work practices that includes rigorous employee selection procedures and performance awards. A one standard deviation increase in Huselid's high-performance index creates an average increase of $27,000 in firm sales per employee, $3,800 in profit per employee, and $18,600 in firm market value per employee. And these results—at least for the 968 firms in Huselid's study—were independent of firm strategy. If such practices are closely aligned with a firm's specific strategic goals, the potential for improved performance is even greater.[1]

Further, employee participation is an effective way to implement other sweeping-change initiatives. Total-quality programs that put responsibility for quality on individual shop-floor workers are twice as likely to succeed as those that rely on top-down management for implementation.[2] Large gains of up to 40 percent and higher in key performance measures such as productivity, finished inventory turns, and gross margins are achieved by companies that combine participation with tools such as lean manufacturing or modular production systems.[3]

But beyond the studies is the simple, common sense fact that in a relentlessly turbulent environment, with rapid and unpredictable changes in markets and technologies, companies must find ways to place great freedom and authority in the hands of frontline employees.

Yet despite the studies, and the clear need for doing so, management has a difficult time embracing the notion of real employee participation. Here is one remarkable indication of this.

Procter & Gamble's Secret—Revealed

Thirty-five years ago, Procter & Gamble began organizing its new plants around self-managed teams that scheduled production, interviewed, and hired people, evaluated their own members as well as managers, and devised their own training programs. The productivity of each plant was astonishingly 30 to 40 percent higher than those organized under traditional hierarchies. P&G then began installing the same system in its existing, older plants, which proved much harder because of stubborn resistance from suspicious managers and workers—yet still resulted eventually in the same level of productivity gains. So clear were the benefits that the company tried to keep this new management approach secret as a competitive advantage.

And yet, as it turns out, P&G needn't have worried: Three decades later, fewer than 10 percent of American employees (probably *far* fewer) work for firms that practice true, systemic employee participation, or what is sometimes called "workplace democracy." Many managers remain skeptical of the idea, or they place more emphasis on other, more easily implemented methods for improving performance. But a number of executives like the idea of substantial employee participation, yet still can't make it work.

Here is a remarkable anomaly. American firms are leaving a clear competitive advantage—one that obviously resonates with our social and political heritage—sitting on the table. Eighty percent and more of Americans who don't work for companies that practice employee participation would like a greater say in their workplaces; perhaps 90 percent of those who *do* work in such places think it's a "good idea." The 100 firms considered the "100 Best Companies to Work For in America" are increasingly embracing employee participation.[4]

Our focus in this chapter will be on what keeps companies from making workplace democracy succeed, even when senior managers support it, and how they can overcome the obstacles. These are questions, it would seem, that are well worth answering in the interest of achieving such considerable improvement in business performance. The answers lie in striking the balance between too little democracy and too much. As the Founding Fathers themselves knew, this is easier said than done.

A TIGER BY THE TAIL

We can start here: Limited or one-shot attempts at employee participation don't work. Hundreds and probably thousands of firms have tried them, but studies show no real results when they do. In companies that do achieve the kinds of performance gains described above, employee participation:

- is long-term and widely dispersed throughout the organization or unit.
- is institutionalized through changes to compensation, training and reward systems, as well as management practices—tangible measures that engender employee trust.
- takes on a life of its own, which is perhaps the most difficult trait for management to accept.[5]

Where employee participation is long-term and deeply ingrained in companies, where it is *systemic*, it becomes increasingly hard to draw the line between "employee issues" and "production issues," for example, or between employees themselves and supervisors or managers. High-tech companies, which are often particularly anxious to embed participative practices into their organizations, can look almost structureless. Work is done by temporary, "vertical slice" groups of managers and employees. Higher authorities or organizational structures don't form them; they form themselves. Executives and managers must learn to relinquish the power and control they're accustomed to exercising.

The results at companies that achieve this can be impressive. At

Compaq, for example, top management's role in product development is now limited to approving the product concept, establishing
design-to-cost parameters, and forming an initial small group to
begin development. After that there are usually no formal approvals
required from top management, even for product launch. The developers act on their own: They're the ones who recognize "this is an
engineering issue" or "this is a manufacturing issue" and then go out
and get the people they need to help solve it. The process moves
through the company "like a shock wave," as one executive puts it,
adding other members as needed from whatever function is required
to work out production, logistics, procurement, publicity, and other
issues. This ability—to add just the right people at just the right time—
is the secret to getting new products into the hands of customers fast,
sometimes in as little as four months. And there's no way such a
process could be controlled by remote authority: The organization
must give employees the freedom to do so themselves.

Unleashing the Forces of Democracy

Such stories are impressive and common among firms that embrace
participation—but they can lead to unrealistic expectations. Managers
believe greater employee freedom and responsibility will result,
by themselves, in greater cooperation and harmony. Unfortunately
there's more to the story.

Management that embraces true employee participation is
unleashing the forces of democracy, for good and for ill, in its organization. It must deal with difficult issues of power, liberty, and rights.
And despite the best efforts of leaders to articulate a common vision
and common purpose, employees in these firms persist in having their
own purposes, forming their own opinions about the business, and
pursuing their own interests, which somewhat surprisingly startles
even the most enlightened management.

When electronic-components maker Solectron decided to implement an aggressive employee-participation program, executives
thought it would be smooth sailing. A pilot program on one production line boasted a 20 percent gain in productivity, plus substantial
gains in quality (and this at a company that had won the Malcolm
Baldrige Award). Further, employee participation would free techni-
cally oriented middle managers to do what they'd always complained there was too little time for—to plan and develop
technology—because they were too busy supervising people. And
there would be little danger of layoffs because the company had
been growing rapidly for years. Nevertheless, many Solectron mid-

dle managers resisted the new regime: They didn't want to lose the status and control they'd acquired!

Conflict seems particularly surprising in firms with substantial employee ownership—yet there it is. Within a year and a half after United Airlines' employees bought the firm and were tossing bouquets at each other and management, pilots and mechanics were waging bruising battles for wage hikes against the CEO they'd picked to head the firm. "Greedy," "unfair," and "selfish" chided pundits with some justification, undoubtedly voicing the opinion of management. The new employee/owners persisted in pursuing their own self-interest. What would it take to make them "act like owners"?

But conflict, the pursuit of self-interest, and the desire to gain or hold power are inherent in human nature. At some point after the initial good feelings and sense of common purpose are established, differences will arise that good communication techniques, exhortations to "trust," or charismatic and visionary leadership won't make go away—and governance should not rest on the assumption they will.

The effort to come to terms with these differences is worth it. Despite well-publicized conflicts at employee-owned firms like United, employee ownership combined with employee participation dramatically improves corporate performance. One particularly thorough study by the National Center for Employee Ownership (NCEO) found, for example, that firms which combine these factors grow 8 to 11 percent per year faster than firms that don't. Several subsequent studies have consistently confirmed both the result and the magnitude of the NCEO study.[6]

The key is to create governance that preserves democracy's ability to unleash individual creativity and entrepreneurism on the one hand, while restraining it's potential to spawn factions and social chaos on the other. The trick is to do so in a way that American employees—skeptical of authority, cynical about HR programs—will perceive as legitimate. The best sources of insight for realizing all these goals are the ideology and tools that established American society itself.

HOW THE FOUNDERS ESTABLISHED "EMPOWERMENT" IN AMERICA

Although there is certainly no easy formula for creating governance that will deal with issues of conflict and power successfully, in the search for principles we can start here: Such issues go to elemental, deeply held values in Americans that we've worked through before.

When they established the nation in 1787, the American founders faced a set of challenges very similar to those facing organizations like United Airlines. The hopes of the earlier Revolutionary leaders that freedom in America would usher in a new age of enlightenment, cooperation, and civic virtue had all gone up in smoke. The states in particular, after 1776, had fallen into chaos; American leaders were horrified that democratically elected legislatures were turning into battlegrounds between opposing factions and acting to oppress their enemies as shamelessly as any British minister ever had—instead of working to further the welfare of the whole. "*We have probably,*" wrote George Washington with emphasis, "*had too good an opinion of human nature in forming our confederation.*" How could such a people ever be organized into a coherent nation that would stop their bickering, much less release their considerable economic potential?

Doing so required American leaders to go back and think through fundamentals, and they responded with concepts of governance extraordinary for their creativity and effectiveness. The key was a radical new concept of power that would seem, at first, only to worsen the situation. But, remarkably, it proved essential to achieving their primary objectives, which were strikingly similar to the needs of organizations embracing workplace democracy:

- restraining excessive democracy,
- strengthening central governance to give it the "energy" needed to form national purposes and act decisively to achieve them,
- doing these in a manner consistent, of course, with the (apparently contradictory) ideals of the American Revolution—most important, with the demands of Americans for greater *freedom*.

The Radical Nature of Power in America

To achieve these objectives, the founders began by grasping what had always eluded the British. There was simply no way to organize Americans without giving them a genuine say, not just over aspects of immediate concern to their lives but in any governance that seeks to wield power over them. This is the line that must be crossed to move away from autocracy, to win both the acceptance and the trust of the people, and to assure them the freedom they would need to fully develop economically.

Indeed as Americans of all sorts engaged in an unprecedented and widespread discussion and clarification about the nature of power, American leaders gradually embraced a bold departure from the conventional concept. Here, at this basic point, the governance they devised differs fundamentally—and radically—from the empowerment practiced by many corporations.

Often, the power conferred on employees is actually a delegation of power, which can be withdrawn. Executives and managers are encouraged to "give" more authority, as well as responsibility, to employees—a concept the founders were very familiar with. That's essentially how the British ruled America; but such power could be, and *was*, withdrawn, almost always with tumultuous consequences.

American leaders after the Revolution recognized the inherent contradiction of such a notion of power in a free society. All power, they concluded, must be in the hands of the people. The people would no longer be *subjects* but *citizens*—each a unit of the mass of free individuals who collectively hold all power. This was not only an elegant way to gain acceptance of a system that would be capable of strong governance, it was the only way. Who else could hold leaders accountable, except free citizens? How else could freedoms vital to the country's development be protected? If power were to be seen by the people as truly legitimate, it could have no other source.

But who, then, are the experts in policy making, the ultimate arbiters? As Benjamin Franklin had tried to explain years earlier to British ministers who were puzzled that the taxes they'd imposed from London were causing riots in America, "Those who feel [the effects of policy] can best judge." Better to inform and educate citizens who participate actively in governance than try to force unaccountable power down the throats of unwilling subjects.

And yet paradoxically, remarkably, placing all power in the hands of free citizens would itself provide the means to restrain excessive democracy, as we'll see in a moment.

Employees as Citizens

Does such a radical notion of power still seem so strange for an organization, or does it give us a glimpse into the future? Wouldn't companies be better off basing their governance on corporate "citizens"?

Notice the effect on corporate performance, for example, when *shareholders* exercise the rights and responsibilities of citizenship, when they take an active role in firm governance, hold management accountable for performance and actively intervene where performance is poor. When the California Public Employees Retirement System (CalPERS), a major institutional investor, does so, the results are extraordinary. The average performance of sixty-two firms pressured by CalPERS went from lagging behind the Standard & Poor 500 Index by 85 percent in the five years prior to intervention, to outperforming the S&P index by 33.6 percent over the five years after intervention.[7]

Further, prospective *new* investors will pay a big premium—an average of 11 percent, for the stock of a company that has "good governance," according to an extensive survey by McKinsey. That is, if it has a strong and independent board of directors that aggressively represents the interests of shareholders and holds management accountable.[8]

While the issue of who are a firm's "stakeholders" is beyond our scope here, shouldn't *employees*–who have a much more intimate knowledge of the firm than shareowners do, and often at least as great a stake in its success–have as much power as they to participate in firm governance?

Margaret Blair of the Brookings Institution has shown that many employees today *have* an economic ownership stake in their firms, even without buying shares. This is particularly true of knowledge workers, who make firm-specific investments by developing specific skills that can't be easily marketed elsewhere. If these employees feel they can't protect themselves from downsizing or bankruptcy, they will underinvest in such firm-specific skills and thus squander opportunities for the company to create wealth.[9]

Many executives in the trenches increasingly realize the importance of getting the input of people before making decisions that affect them—even those decisions normally considered the preserve of top management. This is particularly clear after the restructuring fiascos many companies have lived through in the past several years. Rather than guess how people feel when making the decision, then go around trying to get them to agree (how often does that work for truly difficult decisions?), why not formalize the process of getting their input so management can know where they stand according to fair governance processes, and so the resulting decision will have immediate legitimacy?

Consider Intel's experience where top management continued pushing the company into the memory chip business long after employees had realized it should get out. Intel's management had been fooled by its own "strategic rhetoric," admits CEO Andy Grove. People on the front lines, responding to the market pressures they encountered every day, recognized the need to retreat. For two full years before senior management realized the error, project leaders, marketing managers, and plant supervisors had been diverting the resources under their control away from increasingly unprofitable memory chips and toward more lucrative microprocessors.

Why not strive to create governance that carries out not the will of an individual leader or small group of leaders, but rather "the will of the organization"?

How the Founders Controlled Excessive Democracy . . .

A major concern in attempting to create democratic governance is the fear of excessive democracy. But in building America, the concept of citizenship—the idea that all power is already in the hands of the people—provided the very means both to *restrict* the excesses of democracy as well as to *strengthen* central leadership. Here's how.

In America, citizens would exercise their power—*not* to run things; there would be no "policy making by majority vote"—but instead through a scheme of representation. They would select, directly or indirectly, representatives to make and carry out policy. Thus the founders created not a democracy but a *republic.* While still based on the bold concept of power outlined above, the republic would have safeguards and "filters" for restraining excessive democracy—a concept perfectly acceptable even to liberty-loving Americans.

For example, the Constitution limited the number of representatives in the legislature, increased their length of term, created reasonable qualifications for office holding, and stipulated that some officials be chosen indirectly (the president through electors, for example; judges were appointed by the president and confirmed by the Senate). Indeed, the Senate—a second legislative house with fewer members than the House of Representatives, longer terms, "at large" elections, and a higher age qualification—was itself seen as a restraint on the democratic tendencies of the House. Senators would thus be able to act, as James Madison put it, "with more coolness, with more system, and with more wisdom, than the popular branch."

. . . While Strengthening Governance

This scheme of representation, together with a dynamic system of checks and balances, and not autocracy, were the tools the founders used to strengthen and energize national governance. Keep in mind, these tools did not represent a trimming back of their overarching goal of maximizing the freedom of individuals. Rather the founders simply addressed a new and unexpected threat to that aspiration: Excessively democratic majorities could act as tyrannically as any autocrat, and therefore it was just as important to protect against them too. Thus to create a strong yet republican government for the nation, the founders again went back to fundamentals.

They asked, "What are the primary powers of governance?" They sought answers less from any theoretical ideal, and more from the earlier experiences of the colonies and states, along with their reading of history. The answers they came up with are now familiar to us: the legislature (making policy and laws), the executive (executing policy and laws), and the judiciary (enforcement). But there is nothing magic about such a division. Why did they settle on this particular breakdown and not some other? (It was originally thought, for example, that judges should work for the executive rather than be separate.) Actual experience had shown that this tripartite system was the best way to divide governance. When these particular powers had been held too long or had been too heavily influenced by the same body, it was bad for the state and bad for its people.

The way to achieve energetic governance, then, was to identify those powers that experience showed should be kept separate, and strengthen them by making sure they were kept independent as well. This wasn't rocket science. When colonial governors, for example, had appointed representatives from the colonial legislatures to executive branch offices, the result too often was corruption. The same occurred when judges served at the whim of governors or legislatures rather than for life terms. A comparable situation occurs today when a CEO appoints directors, particularly those who serve on compensation or audit committees—a move now widely acknowledged as one that weakens governance.

Creating a Strong Chief Executive

The founders then buttressed this notion of separation of powers with a system of checks and balances. One of the early mistakes of the American revolutionaries was to create divisions on paper, or "mere parchment barriers" between the respective departments, which were inevitably violated. State legislatures, for example, took to settling private disputes between people in clear violation of their constitutions—a power that should be exercised by more impartial judges. To prevent this in the new national government, the founders placed certain powers in the hands of the various departments specifically to allow each to resist encroachments by the others. The executive, for example, could veto acts of the legislature; in turn, the legislature could override the executive's veto with a two-thirds majority.

These were the tools—a scheme of representation plus a system of checks and balances—with which the founders created a strong national government, and in particular a strong executive. They strengthened the president first by giving him an independent power base. He was selected not by Congress, but by the people through electors; he would represent the people rather than exist as a creature of the legislature. Then, with this strong base of legitimacy and support, the founders conferred suitable powers so that the president could act with all the "energy" he needed. He would be commander in chief of the military and appoint all his own executive-branch subordinates. In combination with the smaller Senate, the executive branch holds all the executive power and much of the legislative power: Between them they make all treaties and appoint all civil and military officers.

Finally, to affirm the ultimate source of power in America and confer legitimacy on its leaders, the whole plan of governance was formalized in a written Constitution that was itself submitted to the participatory process, requiring at least nine of thirteen states to approve. And the founders added a Bill of Rights that further confirmed their commitment to freedom: The power of the state can't be brought against an individual without due process of law, and there are certain rights—such as freedom of speech, freedom of assembly, and equal rights under the law for all people—that even legitimate power can't infringe. Indeed the relationship of liberty and power that emerged in America was this: Liberty was expansive; government should define only its inner boundaries. Power on the other hand must be restricted; its outer boundaries must be set.

How efficient was such a scheme? Keep in mind that when we see gridlock in government and start to shake our heads, very likely the ability of people to act without undue restraint, the ultimate goal of governance in America, has just been preserved. Certainly Americans have pursued important, national goals with great effectiveness: the westward expansion, the Monroe Doctrine, the abolition of slavery, the World Wars, the battles against the Depression and communism, to say nothing of the Industrial Revolution. An absence of democratic restraints on power, on the other hand, might very well have hampered the individual creativity and resourcefulness crucial to the success of all these efforts.[10]

What is abundantly clear is that the new social order created by the American founders freed up tremendous economic energy where it counted—in the people. A dynamic new kind of society emerged in the world, composed of energetic, initiative-taking, wealth-creating citizens, as opposed to the passive subordinates typical virtually everywhere else.

THE NEW CORPORATE REPUBLICS

Create an organization of "citizens"—with the same power and status they enjoy in their communities and nation? As far-fetched as it still might sound, substantial pieces and parts of that concept have been working their way into mainstream American corporations for years. Here we'll see how. Notice the impact in particular on the dynamism of their employees.

Representative Governance at Donnelly

Donnelly Corporation in western Michigan is about as mainstream as a company can get. An automobile industry supplier, it makes rearview mirrors (controlling about 90 percent of the market), exterior mirrors, molded windshields, and other precision glass products. While many American auto industry companies experienced financial crises, downsizing, and bankruptcy during the 1980s, Donnelly was growing at a compounded annual rate of more than 16 percent a year. Over the last decade, while car and light truck production in North America and Europe have been relatively flat, Donnelly's sales have quadrupled: Its "dollar content per vehicle produced in North America" for example, has gone from about $7.50 to over $25. A primary reason for its resilience is a workforce among the happiest and most motivated in the country. Two times Robert Levering and Milton Moskowitz have included it in *The 100 Best Companies to Work for in America*, once as one of the top ten.

Donnelly workers' satisfaction is the result of a remarkable governance structure called the "equity structure," which was organized like a republic years ago by longtime CEO John Donnelly. Each employee has considerable freedom—to learn new jobs, to change job assignments, to control his or her career path. Each factory and office is organized into small teams; every Donnelly employee is accountable not just to a supervisor but, more important, to her team. The teams set their own goals and have broad discretion in how they do their work.

Each team then chooses a representative to a forum for the entire building, called an equity committee, which decides matters of concern to the entire plant or office—such as start time for shifts, lunchroom issues, and vacation policies. Each equity committee in turn chooses a representative to the Donnelly Committee—a sort of employee Senate. Its fifteen or so members include the equity committee representatives together with a senior officer of the company, often the president. The current chairman of the Donnelly Committee, a full-time job, is a former production operator. The Donnelly Committee isn't a decision-making body (to avoid problems with the National Labor Relations Board, which would regard it as a union) but it makes recommendations that carry great weight on matters of general employee concern, such as employment policies, wage and benefit plans, and job-listing procedures.

When the company had to dramatically cut costs in the late 1980s, instituting voluntary layoffs of two to three weeks and actually eliminating sixty office jobs, it managed to do so in a way employees perceived as fair. The equity structure solicited employees for ideas, studied and debated them, and came up with a plan: temporary salary reductions for everyone making over $40,000 per year, ranging from a low of 4 percent up to 17 percent for senior executives. Salaries were reinstated about half a year later, after company performance improved.

This substantial involvement by employees in governance creates a remarkably dynamic workforce. Their conversations tend to be free of clichés or a party line. They offer fresh and original ideas about the business and its future, stimulated by a variety of speakers—from futurists to executives from other firms—brought in to challenge thinking and keep it fresh. When James Womack, author of *The Machine That Changed the World*, came to the company to speak about lean manufacturing, he didn't address only senior executives and plant managers, but a cross section of five hundred Donnelly employees. Twice in the last several years the company has won national awards for having the most suggestions per employee of any company in the United States.

Their experience with the give and take of participation also prepares Donnelly employees to work well with other firms when the company enters into alliances or joint ventures, something the company excels at. In 1986 Honda picked Donnelly to make the mirrors for all its American-made cars despite the fact that the company had never made exterior mirrors and had no plant for doing so. It didn't matter. Honda officials were impressed by the way Donnelly workers get involved, take responsibility and use their creativity and resourcefulness as well as their technical skills.

Equally striking is the reputation Donnelly has acquired among prospective workers. The company has thirteen thousand applications on file, about four for every job. At one plant opening, 150 production jobs generated four thousand applications. Western Michigan hopefuls have been known to camp out in line the night before so they can get their applications in first thing in the morning.

A Bill of Rights at FedEx

Federal Express is known for its highly motivated workforce; one of the main reasons it has one is a particular policy that works essentially as an employee bill of rights. Called Guaranteed Fair Treatment (GTF), and explained in posters and plaques hung throughout the company, it allows any employee who feels he's been treated unfairly to "GTF" his manager, and take the issue all the way to Chairman Fred Smith if he believes it is warranted, all within twenty-one days. Here's how it works.

The employee starts by taking his complaint to his manager first, in an effort to bring it out in the open and settle it on the spot. If the employee is not satisfied with the result, he can then take it to a three-person board of appeal. His boss's manager, the manager's manager, and a managing director have seven days to review, deliberate, and decide the issue. If still unsatisfied, the employee may take it to a panel consisting of the division vice presidents and senior vice presidents, who likewise have seven days to deliberate and decide.

If still unsatisfied, even if all decisions have gone squarely against him, the employee may then take it to a sort of FedEx Supreme Court, a five-person panel consisting of the chairman, the COO (chief operating officer), the senior personnel officer, and two senior vice presidents. If they think the case has merit they will empanel a group of five people, three of whom are peers picked by the employee himself, to hear the case and decide it. FedEx is thus one of the few companies in the world to provide aggrieved employees with the right to a trial by a jury that includes their peers.

Remarkably, the policy is not as threatening to managers as it might sound. When Levering and Moskowitz were researching their most recent version of *The 100 Best Companies*, they asked a group of FedEx managers how many had been taken through the process. Everyone in the room raised a hand, one commenting that anyone who hadn't been "GTF-ed" either hadn't been there long, didn't manage many people, or didn't have a very complicated job. The manager regarded the system as a good "flush out" for resolving issues that might otherwise fester, as well as for helping interpret the company's Policy and Procedure (P&P) manual. "Can anybody read the P&P and interpret it correctly every single time?" he asked, exhibiting a view of leadership in a democratic society that Thomas Jefferson would certainly have approved.[11]

Most important, the GTF process instills in employees the conviction that the company treats them fairly. These disputes are not kept under wraps and "within the family": the company likes to publicize them. One courier told Levering and Moskowitz how she'd been fired for what she regarded as a technical violation of company policy, and filed a GTF. Her boss and both lower appeal panels found against her, but she remained convinced she was right, and eventually won after going through the whole GTF process. But that wasn't the end. Her boss began seeking retribution, doing "everything he could to make life uncomfortable," she recalled. So she filed again, this time for harassment, won again, and this time her manager was relieved of any supervisory duties. "I feel much more secure," she told Levering and Moskowitz, "knowing that if I have been treated unfairly, there is a way to get to Mr. Smith and say, 'Would you please look at this and give me your opinion?'"[12]

FedEx has thus institutionalized a remarkable and powerful aspect of employee citizenship. Smith himself has a deep dedication to the values that arose from the American Revolution—that all power must protect the rights and respect the dignity and worth of each individual. In a company widely admired for the high morale of its employees and their dedication to customer service, he believes that such a clear assurance of fairness is a prime reason they treat the company, and its customers, well.

Accountability of Leaders at GE

A particularly hard obstacle in the effort to place more power in the hands of employees is a boss who doesn't want to give up control. Jack Welch, for example, considered this a major obstacle in his efforts to revitalize GE in the 1980s. Part of the solution was Work Out. Autocratic bosses can often hide from superiors who themselves are overworked, but not from their employees—especially employees encouraged to speak out by top management and who are given a forum to do so. Bosses who are exposed regularly to employees who ask why they have to fill out useless forms, perform meaningless work, or go through unnecessary channels to get something done find it hard to keep oppressing them.

A second important part of the solution was instituting a 360-degree review process, which includes upward appraisals of managers by employees. GE has done away with the ordinary performance review, a superior sitting down with a manager and telling her how well she did. Now GE managers are evaluated on two things. First is whether their business or unit "made the numbers." Second, they are evaluated on how well they adhere to the GE values, which include having a global outlook, the ability to deal with change, integrity, development of personnel, and so forth. An explicit goal of this review is to ferret out autocratic bosses; Welch has stated that the company will not tolerate managers who don't live up to the company's values, even if they do make the numbers. And to determine whether they live up to the values, their subordinates participate in this part of their evaluation. They do so under a sensible system of checks and balances developed over several years.

The manager selects several people to assess his or her performance, including peers, superiors, and also subordinates. The list must be approved by his or her immediate superior—which won't be forthcoming if someone conspicuous is left out, particularly an employee the manager is having a problem with. The appraisals are then compiled by Human Resources, to keep individual reviewers anonymous. The results are used only to assess leadership ability and adherence to values; they do not determine bonuses and promotions. But the leadership and values evaluations have teeth. A study by GE Medical Systems showed that two-thirds of managers who scored in the bottom one-third for adherence to values, as measured by the 360 degree reviews, were gone within a year—tangible proof that the system is helping achieve Welch's goal.

The upward appraisal or 360-degree review process is controversial—a number of companies have tried and abandoned it. But Welch, a natural social architect, recognized what the American founders knew: In America, leaders must be accountable to those over whom they wield power. Rather than throw the process out when it runs into difficulties, GE is finding ways to make it work. And the results can be beneficial not just to employees, but to enlightened bosses as well.

A School for Leaders

Every year Federal Express conducts a Leadership Survey, similar to GE's appraisal process, that includes input from employees. And the Survey matters: It determines whether the company's top three hundred or so managers get bonuses for the year or not. Several years ago, a director of invoicing named Cyndi Henson was badly stung by a mediocre score on the Survey from her own managers two levels down. She decided to call a meeting with them, and was quite nervous because they were clearly upset with her. "I didn't know whether to have my boss there, or their boss . . . or security!" she later recalled. The managers at the meeting hit Henson particularly hard on the question: Does your manager's boss give you the support you need? "To be honest," she says, "it was rather devastating. I thought I'd given them plenty of support; I was astonished that they thought I hadn't."[13]

Without knowing it, Henson had grown remote from her employees, the result of two distractions: a sick child at home, and the need to gear up for a new quality program being installed companywide at work. The meeting itself made for a very intense day. Fearful of retaliation, the managers initially wouldn't speak up, but Henson gradually persuaded them that she simply wanted to identify the problem and fix it. Slowly they began to furnish her with examples of objectionable behavior.

For instance, Henson had a habit of raising her hand "like a stop sign" when she wanted to end discussion in a meeting. "I realized," says Henson, "that I gave the same signal to my three-year-old son when I wanted him to calm down. They thought it was paternalistic." That broke the ice. As they talked, Henson and her managers, mostly mothers themselves, began seeing each other as real people with pressures at home and work. Henson vowed to keep in touch with their concerns; she would start by eliminating the offending gesture. In turn, she asked them to raise any problems they had with her at the time they occurred, and not months later on the yearly survey. Henson aired other complaints of her own as well, pointing to decisions the managers were delegating up to her that they should be making themselves.

Henson and the managers extended this dialogue they'd started in a series of two-hour monthly lunch meetings, off-site. Held over several months, the meetings helped improve morale in her department and resolve problems, as well as improve her leadership score on the next evaluation. They were crucial to smoothly implementing her division's portion of Federal Express's new total-quality program.

Pleased by the improved relationship with her managers, Henson applied the same responsive approach to a second trouble area, a group of invoicing employees in her division. "They'd been through four or five managers," said Henson. "It was a very low morale situation."

Henson and her managers asked the disgruntled employees to address a festering problem: too many backlogs and too much overtime. They then confronted the more serious underlying issues in some frank meetings. "They asked us a series of tough questions," says Henson. "They knew managers had flexibility in their work hours. They wanted to know why they had to be at work at 5 or 7 A.M. Didn't they have sick children too and emergencies in the night?"

Henson worked with the invoicing employees to devise flexible work hours, including a procedure to swap hours with co-workers when emergencies came up. Their new flex-time plan worked so well it was replicated throughout Henson's division with great success. Overtime and backlogs were entirely eliminated, saving $2 million the first year. Employee satisfaction shot up, as did customer satisfaction (a connection not lost on Henson). In the process, average billing time fell from more than seventeen days to less than eleven.

Such encounters were more than the boss having some heart-to-heart talks with her employees. Henson's behavior and policies changed, and improved, because her employees had the ability to hold her accountable in meaningful ways, and because Henson was smart enough to respond to their input. The next year's survey reflected a major change in Henson's division. The overall Leadership Index for her division shot up from a mediocre score in the 70s to the low 90s, a remarkably fast improvement for a seven-hundred-employee operation. Bosses who shun any suggestion of being accountable to subordinates might reflect on Cyndi Henson's experience. She was promoted a few years later to vice president of worldwide customer service.

None of this is to say that the 360-degree review is a panacea. In some companies, peers "brother-in-law" each other's evaluations so that everyone looks good. At others, unchecked bosses sometimes bully subordinates into favorable reviews. And where reviews by subordinates are used to determine a specific boss's pay and promotion, they can become overly politicized. (At Federal Express, the surveys are lumped together into a single, companywide Leadership Index for determining bonuses for all top managers as a group). But the 360-degree review deserves the effort, because companies like Federal Express and General Electric that are using and benefiting from them are on to something fundamental, a basic function of good citizenship.

And when a boss like Cyndi Henson uses them as a tool to better understand her impact on subordinates, they can lead to dramatic improvement in leadership. "I wouldn't be vice president today if it hadn't been for these changes. It prepared me for my current position. I learned from the experience and grew both personally and professionally."

6

The Federalist

Building Global Enterprises on Individual Initiative

A rapidly expanding company wants to exploit opportunity—in a growing industry perhaps, or in promising regional markets, or with an exciting new technology. To succeed, it will have to resolve a familiar set of paradoxes: It will need to be both local and global, large and small, radically decentralized yet with central reporting and control. For example, it will need a strong headquarters that can move resources quickly to new areas and make sure they generate sufficient financial returns, while giving plenty of autonomy to business units that in turn must give plenty of freedom to their employees to react to local conditions.

How can a company acquire such traits in a way that continues to build on the fundamental premise of this book: that its success will depend ultimately on tapping the initiative and creativity of individual employees—a large number of whom are independent-minded and averse to hierarchy? Like so many governance issues facing companies today, this one is nothing new.

America faced precisely the same challenge in 1787: how to unite three million increasingly diverse, independent-minded Americans in thirteen highly autonomous states into a cohesive whole with a powerful center—in a way that would best exploit the fabulous opportunities that lay before them. And like many corporations, America at that time was suffering from "the tyranny of the small business unit," which threatened to weaken the whole or even tear it apart. In particular the individual states were behaving irresponsibly and giving no thought to the good of the nation, in part owing to the weakness of the central government under the old Articles of Confederation. They preferred to squabble and take advantage of one another rather than cooperate.

While Americans recognized the need for a vigorous central government, they would never accept one that infringed in the slightest on their liberties or otherwise appeared too powerful. The solution the founders devised—federalism—has proven one of the great innovations in practical governance. It united a disparate group of states into a cohesive and strong nation, and provided a remarkably adaptive and flexible framework for America's fabulous expansion. The same system that governed a few million souls in thirteen states huddled along the Atlantic coast before the age of steam engines now governs nearly three hundred million people in fifty states in the age of cyberspace, all under a Constitution that fills about ten pages in a standard-size book.

This solution was so powerful it is now being rediscovered by a growing number of companies as they expand globally, such as Coca-Cola and General Electric—as well as by such excellent foreign firms as Asea Brown Boveri, Royal Dutch Shell and British Petroleum—and has become a subject of increasing interest to management writers.[1] Even better, it fits and naturally extends the concepts described in previous chapters.

MANY CENTERS OF POWER

What held, and still holds together a society as spread out and diverse as our own? Any notion of an autocracy, tying everyone together through an elaborate hierarchy to the top, was out of the question in America. Any system devised by the founders would have to rest, first and foremost, on the concept of citizenship and its fundamental precept that America would thrive best if it maximized the liberty of individuals. The solution they devised would have to be true, in other words, to the spirit of the American Revolution.

Federalism does away with any notion that all power is placed in the hands of a single person or entity sitting atop a hierarchy. Federalism has *many* centers of power.

Unifying power is wielded not at the top but at the *center,* where power is not absolute but limited to a few, specific provisions. The U.S. Constitution, which describes all the powers wielded by our own central government, can be read in an hour. And the specific purposes served by those powers could themselves be described in a single sentence—as in fact, they were. All powers not specifically granted to the center are reserved to the local units. The 10th Amendment, for instance, reserves to the states or to the people all powers not delegated to the national government.

Jack Welch captures the federal spirit when he says, "I have only three things to do: choose the right people, allocate the right number of dollars, and transmit ideas from one division to another with the speed of light." As to how individual GE businesses should price their products, or meet equipment needs, or whom they should hire, he has nothing to say. When British Petroleum "went federal" in 1990 to better manage its increasing global sprawl, headquarters proposed a list of twenty-two "reserve powers" to retain. But even that list was pared back to just ten after discussions with the business units.

Although the center's powers are limited in a federal system, *within* those powers the center is supreme, to prevent excessive local autonomy—or in corporations, the tyranny of the small business unit. The U.S. Supreme Court, for example, can strike down any state law that encroaches on federal authority. And if state authorities defy federal law the president can call in federal troops to enforce it, as Dwight Eisenhower did to desegregate the schools in Little Rock, Arkansas. The fact that the center's power is limited doesn't mean it is weak; a federal center can be quite strong where and when it needs to be.

For example, clearly a prime responsibility of the center in a corporation is the financial performance of the company as a whole. Despite its freewheeling entrepreneurial culture, 3M's headquarters sets rigorous financial standards that its operating units must meet, maintains a standardized reporting system they must all use, and forbids them by directive to create their own system. 3M managers must submit detailed financial budgets at each stage of the product development process. Some managers complain that they seem to spend all their time preparing the budgets, but even they agree the system seems to work.

Not De*centralization but* Non*centralization*
This federal division of power into many centers is neither rigid decentralization nor absolute centralization—but rather flexible "non-

centralization." Power in a federal system can *flow* to where it's needed when it's needed.

A company might decide, as Owens-Corning did in China, that headquarters should keep hands off local decisions. In China local officials tend to be the decision-makers; if local Owens-Corning managers have to keep checking back with headquarters they are apt to lose face. Or a company might decide to centralize certain decisions, as IBM and Ford have done in their global operations. IBM chairman Louis Gerstner wanted major European customers (who are increasingly centralized) to be able to computerize their entire operations by dealing with just one IBM office, rather than getting bogged down dealing with perhaps twenty. And in a move that defied conventional wisdom, Ford eliminated separate country units for their different car models, engines, and parts, to create single world models that can achieve very large economies of scale. Whether either decision was right is less important than whether both organizations can continue to move power flexibly as answers emerge or conditions change.

Nimble foreign firms are proving quite adept at this as well. When ABB was first formed in the merger of Asea and Brown Boveri, the new headquarters imposed tough performance standards throughout the company, under a uniform reporting requirement. Headquarters wanted only two pieces of information from each of the company's four thousand profit centers: financial results and the number of employees. And big trouble loomed for the unfortunate manager who failed to meet the expected numbers. "The current level of performance is unacceptable," wrote one boss to a profit center manager. "I will not accept excuses. When I arrive next week, be prepared to discuss in detail your steps to improve profit to agreed levels and to reduce inventory by 16 percent within 3 months."[2]

Managers naturally complained about so onerous an exercise of power, but headquarters had a compelling justification: Many of ABB's major markets were in recession shortly after the merger, and the company therefore had to emphasize results immediately. But ABB also proved adept at relaxing headquarters' hold over the profit centers, when appropriate. In another initiative to help them exploit more opportunities, headquarters required the profit centers to share important information on such matters as customer needs, best practices, and process performance. But this time there was no uniformity requirement; each account manager could gather and report information any way that made sense to them, a practical acknowledgment that if headquarters tried to require uniform reporting, there would be "many chuckles," as one staff executive put it, "but little compliance."[3]

The essence of the federal outlook is a healthy suspicion of power. Power is divided not only among many centers in a federal system but also within each center, using a system of checks and balances. The Constitution, as we've seen, divided the national government into a legislative, executive, and judicial branch—each with the ability to resist excessive use of power or encroachments by the other two. Federal organizations thus build on and preserve a fundamental tenant of citizenship: The sum total given to all centers of power, and to each "branch" within each center, is finite and specified. Individual employee-citizens have the remainder, and thus the freedom and responsibility to act or decide for themselves on all matters—except where specific provisions, set by accountable leaders acting within a limited range of authority, prevent them.

Therefore, the real strength of a federal organization comes not from an all-powerful leader at the top, but from the extent to which individual people throughout the organization identify with it and feel attached to it. A major issue becomes: How do you get unity and emotional attachment to the enterprise when its most dynamic members are often rugged individualists?

Must the emotional appeal so essential to the American concept of community be sacrificed in a large organization because it's too big, too impersonal? Not necessarily. Think for a moment about the pride and loyalty the United States still engenders in Americans, despite our diversity and the extent of our sprawl. It wasn't always so. At first, Americans from different states felt little if any bond with each other. The same is often true in large companies: Employees tend to identify with their immediate unit or division, where they know more people and have more of a say, but they feel little attachment or loyalty to the organization as a whole.

Binding Employees to the Largest Organization

American federalism solved this. The founders created a separate "citizenship" in the nation as a whole, exploiting an unexpected and powerful aspect of human nature: People can feel strong loyalty to more than one entity—for instance, to their nation as well as to their local community and their state. You needn't force them to choose, or even to divide their loyalties.

GE created this sense of twin citizenship among senior business managers–calling it "integrated diversity"–when Jack Welch wanted them to cooperate more and take a greater, companywide perspective. To achieve this, he created a particular type of top management team and gave it a name: the Corporate Executive Council (CEC), which was composed of about thirty leaders of General Electric's main businesses plus a few top staffers. Its mission is corporatewide and long-term: to set GE's goals and devise and implement strategies to attain them. Thus Welch expected the head of GE Plastics, for example, to spend a significant part of his time thinking and acting as a citizen of GE as a whole.

He uses a variety of means to instill this new sense of second citizenship. The CEC performs real work; there are no routine presentations or scripted agendas, thus providing its members with real experience of this principle in action. Performance at CEC meetings is a primary basis for promotion, and executives who dismiss its importance don't last long. This makes the concept of dual citizenship concrete; CEC members have explicit responsibilities both to their individual businesses and to GE as a whole.

When a global inflation scare arose a few years ago, CEC members noted how economists were always late with forecasts because they relied on old data. Members agreed to set up an informal internal network to inform each other about breaking price changes in their industries. As a result GE gained a far better handle on how to price products than its competitors had. And in contrast to a bureaucratic initiative that would have lasted forever, the internal network was halted as soon as the inflation scare passed.

Meddling Citizens

CEC members delve deeply into one another's businesses at meetings, bluntly raising issues and making suggestions with full information about one another's financial position. This is a radical departure from ordinary protocol at most companies, but clearly vital if their status as corporatewide citizens is to be authentic. As a result, the business heads began acting with increasing responsibility where they might not have before.

In a disastrous effort to build its own advanced rotary compressors, for example, GE Appliances lost $250 million (fully half of the whole company's increase in net income for the year). Under the old system, GE's chief financial officer would have called other business heads and requested their help in making up the difference. Their usual response would have been: "I've got my own problems." When Roger Schipke, then Appliances head, presented the problem at the

CEC however, members thought more in terms of the whole enterprise. Bob Wright, head of NBC, noted that the network's ad sales were doing well and that earnings might be up an extra $30 million which could be spared. Brian Rowe of Aircraft Engines offered to send a dozen compressor engineers to help with the problem, and without saying so explicitly, at Aircraft Engines' cost. The result: Appliances got the funds to work out of the problem, Schipke kept his job (he went on later to become CEO of another company), and GE wound up with a 16 percent increase in net income over the previous year.[4]

A Structure That Expands

Twin citizenship instilled under democratic principles also helps solve a newer and particularly knotty problem—how to absorb overseas subsidiaries, staffed largely by nationals who don't feel they have anything in common with the company or vice versa, in addition to confusing differences in culture. A common sentiment from a U.S. regional manager goes something like, "Market some product made in a European facility? We're not giving them business over our own people."

GE Medical Systems (GEMS) solved this with an adaptation of the CEC, which it calls the Group Operating Council. Its purpose is to unify business centers in Milwaukee, Paris, and Tokyo, each of which represents separate offices widely scattered throughout the world. In setting it up, GEMS CEO John Trani gave the older U.S. office in Milwaukee no more representation than the other two offices, even though it accounts for more than half of GEMS' sales, thus preventing the older office from dominating. Like the CEC, the Group Operating Council (GOC) is not just for show. Trani gives the Council enough authority to commandeer all the people and resources it needs, under a companywide charter to "maximize global opportunity."

Because everyone's interests are protected, the GOC has created greater cooperation between global offices. At one meeting, representatives from GEMS Europe described a practice they'd been using to devise much better strategy: Don't rely on field reports to understand customer needs, get headquarters executives out of their ivory towers and into the field for periodic, in-depth visits with customers. The method was adopted by GEMS worldwide and Trani likes to point out that it didn't originate at GEMS' U.S. headquarters.

Marc Onetto, general manager of Global Tubes and Detectors, explains why he benefits from such corporatewide citizenship. "What does my business have in common with GE's nuclear fuel business? On the surface, nothing. But we had a problem with foreign particles in our tube production facility–and one of my engineers knew that the nuclear-fuels people are expert at ultraclean environments. We learned and adapted best practices from them, and solved the problem. Our relationship with them–built up through such interactions as the GOC–was a big help in this."

Other methods companies use to instill this sense of second citizenship, not just among managers but throughout the ranks, include symbols and communication. A number of effective CEOs make themselves highly visible to the public, publishing articles and books and interacting with outsiders, in part to embody and reinforce the corporate identity in the minds of employees. Business cards include the company "flag" or logo–such as the famous GE "meatball"–in addition to the name of the small business unit. Common standards are adopted, such as units of measure, a common language (typically English) so that people can easily understand each other and interact, and a companywide information system developed to allow people everywhere to communicate. Shared company values and mission statements are created through a process of broad participation, as Johnson & Johnson did when it recommitted to its Credo, or as GE did when it created its current values statement.

THE KEY TO A FEDERAL
ORGANIZATION'S STRENGTH

Beyond symbols, the best way to instill this loyalty-creating notion of twin citizenship is to institutionalize it: Have the center, which represents the organization as a whole, act directly on employees. This is a primary reason the United States succeeded so well under the Constitution after nearly failing under the Articles of Confederation, but a distinction often lost on organizations and management writers today.

Under the Articles of Confederation, the United States was merely a confederation of independent states, a nerveless whole lacking the strength either to govern its people or protect them from external threats. The primary reason: The national government couldn't act directly on the people; it had to go through the states, which, naturally, were jealous of their own power and therefore kept the center weak. To give the nation strength and an identity in the minds of the people, the Constitution allowed the national government to act directly on individuals. It could tax them, for example, and they in turn could elect certain of its officials–such as congressmen, directly, or the president, through a separate electoral college—without going through their state legislatures. This direct relationship, built on a foundation of liberty, created a strong emotional bond between the national government and the American people.

Abraham Lincoln proved how strong this bond was in the Civil War just seventy years later, confounding Southern leaders: To their surprise, Massachusetts shopkeepers and Illinois farmers in the North were willing to fight just as hard to preserve the young nation as their South Carolina and Virginia counterparts were to protect their centuries-old ancestral states.

That important federal trait is being rediscovered "in the arena" by a group of "transnational" corporations. That term was coined by the Harvard Business School's Christopher Bartlett and the London Business School's Sumantra Ghoshal in an impressive study of twenty large, vigorous global competitors like 3M, Intel, Lincoln Electric, Andersen Consulting, and General Electric. What makes their study particularly fascinating is that it includes several firms from Europe and Japan, such as ABB and Kao, who are themselves discovering the power of this same federal principle.[5] It allows even far-flung, massive organizations to build on the initiative and creativity of individual employees. Here's a sketch of how they are doing so, from the grass roots up.

Steps for Building Large Enterprises on Individual Initiative

The organization is formed (or restructured) into many small units, even if it has hundreds of thousands of employees. ABB, for example, has hundreds of small business units, each a separate legal entity with its own balance sheet and P&L statement, averaging about two hundred employees each. Every member of the unit knows everyone else. Similar structures exist at 3M and Johnson & Johnson.

The goal of each business unit is simple: to pursue growth opportunities within a broad, easily understood company strategy. Only three key management roles are recognized. The most important is the *entrepreneur*—frontline people whose job, in a phrase, is to "pursue opportunity." Everyone else must assist and further this, or as one transnational computer company puts it, "everyone in the company works for the entrepreneurs." *Coaches* in senior management support and help develop entrepreneurial initiatives, and review their progress. *Leaders* at the center, who are responsible for overall strategic goals, provide broad boundaries within which frontline people have free reign to operate, while setting highly demanding performance standards that they must meet.[6]

This collection of perhaps hundreds of small business units is no loose and "nerveless" confederation. A vigorous center, acting directly on individuals under democratic principles, creates a strong companywide identity.

Suppose "Sasha," a manager in a regional office, thinks her company can challenge a supplier that is currently dominating the region. A "board" will be created, chaired by her coach and acting somewhat like a small company board of directors on behalf of the center. She'll select the rest of its members in consultation with her coach, from the pool of other coaches based on the talents, experience, or resources they can bring to the effort. Sasha may also go outside the company if needed, to get customer representatives, say, or university professors on her board. This provides a restraint on coaches, to keep them from lapsing back into the familiar role of boss.

The board will review and challenge Sasha's plans, review her budget, and monitor subsequent performance against the agreed plan and budget. Budgets are "sacrosanct," a creature of contract. Once agreed to, Sasha will be sure of getting the funds—no one in senior management can block them—unless she demonstrates an inability to live up to the contract.

The budgeting process provides another logical way for the center to act more directly on, and thus reinforce its connection to, individuals. In a traditional division structure, budgets cascade down through each level of the hierarchy, with each level expected to meet its aggregate goals. In such a system, one high-performing unit can lose budget dollars suddenly when a poorly performing peer runs into trouble. But in the transnationals studied by Bartlett and Ghoshal, the center acts directly on each unit, adding to or withdrawing money according to its individual performance. All the way up to senior management, each unit's budget is approved and its performance is judged individually.

A Federal Integration

But what ties the entrepreneurs like Sasha and the individual business units to *each other*? In an autocracy of subordinates with one supreme power, everyone is connected to the top—via an elaborate hierarchy—with ties of dependence and subordination. In a federal system of employee-citizens with many centers of power, everyone is connected not just to the center, but to each other in a vast communications network whose links are based on common interests. Thus ties of autocratic dependence are replaced with a federal integration.

A remarkable model for this federal principle is provided by, of all firms, a Japanese company called Kao—a highly creative household-products maker that has won some impressive battles against Procter & Gamble and Unilever. Its technology and design innovations in the "Merries" line of disposable diapers, for example, reduced P&G's market share in Japan from nearly 90 percent to less than 10 percent.

Kao depends on extensive integration for its product creativity, achieved in part with elaborate information systems. One system, for example, compiles and analyzes all telephone queries and complaints from customers, providing everyone in the company with a "window on the customer's mind" to prompt fine tuning of products and packaging, as well as ideas for entirely new products. Such extensive systems allow frontline managers, rather than middle or senior people, to integrate their unit operations with each other and with the company as a whole.

Equally important to Kao, perhaps even more important as an integrating mechanism, is face-to-face interaction. The company has an extensive system of intrafunction, interfunction, and interbusiness meetings to promote the exchange of ideas and joint projects. These include "Open Space" meetings that anyone can participate in, which prompt not only participation but also network-building among frontline people, giving them access to companywide expertise and resources that they can leverage. In Kao's respected R&D organization, different labs host monthly conferences to bring young researchers—who can nominate themselves to attend—to exchange and disseminate ideas. Such collaborations have produced innovations, like an emulsifier produced jointly by three labs that was essential to the success of Sofina's, which became Japan's leading cosmetics brand.

A notable aspect of Kao's internal governance is its commitment to American-style democratic values. Senior managers are responsible for disseminating and instilling them, including: absolute equality of human beings, individual initiative, and rejection of authoritarianism. Free access to all information for everyone is a core value of the company. So is a spirit of egalitarianism: Chairman Yoshio Maruta and top management share a single floor and a pool of secretaries at company headquarters, which contains a large, open space with conference tables, overhead projectors, and lounge chairs. Anyone can, and often does, join in any discussion and contribute as an equal regardless of who has formal responsibility for the matter at hand. That same scheme is duplicated at units and labs throughout the company.[7]

GETTING AMERICANS TO COOPERATE

None of the above should be mistaken for any claim that a federal organization of employee citizens, for all its advantages, will lead to organizational bliss–especially with a workforce of independent-minded Americans. While such concepts can help free up employees and energize workforces, what about *cooperation*? American employees in particular are going to continue to form their own opinions and pursue their own interests. If the forces of democracy are truly unleashed, what then will solve the very difficult problem of holding the enterprise together?

The Problem with Teams

The frequent answer: teams. Teamwork has become something of a chimera for corporations seeking to remove causes of discord and improve cooperation. Unfortunately it doesn't always work very well. A. T. Kearney found in one study that fully seven teams in ten fail to accomplish the desired result.[8] One of the primary reasons is distinctly, and persistently, uncooperative behavior: The team's efforts are blocked by other, entrenched power sources, or factions, in the organization, such as middle managers who feel their authority threatened by an upstart factory floor team. Another reason is cooperation–of the wrong sort. The team merely replaces one form of coercion, top-down control, with another that is hardly more suited to freeing people up–namely, peer pressure.

Management exhorts employees to embrace a collective purpose. Team members are expected to put aside individual interests and preferences for the good of the team; they must find consensus. The team therefore becomes just as stifling to individual creativity as top-down control. Team members might grow frustrated, for example, when an essential and highly talented but also iconoclastic employee refuses to "go along." Time and money are then wasted on esoteric training in subjects like conflict resolution or team dynamics, as opposed to real work. The result is often mediocre decisions whose primary virtue is that they preserved group harmony and good feelings–at the expense of genuine creativity and excellence.

The "Rat System" at Ethicon

But *does* teamwork and a strong emphasis on cooperation by management achieve even these results? Do they really build harmony and worker morale? In a revealing study, Guillermo J. Grenier examined these issues in a plant owned by Ethicon, a suture-making subsidiary of Johnson & Johnson.[9] Johnson & Johnson management, of course, is exceptionally enlightened, which perhaps highlights the flaw in depending on teams to bring harmony to a workforce of Americans.

Ethicon's New Mexico plant was organized around teams (in particular, quality circles) within a flexible, participative environment. Employees were given a substantial voice in decisions about hiring, firing, evaluation, and disciplining. Management expected such measures to create nothing less than a new vision of work in America, based on unity, cooperation, purpose, and inspiration. This sounds good and appears to be in keeping with a federal outlook, but there was a distinct fly in the ointment.

To management's considerable chagrin, at least a third of Ethicon's employees and possibly many more favored unionizing the plant. And this despite the fact that they'd been quite impressed by a company so committed to cooperation, and even though Ethicon had located in the Southwest primarily to avoid unionization—which employees knew when they came to work there. That created a bind: Ethicon was determined to keep the union out but could not appear to control the outcome in a facility so highly touted for its participation and worker empowerment.

This led to a distinct shift in the outlook of Ethicon's management toward its teams. Any expressions of individual or separate interests were increasingly frowned upon. Beneath the veneer of cooperation and good feeling a disturbing reality emerged, and management began to turn increasingly to manipulative techniques.

A plant psychologist was used to co-opt team facilitators toward management's point of view, then to create peer pressure against "counterproductive behavior" by employees, which included any expression of discontent with Ethicon or support for the local union. Pro-union workers were labeled as losers and otherwise deprived of status and respect. New hires were carefully screened to find "team players" and exclude anyone who was pro-union. Gradually the feelings of cooperation deteriorated, as the team system became known among the plant's union supporters as the "rat system."

The strategy "succeeded"; the union lost the election by two to one. But did it really work? The team system at Ethicon resulted in nothing that remotely resembled harmony. To the contrary, it left a sharply divided workforce, a third of which felt humiliated and besieged—"like being attacked by a pack of wolves" as one employee put it. Ethicon employees knew when they hired on that the company wanted to avoid unionization, but changing one's mind to further one's own interest is what free people do.

If the idea of governance based on teams and depending on the formation of collective purposes and opinions seems somehow fundamentally out of step with American society and the natural forces of democracy, that's because it is.

How Democracy Played Out in America

Management that embraces teams and urges employees to put aside their differences in the name of cooperation borrows from the Founding Fathers themselves, who believed that leaders in America who could create common interests, common purposes, and common outlooks among the people to bind them together would have to emerge before republican governance could work.

But in fact that's not the way things worked out at all. Far from developing a common interest, something like the opposite occurred among Americans in the new United States, to an extent startling and unsettling to their leaders. Society became atomized, it celebrated the individual, and its dominant feature became the overt and unabashed pursuit of self-interest.

As for the emergence of a common outlook and common opinions, again far from it. Something like the opposite occurred here too. Conservative American leaders clung to the idea that truth was fixed and universal, that its principles could be discovered by educated and enlightened men. But a different view of truth emerged among the people: a growing dismissal of elite opinion in favor of the common, ordinary judgment of individuals, along with a growing conviction that everyone had eyes, ears, and experiences of their own and could form opinions deserving as much respect as those of experts and scholars. What other concept of knowledge would work in a fast-moving and democratic environment except one that was fluid, adaptable to change, specific to individual circumstances, and that could keep itself up-to-date and current?

This doesn't mean that truth couldn't be determined in matters of general concern—only that its determination was taken out of the hands of the elite and democratized. Truth and knowledge in America thus took on a profound new quality: They became "the creation of many voices and many minds," notes historian Gordon Wood, "no one of which was more important than another and each of which made its own separate and equally significant contribution to the whole."[10] This is a concept very much like that experienced by Intel as it wrestled with its memory chip business. This meant of course that error would enter into the public discourse at times, but as Thomas Jefferson noted, this should prove no danger to a free society where "reason is left free to combat it."

As democracy took hold in American society it gradually became clear that no one was in charge of the great, bustling, and booming enterprise. The result was nothing like what the Founding Fathers had envisioned. Indeed, they grew increasingly concerned, if not appalled, by the outcome. George Washington died thinking America's republican experiment had failed—destroyed by the emergence of party spirit. Alexander Hamilton wound up feeling a stranger in his own land. The always optimistic and democratic-minded Jefferson despaired in his last years over what democracy had wrought, and over how the ordinary people in whom he'd placed such faith were not becoming more enlightened or more rational, as he'd hoped and expected. Even that astute student of human nature, James Madison, had guessed wrong. Madison believed that the system of representation he'd helped create would encourage people to select "neutral umpires" for leaders—men who would govern for the good of the whole while wisely mediating the conflicts between contending factions.

But grassroots Americans wound up rejecting any such notion. Professor Wood describes the rise of hard-nosed, up-from-the-ranks men like Pennsylvania's William Findley who skewered the pretensions of America's would-be philosopher kings. In the debate over the new Bank of America, the wealthy merchant Robert Morris assumed the pose of Madison's above-the-fray leader who was acting only on behalf of the whole community. The Scotch-Irish ex-weaver Findley destroyed his pose: Of *course* Morris and his allies had an interest in promoting the bank, they were *shareholders!* Further—and this was a radical concept that emerged in American democracy— there was *nothing wrong* with them, or anyone else, seeking to advance their own interests provided they were above board about it, as Findley and his allies intended to be.[11]

A new line of thought emerged in America that rejected the Founders' notion of all-wise, disinterested leaders who would anticipate the needs and balance the desires of so fragmented and diverse a society as ours. Only people who actually share a particular occupation or interest could adequately speak for that occupation or interest—this became the criterion Americans used to select their leaders.

An Amazing Harmony

Yet—and here is the important point—despite the increasing absence of a collective, organizing purpose supplied by leaders or institutions, or of widely shared opinions and traditions, cooperation did emerge among people to an astonishing extent. It utterly defied the conventional wisdom that a society which lacked collective goals would surely fly apart and sink into chaos. To the contrary, an amazing harmony and order settled over the bustling American beehive as Americans got down to the business of developing what would soon become the richest economy in the world. How?

Republican government had freed people from oppression, whether by autocrats on the one hand or excessive democracy on the other, and provided them with a continentwide, market-based infrastructure to enable them to create wealth and pursue happiness. They cooperated to an astonishing extent, not because a strong leader articulating a collective purpose was in charge guiding their moves–but for a much better reason: They recognized it was in their interest to do so.

Of course Americans disputed, fought, litigated; these traits are in our nature. But think of the cooperation needed to transform a backward, agrarian economy into a continentwide marketplace in so short a time–the new relationships that had to be formed, the cooperative ventures undertaken, the enterprises launched. And yet none of this was orchestrated by visionary leaders setting common goals and purposes. Central authorities didn't plan and direct the effort to develop the nation; instead it was the initiative of citizens, who actually took seriously the idea they were free to think and do things in their own way, including pursue happiness, who did so.

They were the ones who besieged legislatures for internal improvements like roads, ferries, and bridges to facilitate their enterprises, and for corporate charters to pursue them. Prior to the Revolution only six corporations had been chartered in America in 150 years; over the next fifty years, an average of forty corporations per year were chartered–a phenomenon unknown in autocratic Europe. Massachusetts alone had thirty times more corporations than existed on the entire continent. Democracy and the new order of citizenship transformed even stodgy American farms into hustling, thriving businesses that engaged in trade, merchandising, proto-industrialization, and manufacturing in addition to farming.

Previously, the purpose of society had always been to find great and wise leaders to take control of the ship of state and steer it toward a collective destiny; the interests and the happiness of individuals were secondary. The Founding Fathers' great legacy–and this was partly unintended–was the creation of a society that allowed people to take control of their own destinies, which included pursuit of their own personal happiness. Great visionary leaders were no longer in charge as society took on a life of its own.

This experience suggests to managers that perhaps they shouldn't worry so much about articulating soaring visions or collective purposes in order to somehow generate cooperation. Instead, they should look more to making sure it actually *is* in people's interest to cooperate, not because they're on a team, but because artificial barriers between them and the marketplace have been removed. That, at least, was the key to fostering cooperation in America when the forces of democracy were first unleashed.

Engaging Self-Interest While Attacking Passivity at Cin-Made

Americans after the Revolution were eager to embrace their new market economy. Getting people to face the realities of the marketplace is a challenge more typical of our times, given that employees have grown too accustomed to being taken care of by paternal organizations. Here's a delightful example of a company that overcame this reluctance—and found the cooperation that eluded Ethicon.

In 1984 Robert Frey and a partner bought Cin-Made Corporation, a Cincinnati maker of mailing tubes and other cartons. Cin-Made turned out to be on the fast track to bankruptcy: It was losing $30,000 per month and had serious worker morale problems together with a hostile labor union. Morale wasn't helped when Frey, who now acknowledges his arrogance, not only cut wages to stop the losses but berated employees by telling them their jobs were easy. When they struck, he beat their union back to make the cuts stick.

But Frey's "victory" left him with a beaten and humiliated workforce that now despised the boss, and the company continued to bleed money. Eventually Frey—who'd learned that his employees' jobs were *not* easy when he tried to do them himself during the strike—realized that his star was hitched to his workforce. Cin-Made plant workers were better qualified than he to plan production, for example, or solve workload and operational problems, or control costs and cut waste. How could he get their cooperation? His efforts to exhort them to do better were getting him nowhere.

What finally worked for Frey was to embrace this approach: to establish a clear cause and effect relationship between the money employees earned and the profit the business made. He wanted employees to think of work not as doing a job but as helping the company succeed. He achieved this with a comprehensive infrastructure—notice that it didn't tell people what to do, it caused them to encounter the marketplace.

Frey installed an aggressive profit-sharing program, after making an extensive study of such programs and why they often fail. The program he finally devised was not a watered down version, with no clear connection between work and profits. Frey allocated fully 35 percent of Cin-Made's profits to the program: 18 percent for workers and 17 percent for managers. He then cut out all raises and bonuses. Further, there would be no wage increases (beyond restoring the earlier wage cuts); he was determined that from now on employees would earn more and prosper only as the company did.

Frey coupled this program with new power for employees and new tools with which to exercise it. He opened the company books to both workers and their union, and not just to inspect or audit but to study and master. He provided workers with more and more complex information on factors they could control—like productivity, scrap rates and profit projections. Increasingly he expanded the responsibilities of the best workers; now when managers sit in on meetings, they typically do so only to provide input. When Cin-Made's central planning unit proved ineffective in keeping up with changing customer needs, Frey assigned worker committees to do the planning. He also began allowing workers to interview and have a veto over all candidates for jobs, including managers.

The whole process was far from smooth. Cin-Made employees had long been accustomed to more conventional, paternalistic management. They didn't relish the new responsibility; Frey had to force it on them. He began by instituting monthly meetings with factory workers in which he would raise pointed issues: How can we cut waste on this run? How should we distribute overtime on that order? When suspicious (and often still hostile) workers refused to answer, rather than conclude that empowerment doesn't work and return to his autocratic ways, Frey would throw a temper tantrum until they did start coming up with ideas. What a contrast to the typical autocrat—Frey would demand that his workers do things *their* way!

Eventually cooperation began to flourish at Cin-Made, because employees grew increasingly convinced it was in their interests to cooperate. The results were extraordinary. Cin-Made averted imminent bankruptcy and survived. Productivity rose by two and a half times in the decade following Frey's purchase of the company. Profit-sharing augmented worker salaries by 36 percent. Best of all, Cin-Made workers now push for more responsibility—the result of a growing sense of citizenship—a change Frey describes as "electrifying." For example, full-time employees who once shunned any responsibilities now monitor the work of temporary hires as a matter of routine. Strict adherence to job descriptions is a thing of the past. Absenteeism is rare.

Frey candidly states that sometimes employees blow the decisions they're now responsible for making (though, he adds, not as often as he would). But, as he puts it, that's not the point. The point is that when they do make mistakes, they now learn from them and grow rather than point fingers.

7

A Philosophy of the Unexpected

How Americans Find Opportunity

The executive recalled how consultants had sold a comprehensive re-engineering program to his boss, who was under pressure to "grow" the business. They "just seduced our CEO," he recalled, by saying that the program would "solve all his problems" as well as put him on "the cutting edge of business management." The consulting team used "templates," and the rule was "you can't vary from the templates"–even though no one in the company was quite sure how the whole program would ultimately fit together. When employees began to realize that the program was overwhelming the organization, they were afraid to speak up: The consultants would paint them as "resisting change" or "clinging to the past."

Despite spending in the millions, the business's re-engineering effort failed, having made no real impact on cost reductions or revenue growth. Instead it contributed to the loss of employee confidence in senior management and eventually the CEO was fired, primarily for not growing the business.[1]

The failure of such programs, often on a massive scale, has been the subject of countless articles and books, with more on the way.[2]

The problem, however, is not with the concepts themselves; many of them can provide useful insights—to some companies, in certain situations. The real danger is our sometimes excessive faith in "knowledge professionals" offering "thought leadership" and the ability to "solve any problem" using sophisticated abstract tools at their disposal. Such an outlook toward business completely departs from the clearer, simpler, more direct way Americans have ordinarily viewed the world throughout our history.

Here and in the next two chapters, we'll ask, How do Americans naturally think, how do they normally learn? How do they typically recognize and exploit opportunity? How do they instinctively interact with the world to make things happen and get things done? What was the outlook that originally unleashed the creativity and entrepreneurism of Americans—before they were deluged with a flood of management programs, systems, theories, and procedures?

Recapturing a "New" Style of Thinking

Any notion that business is an abstraction, that great organizations must be built according to sophisticated theory, is far from cutting edge. To the contrary, such an outlook bears a striking resemblance to the way seventeenth- and eighteenth- century Europeans related to the world—a stifling society our American forebears wanted more than anything to escape! The autocratic Europeans believed that every great institution required a foundation of sophisticated theory: Successful government required a deep political philosophy, national wealth a profound economic theory, satisfying religion a systematic theology, and so forth.[3]

That's not the way thinking and action developed in America as Americans strived to master and exploit a strange new environment. The nation's founders, such as Madison, Hamilton, Jefferson, and Adams, though exceptionally learned themselves, grew more and more willing to adjust and adapt the theories they'd mastered to the novel environment they encountered. They never used theories, like the reengineering consultants above did, as rigid templates from which they couldn't vary. Political theory provided only one source of ideas—and an increasingly less important source than experience and observation—to meet the unprecedented and complex challenge of building the republic.[4]

Far more important to that effort was their remarkable capacity— and this trait was shared widely by Americans—to extract insight, and opportunity, from the circumstances at hand. The contrast between their way of relating to the world and that of Europe's professional thinkers was captured best when the Abbé Nollet, one of Europe's most advanced physicists, dismissed Benjamin Franklin's scientific discoveries as "mere" observation. (It was Franklin, of course, not Nollet, who revolutionized the science of electricity with his acute observations.)

Creating Their Own Theory

More useful in America than sophisticated learning was an open and unencumbered mind.[5] Americans became highly receptive to the new, the unanticipated, the startling. Rather than look for what was expected or predicted in order to confirm some favored theory, they looked for the *un*foreseen and *un*expected as a prime source of opportunity to exploit. Such an outlook took the job of thinking out of the hands of remote professional thinkers and put it in the hands of ordinary people dealing with the situation at hand. The worldview of Americans was a philosophy without philosophers, as historian Daniel Boorstin has pointed out; it was, in his wonderfully suggestive phrase, "a philosophy of the unexpected."

Much of what built America itself, for example, contradicted the "best" thinking and most "cutting edge" theories. Rather than adopt abstract theories wholesale to build the nation, the founders created their *own* theories—such as Madison's federal republic, or Hamilton's system of public finance—that fit America's unique circumstances and distinctive people. And to create them they relied most heavily on experience and self-evident observation, in particular, the experiences of the state and national governments in the decade or so after the Revolution, experiences in which many of them had personally participated. Some of the more cerebral founders, such as James Madison, hungry for knowledge grounded in actual experience, studied history in an effort to learn from the experiences of others.

More impressive, and more important, a philosophy of the unexpected encouraged Americans to challenge their *own* assumptions and beliefs, no matter how cherished. The American Revolution had created its own dogma, its own templates, of how a society should be built: Executive power was bad; strong national government was dangerous; power in America should be left to the legislatures in the states, elected every year or two to keep them closely accountable to the people. Such a system, thought Americans, would usher in an era of virtue and political harmony unprecedented in the world.

But when it didn't and unruly mobs began taking over the state governments, the founders coolly reversed all those assumptions and fashioned a strong national government to control the states, with a strong executive and elaborate checks and balances to keep Congress under control. Only when they did so—when they were willing to challenge some of the Revolution's most honored beliefs—did the nation begin to realize its tremendous economic potential.

This outlook of regarding the new, the unforeseen, the surprise, the unexpected as potential opportunities to exploit rather than mishaps to fear, which was so essential to building the nation, is at the heart of America's extraordinary entrepreneurism.

INNOVATION IN AMERICA HAPPENS "UNEXPECTEDLY"

To exploit the opportunity offered by the new world, Americans throughout history have valued most the knowledge that comes from:

- unexpected successes,
- unexpected failures (which are often more instructive),
- unanticipated changes in customers or markets,
- unforeseen changes in technology,
- mistaken or obsolete assumptions.[6]

When the Puritans arrived in Massachusetts Bay, they were astonished by the richness of the sea—an abundance of mackerel, cod, bass, lobster, crab, oyster, and more that was, wrote one, "almost beyond believing." They had come expecting to farm but when the New England soil proved too rocky and infertile, they exploited this unexpected opportunity. Thus was established one of the great patterns for innovation in America: recognizing the unexpected fact or event and making something out of it. "The sea," wrote Boorstin, "helped New Englanders find resources, not in the land, but in themselves and in the whole world."[7]

The sea-trading industry that emerged from fishing in New England was in essence the business of capitalizing on the unexpected. Yankee traders would look for bargains at any port they happened to call on. They might ship to Buenos Aires at a moment's notice whatever was suddenly in demand there, or divert a ship from Canton to Calcutta if an abrupt storm or war made the trip unsafe. They might jettison an entire cargo, or an entire ship, if it became apparent the voyage couldn't make a profit. Or they might scramble to find and ship huge amounts of American ginseng to China if they learned that demand there had suddenly soared.

This penchant for the unexpected is a story repeated again and again as America developed and Americans got ahead. When John Jacob Astor noticed that returns on the property around his head-quarters in New York exceeded those of his main business, the fur trade, he launched a spectacular career developing New York real estate. When J. P. Morgan observed the unanticipated influx of immi-grants from Europe, he recognized the workers that American facto-ries would need to compete in the Industrial Revolution, and estab-lished an international banking center in New York to finance them. Meanwhile the world's dominant financiers, the Rothschilds, dis-missed the European immigrants to America as "riff-raff"—and got left behind.

Great Enterprises That Weren't Planned

A continuing thread in the development of our greatest enterprises, and the failure of their competitors, has been this openness to the unexpected. When a lab assistant accidently left a burner on in DuPont's polymer research lab, the chemist in charge noticed that the material in the kettle had somehow congealed into fibers—exactly what they'd been looking for! Although it would take DuPont scien-tists several more years to figure out how to make Nylon intention-ally, still they recognized and built on this entirely unexpected event. The same accident had happened several times, and earlier, at major German chemical companies, but they had dismissed it each time because they hadn't planned the experiment.

After World War II, IBM and its competitors made computers designed solely for scientists such as astronomers. Quite unantici-pated by anyone, businesses began buying the machines for entirely mundane uses like payroll. At the time, Univac made not only the most advanced computer but also the one most adaptable to such business uses; nevertheless it shunned corporate customers, fearing they would "demean" its sophisticated product.[8] Not IBM. Not only did it do everything possible to meet this surprising demand, such as training programmers for business uses, it also threw out its own computer design and adapted Univac's. What distinguished IBM's Thomas Watson was not that he somehow anticipated the emerging business use of computers; he was as surprised as anyone. What made IBM successful was Watson's openness to an unexpected turn of events.

3M has a history of paying special attention to the different, the unusual, the unexpected. In 1920 an obscure inventor named Francis G. Okie wrote to several mineral and sandpaper companies request-ing samples of their sandpaper grit sizes. But only one, 3M, bothered to respond, and did so even though it didn't sell raw materials for sandpaper and thus had no apparent business to transact with Okie. 3M's CEO William McKnight didn't foresee a market for a new technology at that point–he simply wanted to know why this man Okie wanted grit samples. As it turned out, Okie had invented a revolutionary waterproof sandpaper that 3M quickly acquired rights to and sold as "Wetodry" to automakers and paint shops around the world. An additional find was Okie himself, whom McKnight hired and who became a key inventor of 3M products until he retired nineteen years later.[9]

Superior entrepreneurs look hard at common assumptions, explicit or hidden. Discount retailers "knew" that small, rural towns couldn't support large stores. Wal-Mart achieved explosive growth precisely by putting stores in small, rural towns and remained virtually untouched by competition until it was doing $400 million in sales. Ted Turner created a successful news channel, CNN, without star anchor people.

A Window of Opportunity

Perhaps the most profitable insight of the last decade occurred because Microsoft's Bill Gates was open to the unexpected. At the time, Microsoft was collaborating with IBM to develop the successor to DOS–Microsoft's operating system then used in most PCs, including IBM's. Most people would have been thrilled to collaborate with one of the most respected and powerful companies in the world. Contrary to legend, IBM had not been caught napping by the PC revolution; the company had set up competing task forces as early as 1977 to develop a personal computer, came out with one in 1980, and by 1983 was the industry leader (although it never achieved anything like the dominance it had enjoyed in mainframes). Further, it now had four teams on two continents working on the successor system to DOS.

But Gates noticed something unexpected. During one break from a meeting at IBM, he looked around and saw several PCs used by IBM employees; none was less than seven years old! "This tells me more about IBM than I've ever seen," he thought, crystallizing his own growing frustration with the company: that it seemed too slow in its responses to a market as volatile as personal computers.[10] A lot of people would have discounted the surprising evidence in front of their eyes, but not Gates, who grew less intimidated by IBM's huge development teams and eventually regarded them as just more IBM bureaucracy. He decided then to go it alone on the new software, and the result was Windows—the most profitable operating software yet developed. Within five years Gates's still little company was actually worth more on paper than IBM.

THREE MONEY-MAKING PHRASES

Here are some phrases that have helped stimulate this kind of fresh thinking, allowing people to get beyond conventional wisdom, buzz phrases, and hidden assumptions to find opportunity in unexpected events. The first is to ask, even in the midst of apparent failure, "where's the opportunity?" This was the key to the success of the United States itself.

"Where's the Opportunity?"

Americans were shocked and dismayed after the Revolution when the states began to spin utterly out of control. Factions composed of society's "rabble" began forming and taking over the legislatures—not to establish virtuous government but to oppress their enemies by confiscating their property, canceling legitimate debts, and even settling private disputes and old scores that belonged in courts of law. With the states trampling so outrageously on individual rights, how could the founders ever make the case for creating a strong national government? But rather than bemoan the decline of virtue throughout the land, American leaders looked for opportunity in the midst of calamity—and found it.

In fact, they saw factions—the cause of all the disruptions in the states—as *key* to bringing order and stability to the national government! States like Rhode Island or even Massachusetts were small enough for such groups to join together and take over the government, but the United States was much too large and spread out, and contained too wide a variety of interests for that to happen to a national government. Contrary to all conventional wisdom, the trick to stabilizing government in America was not to somehow suppress factions—impossible in a free society anyway—but rather to *include* so many of them over so great a territory that they could never combine to form a majority with an interest adverse to the country or its people. This was the source of James Madison's famous "enlarge the sphere, balance the interests" formulation.

Indeed, so confident were the founders in the stability of a national government constituted this way, if done carefully, that they gave it powers to subdue the unruly states, which were previously regarded as the true bastions of liberty. And the founders' new system, contrary to the expectations created by revolutionary dogma, worked superbly. Property rights were quickly secured and the people were left alone to go about the business of building wealth for themselves and the nation.

That outlook—of being open to opportunity even in the midst of apparent failure—has been vital to America's economic growth as well. Indeed, "Failure is our most important product," as one great business leader, Johnson & Johnson's R. W. Johnson, Jr., liked to put it. The company has a long history of losing ventures, from "kola stimulants" to colored plaster casts for children to heart valves— together with over a century of unbroken profits. Perhaps its most famous product, its soothing Baby Powder, was created to respond to an unexpected shortcoming in its medical plasters, which were irritating patient's skin.

This isn't to encourage carelessness. But where failure occurs despite careful planning and follow through, it often indicates fundamental change and therefore opportunity. The most famous failure in automotive history—the Ford Edsel—was, contrary to legend, meticulously planned and marketed to challenge General Motors' higher-end models. Less well known is that Ford planners paid close attention to the failure, rather than dismissing it as an aberration, and found that something fundamental had changed in the car market. Their investigation uncovered a dramatic shift away from the income segmentation of the market pioneered by GM and toward a "lifestyle" segmentation. The new knowledge Ford gained from the Edsel's failure resulted in the creation of the Thunderbird and later the Mustang, two of the most successful models in automotive history.

At times we regard failures like the Edsel as a sign of American bumbling—our inability to properly plan and strategize. Other societies seem to have more of a knack for this. It is still widely believed, for example, that the Japanese invasion of American markets was the result of superior foresight and brilliant master planning by central ministries. Why can't we be more like them?

The Japanese Were More Like Us

But in fact, the Japanese succeeded in invading foreign markets by acting more like us! Contrary to widespread belief, Japan's ministries did not foresee the invasion of American markets and pick "winners" to carry out their plan. In fact the Ministry of International Trade and Industry (MITI) and the Ministry of Finance performed dismally, consistently supporting losers while winners like Honda and Sony had to fend largely for themselves.[11]

And these winners did not succeed by brilliant foresight. Honda, for instance, fell flat on its face in its first attack on the American motorcycle market. Nissan had to be pushed into the American car market, and arrived with a heavy, slow, boxlike model that seemed almost designed to fail, which it did.

Successful Japanese companies, however, often *did* demonstrate the ability to find opportunity in the midst of such failure. Honda, for example, came to America with no master plan beyond simply trying to sell something in a huge market. There was no discussion of profits by Honda's top management, and no deadlines to break even; the company simply hoped to gain 10 percent of America's import market. As for state support, the Ministry of Finance approved a piddling $250,000 in financing. Honda's secret was its deft responses to a string of entirely unexpected events, many of them failures.

Honda opened its American invasion with its larger 250cc and 350cc models, which promptly flopped; they were too puny for American-scale speed and distances, and broke down too often. Meanwhile its Los Angeles office began getting calls about the little 50cc Supercub, or "Moped," which Honda employees had brought from Japan to run errands around the city. Honda executives figured the Mopeds had no market in America, and in any case might hurt the macho image the company was striving for. But to their complete surprise, Angelinos were quite interested. To their further surprise, the callers weren't the usual motorcycle dealers but Sears, sporting goods stores, and bicycle shops.

Corporate graveyards are strewn with companies that ignore such surprising events, but Honda went with them. Later it adopted a punchy and effective ad campaign: "You meet the nicest people on a Honda," a final repudiation of its original macho image. Spurred by the Moped, Honda sales went from half a million dollars in 1960 to $77 million in 1966. The next year, its share of the entire U.S. market (not just U.S. imports) was a whopping 63 percent. The product, the distribution network that launched Honda in America, and the "nicest people" ad campaign, were all the result of being open to the most unexpected, and unsettling, events—by asking "Where's the opportunity here?"

"But Why?"

The second way to uncover unexpected opportunity is to carefully study established practices or the conventional wisdom and ask, "But why?"

When American leaders met in Philadelphia in 1787 to restructure the United States, much of what they wound up doing contradicted the "best" thinking. Most leading political thinkers, including the famed Montesquieu, held, for example, that republics must be small; but James Madison worked out a scheme to make America a republic that depended on being large. All theorists, including John Locke, held that political power couldn't be divided; but the very essence of American federalism was to divide power with abandon. Present them with the most widely accepted piece of conventional wisdom, and they'd ask, "But why? Does it apply to our particular circumstances?"

Even when it does fit, it's still worthwhile to ask the question. Sam Walton spent countless hours roaming Kmarts, found out that most of that discount retailer's practices *did* made sense—and adopted, improved, and extended them. But very often the answer doesn't make sense, and that can point the way to substantial opportunity.

When Lamar Muse, Roland King, and Herb Kelleher created an airline to serve economy-minded, short-haul business travelers in Texas, they had no trouble distinguishing Southwest Airlines from other carriers. Most of what the major carriers were doing made no sense for Southwest's market. They were falling all over themselves, for instance, to provide frills to passengers: fancy meals, lots of attendants, in-flight movies, vacation packages. Southwest offered low ticket prices, highly dependable service, and no frills: no meals (peanuts and crackers only), minimal attendants, no assigned seats, not even baggage transfers. Other carriers had three pilots in the cockpit; Southwest uses two. Other carriers used the hub-and-spoke system; Southwest flies directly to its destinations. Others use a variety of aircraft models; Southwest flies only the efficient Boeing 737 to save on parts, maintenance, and mechanics' training. Other airlines are hooked into travel agents' reservations systems; Southwest refuses.

The very act of scrutinizing an industry can suggest an entirely new market, as well as ways to exploit it. Companies, like people, fall into bad habits they can't change. This creates opportunities for someone else.

Gourmet Coffee and Financial Software for the Masses

Howard Schultz wondered why his own employer, gourmet coffeemaker Starbucks, didn't try to sell to a broader market. Fifty percent of Americans drink coffee every day and most of it is bad—instant, freeze-dried, or perhaps percolated from grounds out of a tin can. Why not make good coffee widely available? Further, with alcohol consumption and the popularity of bars on the decline in America, why not expand the traditional gourmet coffee shop into a sort of coffee bar?–an idea inspired by a trip to Italy where Schultz had observed the locals' fondness for conversation over coffee at neighborhood cafes.

But Schultz's bosses dismissed the idea as a diversion that would not add value. So in 1987 he got together $3.8 million to buy his company's six stores, tried out the concept (it finally began winning acceptance in 1990), and in less than five years had built one thousand stores that were bringing in total profits of $35 million a year.

Often industry outsiders are the ones who can best spot the bad habits of industry leaders, and ask, "But why?" When Scott Cook, a former brand manager for vegetable shortening at Procter & Gamble, was looking for a business to start in the early 1980s, his wife complained one day that doing the monthly bills was taking more time and becoming more difficult. Cook figured that plenty of other people must have the same complaint since his wife was a computer marketing consultant with an M.B.A. from the University of Wisconsin. Cook then studied the available home finance software on the market and found a major anomaly: They were all too complicated, filled with technical accounting terms even computer nerds couldn't get the hang of.

Cook therefore decided to create Intuit Inc., whose first product was Quicken, a supremely easy-to-use home finance program with a main display that looked like an ordinary check. Quicken would eventually dominate the household market, becoming so associated in people's minds with making a tedious process simple and fast that when QuickBooks was introduced for small businesses in the early 1990s, its programs became top-sellers immediately. And this despite facing a host of very savvy competitors, including Microsoft. (Indeed, Microsoft seriously discussed buying the company from Cook for a reported $1.5 billion.)

Challenging Giants

Perceived inadequacies of your own company, or "barriers to entry" posed by industry leaders, might be nothing more than accepting as gospel some industry practices you should question instead. Fledgling Dell Computer, started by Michael Dell in his University of Texas dorm room in 1984, couldn't hope to match IBM's direct sales force or Compaq's dealer network. But so? Both of those capabilities represented traditional ways of marketing products; PCs were different. Why not advertise in the burgeoning PC magazines that "geeks" liked to read, and sell direct to them over the phone. After all, Dell and his employees, who were geeks themselves, knew much more about computers than PC store clerks did. And while sending a computer through the mail isn't cheap, neither is maintaining an elaborate distribution network.

Manufacturing according to sales forecasts—the standard practice used by companies like IBM, Hewlett-Packard, and Compaq to make PCs—was also questionable to Dell. People's preferences, in terms of the capacity and features they want and the price they'll pay, vary widely, to say nothing of the rapid advances in technology that can make a model obsolete fast. If Compaq or IBM misses a forecast by the smallest margin, they can be stuck with thousands of machines they can't sell, as well as tens of thousands of components they can't use. Why not build to order instead? Dell found that doing so isn't much harder than mass manufacturing, and that it doesn't take much longer to fill orders than shipping out of an inventory does, but it does allow the company to charge 15 to 20 percent less for each machine.

The business model created by challenging such industry conventions has proven exceptionally well suited to today's economy. As of this writing, Dell was already doing $4 million worth of business per day on the Internet, while most companies are still trying to figure out how to make any money at all there. A purchasing manager who needs, say, five engineering work stations can go to Dell's Website, specify the configuration he wants, see what it will cost, place his order, have his company billed, and receive them, all in five days.

"If Only"

Thomas Jefferson's famous embargo of English manufacturing provides our third money-making phrase. When Jefferson imposed it, New England shipping was virtually destroyed as "forests of dead masts gradually filled once flourishing harbors."[12] The situation became even more bleak when outright war erupted in 1812. However, the thoughts of many New England sea merchants turned not to despair, but to seemingly fanciful opportunity—even wishful thinking. "If only we had factories here," they thought. It was true they could no longer trade with England, but it was equally true that England could no longer sell its manufactures to America. If America had its own textile factories, the New Englanders could use their ships to take Southern cotton not to factories in England but to new mills in Philadelphia, perhaps, or New York.

This led to more wishful thinking. Since no one else was building textile factories in America, why not build our own? It was a bold idea, and brilliant: The New Englanders could not only keep their ships employed, they could also use their knowledge of merchandising and trade to sell the finished goods. Thus was born the American factory system, arguably the single most important event in the transformation of a rural economy into a modern industrial one, with the epochal changes it created in capital, labor, and cities. It was achieved by New Englanders engaged, as Alexis de Tocqueville said of their forebears, in "the dreams of fancy and the unrestrained experiments of innovators."[13]

A few years ago PacBell executives noticed a variety of promising new technologies appearing on the scene. Yet the company wasn't taking advantage of them because its own employees hadn't anticipated their appearance or planned for their use. Executives weren't sure *how* the company could exploit them but believed ways could be found to do so if the right PacBell employees opened their minds to the possibility.

They therefore asked a particularly creative senior manager, John Lewis, to form a team with a broad, open-ended goal: Think of ways to substantially increase productivity. There were no detailed instructions, no real guidance like "cut the costs of purchased items in your area 5 percent." Some managers would dread such an assignment, but Lewis relished the challenge.

Realizing he would have to find ways to encourage new thinking, he scheduled a few days for his team to meet offsite. To avoid getting mired in the same old PacBell problems, he started by "firing" everyone on the team including himself, in order to encourage a fresh-start atmosphere. He had everyone imagine they'd just inherited a phone company from a forgotten uncle. They could run it any way they wanted to, subject to only one constraint required by reality: "Uncle Herman" hadn't left enough money for a new computer system. Otherwise, they were free to do anything they wanted with "the company."

Still, team members got bogged down in the PacBell culture, speaking in corporate acronyms and reverting to familiar ways of thinking. Lewis attacked that by imposing a twenty-five-cent "cocktail fine" for each use of PacBell-speak, which helped "though we did have many cocktails," recalls Lewis. Soon the acronyms and buzzwords cleared up and fresh thinking came more easily.

With the team more receptive to creative approaches, Lewis began encouraging them to start sentences with a variation of "If only"–by saying "I wish." No holds were barred; what in the best of all worlds would they like to see "the company" do, subject to the one constraint? After some initial hesitation, team members began to catch the spirit and eventually one came up with a winner: the "wish" that whenever a customer called with a problem, the first person who answered the phone could solve it rather than switch the call to various people until it lands in the "right" department.

This was a difficult goal: PacBell office workers would need fast, easy access to numerous databases—a tough problem without expensive new computer systems. But it was also dramatic and worthy, and enthusiastic team members tackled it with a gusto that generated a stream of new ways of thinking about the business. *Now* they began finding ways to bring together the new technologies PacBell had never figured out how to exploit before—not because the team asked, "What are some ways to exploit this technology?" but rather because it had a worthwhile challenge and wanted to use every available tool to meet it.

Feeling less constrained by previous practices, the team also felt free to work outside PacBell's existing organizational structure. In four weeks they confidently brainstormed a new PacBell company, which was later called Infotel. The result: Infotel did not quite reach the original "I wish" goal, but made substantial progress toward it. Heavy manuals and cumbersome forms, as well as most customer handoffs, were eliminated. Customers could get call waiting activated in seconds rather than hours. When one customer's daughter knocked over a fish tank and shorted out a line, repairmen arrived before the customer knew the line was dead.

The team also went to work to develop a first-rate software program that would eventually allow individual customer service reps to handle almost any call, whether from a customer questioning a bill, reporting trouble on the line, or inquiring about new services. And it was able to achieve this revamped—and much more productive—customer service operation by jerry-rigging the old computer system rather than buying a new, easy-to-use but expensive one.

8

We Hold These Truths to Be Self-Evident

How Americans Exploit Opportunity

A group, or team, or division tackles an ambitious project—to open a new market, devise a new process, develop a new product line, or exploit some other source of opportunity. They've given it careful thought, discussion, and planning; morale and confidence are high. But, however great the potential of the new effort, however exciting its prospects, one thing is sure: Things won't work out as planned. The final result will bear little resemblance to the original concept, particularly for an effort that is truly novel. People will have to learn, adapt, and reformulate the original concept as they go; indeed, their ability to do so will be key to the project's success.

Here we'll ask, How *do* Americans learn—naturally? How did they normally interact and adapt to their environment, before they were inundated with management themes and buzz phrases? After all, they have a long history of creating technologies, establishing communities, building businesses and industries—even creating a nation. Here we'll see how they did so, and how some organizations are recapturing an extraordinary source of wealth creation.

YOUR BEST SOURCE OF KNOWLEDGE

Perhaps the most recognized sentence in American history begins, "We hold these truths to be self-evident. . . ." In his original draft of the Declaration of Independence, Thomas Jefferson wrote "We hold these truths to be *sacred and undeniable*" (italics added). It was probably Benjamin Franklin, the down-to-earth businessman and politician, as well as the best experimental scientist in America, who suggested the change to "self-evident."[1] It was readily accepted by the more philosophical Jefferson as well as the rest of Congress.

The founders were emphasizing that even the most important truths aren't sacred or mysterious, understood only by some higher authority. To the contrary, they can be readily perceived by anyone. The Revolution fostered a major step in the development of thinking and action in America. Franklin, Jefferson, Thomas Paine, and the other American revolutionaries believed that it was absurd to look to higher authorities in order to understand how the world works. Nature's laws could be discovered by anyone intelligent enough, using reason and experience.

Franklin in particular should know; he proved this himself repeatedly, often to the astonishment of learned experts.

Focus on the Self-Evident

After Benjamin Franklin retired from business and grew interested in the new phenomenon of electricity, Europe's professional scientists scoffed—this man Franklin was a businessman and political operative with no academic credentials. Yet he would confound Europe's professionals by discovering what they'd been unable to, that electricity is a fundamental force of nature, the same stuff as lightning, thus uncovering perhaps the most important technology in history. To a great extent he did so simply by focusing on the self-evident.

At that time electricity was thought to be merely a curiosity created by rubbing glass bottles or thick carpets with one's feet, useful only for parlor tricks. But impressed by the wallop an electrical charge could pack, Franklin suspected there was more to it than that. He wasn't the first to conjecture that electricity might be the same stuff as lightning, but he was the first to believe and confirm it.

Europe's leading scientists approached the question by reasoning from existing theories and concluded, wrongly, that electricity and lightning were unrelated. Franklin, on the other hand, who had less than a second-grade education and was largely ignorant of theoretical science, investigated the issue by experimenting–a process whose methods he *had* studied closely.² And many of his efforts amounted to "trying a lot of stuff and seeing what works." For instance, to figure out how to discharge an electrically charged metal ball, he and his fellow experimenters tried everything from pouring sand over it, to breathing on it, to blowing smoke on it from a piece of burning wood, to holding a lit candle near it.

What caused Franklin to think that electricity was indeed a form of lightning? By simply focusing on the self-evident, observing what anyone could notice, and reasoning in a way that anyone could understand. In the course of his experiments Franklin noticed that this new stuff looked and acted, on a small scale, just like lightning; today we might say it passed the "duck test." He noted that both gave off the same color. Both moved "swiftly," and in a "crooked direction." Both could ignite flammable substances. Both gave off a sulfurous smell, and so on–to a total of twelve common, readily observable properties. Only one thing wasn't known to Franklin: He'd found that a sharp metal rod would draw off an electrical spark from a charged ball at a considerable distance. Would such a rod do the same with lightning from a cloud? Since they had all other properties in common, Franklin thought it likely they would also have this in common and concluded his journal entry that day with, "Let the experiment be made."

Similarly self-evident observations suggested his superb kite experiment. There were no buildings in Philadelphia tall enough to get a metal rod close to any clouds passing by, so he tied a sharp piece of metal to a kite and flew it in a thunderstorm. The result, as we know, confirmed his guess: The tools scientists were creating to generate electricity (Franklin himself invented, and named, the electric battery) were harnessing an awesome force of nature that could one day be put to humanity's use. And in a telling difference between the pragmatic Franklin and the overly theoretical Europeans, the Abbé Nollet, the most respected European expert on electricity (the same one who had dismissed Franklin's discoveries as the result of "mere" observation) tried to prove him wrong with theoretical arguments. The worldly Franklin declined the challenge, preferring to let his results speak for themselves.

This simple emphasis on self-evident observation has been essential not only to America's intellectual and technological development, but to its economic growth and in particular, to Americans' ability to exploit opportunity.

Do the Obvious Thing

We've seen how New England merchants recognized a major opportunity, even in the face of apparent disaster, when Thomas Jefferson's embargo shut off their trade with English factories. But how did they successfully *exploit* it? This wasn't easy either, from one standpoint.

After all, how could they possibly expect to build their own factories in Massachusetts? Europe had been manufacturing textiles for decades—but there was no comparable organized manufacturing system in America, no knowledge of technology to build the machines such a system would need, and no tradition of crafts to furnish trained people to run them. Had an English manufacturer tried to set up operations in America based on English experience, he would have been completely stymied.

Yet in only a few years, European visitors to Waltham and Lowell, Massachusetts, were astonished to see thriving textile factories in the American "backwater." Indeed, they were clearly superior to anything in Europe. How did the Americans do it? To a large extent, they'd simply tried the obvious thing. When the Europeans looked closely at these flourishing new factories they weren't struck by their novelty or inventiveness, but instead wondered why no one had thought of such things before.

For example, in England, the textile manufacturing process was highly decentralized. The reason? Because of sharp traditional distinctions between crafts such as spinning, weaving, and dyeing, and also because water rights were heavily fragmented, which made it impossible to get enough water power in one place to run all the machines. Thus manufacturing in England was typically scattered around many different sites.

But the Americans completely ignored that aspect of the English system, thoroughly centralizing their own factories. Unlike in England, plenty of large sources of water power were available in New England. One friend of the Lowell developers blithely asked why they didn't just buy up the Pawtucket Canal; it would give them the whole power of the Merrimack River with a fall of over thirty feet. Such a suggestion would have astonished any English manufacturer, if he took it seriously in the first place. But the suggestion made perfect sense on its face to the Americans, who proceeded to do just that.

With such a massive power source in one place and free from European cultural constraints, the first American factory builders put all processes under one roof from the first. They simply saw no reason why an operation couldn't be set up, contrary to what they'd seen in England, at a site where raw cotton could go in one end and finished cloth ready to ship would come out the other.

As for the technology needed to build the machines, where did that come from? Not by invention; the early American textile industry would devise few new processes and completely fail to invent manufacturing machines or even improve them significantly. The knowledge required for such technological breakthroughs was still lacking in America. So the American factory builders again did the obvious thing; they went to England and filched theirs. Francis Cabot Lowell, for whom the soon-to-be thriving manufacturing town of Lowell was named, learned manufacturing processes by visiting English cotton mills under the ruse that he was traveling to improve his suddenly poor health. Indeed the Americans grew adept at smuggling English knowledge, enticing the brilliant English engineer Samuel Slater to stow away to America and build cotton spinners here.

Seattle-based Price/Costco, Inc. has put that same outlook to work—that is, simply focusing on the self-evident and doing the obvious thing—to exploit opportunity in, of all places, the English retail market. A Costco manager, Paul Moulton, noticed that British retailers were living off the fat of the land. How? Not by commissioning a sophisticated study but simply by pouring over their annual reports. British supermarkets, for instance, were grossing a hefty 7 to 8 percent on revenue (versus the 1 or 2 percent typical in America at the time).

Moulton then took a close, firsthand look at British retailing by making site visits to virtually every type of store: supermarkets, department stores, furniture stores, cash and carries. From straightforward observations made during those visits, Costco's strategy for invading the British market took shape. A simple walk through the aisles of British discounter Makro, for example, revealed prices 25 to 40 percent higher than Costco needed to charge; it could sell a Sony TV listed at $245, for example, for $150.

And to learn what Britons buy, Moulton simply looked for patterns on British store shelves. He was struck, for instance, by the extraordinary amount of space devoted to junk food, much more than in America, particularly for potato chips, candy, cookies, and other sweets. Moulton would find a place for them on Costco's shelves too.

Casual conversations with workers (Moulton found they'd open up to an American) laid the groundwork for a personnel strategy. British workers told Moulton how much they made, what working conditions they expected, and how they would like to fit financially and organizationally into a Costco store.

This isn't to say Price/Costco's British invasion is proving to be a bed of roses. Expenses in Britain are high, local shopkeepers are a formidable political force, and British shoppers are not traditionally as price-conscious as Americans. But here's another fact Moulton picked up on his visits to England: British retailers act as fat as they look on paper. Visits to their corporate headquarters revealed opulent offices on pricey property, together with bloated staffs. Moulton noted that one maintained a corporate staff of two thousand where a comparable American firm would get by with half that.

Moulton made one other valuable discovery while looking around London. Costco Europe headquarters is now located in a cheap-rent, working-class suburb of London as opposed to the gilt-edged locations of its competitors. After setting up a small office to share with three subordinates, surrounded by metal desks and beat-up filing cabinets, Moulton remarked, "It's cheaper out here." Costco Europe's prospects continue to look solid because it was established by a hands-on manager who based decisions on what he saw and heard with his own eyes and ears. As Moulton puts it, "My best information doesn't come from data; data doesn't tell you why."

RECAPTURING AMERICAN PRAGMATISM

What can go wrong with thinking when decision-makers confront a new situation? How does the sort of fresh, dynamic creativity exhibited by a Benjamin Franklin, a Francis Lowell, or a Paul Moulton get stifled? Very often it happens something like this: A problem lands on a decision-maker's desk. To handle it, he breaks it down into its parts, classifies, or pigeonholes them, and then solves the pieces by applying the applicable theoretical tool. That gives the problem a nice familiar look. "This is a routine accounting problem," or "This conforms to the proper sequence for new product development," or "This is just like that situation we had in Chicago."

Such thinking is based on the dubious notion that unchanging principles underlie business, and that managers must seek out highly trained experts with elaborate theories to explain them—to show how, for instance, strategy, or financial management, or product life cycles work. But that outlook is rooted more in European traditions than in our own.

That's *not* how thinking developed naturally in America; Americans dealt with a novel, rapidly changing, and democratic environment that seemed to follow no rules. Rather than a theoretical approach to thinking and learning, Americans moved toward a more pragmatic approach, best articulated by Charles Pierce, William James, and the great educator John Dewey.

They urged philosophers and professional thinkers to acknowledge what the American experience had shown time and again: The search for nature's timeless essences and unchanging laws, the fundamental principles on which the universe is built, is futile. The process of breaking situations down into distinct parts, applying the "correct" theory, and putting the pieces back together into a whole doesn't reflect reality anymore than gluing together the pieces of a broken mirror does. Such an outlook assumes that different situations, properly broken down and analyzed, are essentially the same.

But a much different way of thinking and interacting with the world developed as Americans built the country. American pragmatists regarded each circumstance as unique; it has to be understood on its own terms and within its own particular context. No generalized theory can possibly capture the intricacies, the unique subtleties inherent in any complex real-world situation. Rather than break a problem down into familiar-looking parts in a false quest for simplicity, the pragmatist "builds it up" by asking what makes it and the context in which it occurs different. Rather than emphasize the distinctions between the various pieces of the puzzle in order to compartmentalize thinking, the pragmatist looks for their interconnectedness, for how they relate to each other, to the whole, and to the larger environment. This is a key to understanding reality, and to exploiting the opportunity it presents.[3]

Here's one approach that can stimulate such an outlook, illustrated by a consummate American pragmatist to deal with one of history's greatest challenges.

Don't Follow the Book . . .

Had George Washington relied during the first year of the American Revolution on "the book"–the accepted theory of fighting war in his day–he, and the country, would have been sunk. Instead he threw the book out and found a better way to deal with the daunting task he faced. Here's how.

According to the book, wars were won by defeating the enemy in a single all-out, decisive battle or a "general action." In addition, armies were expected to protect major cities at all costs. To this "knowledge" the Americans had added their own "lessons learned" (wrongly, as it turned out) from their early successes against the

British—that amateur militia could rise to the defense of their homes and rout British regulars at a moment's notice, as they had at Concord, and that entrenchments were the secret weapon for inflicting huge casualties, as they'd been at Bunker (Breed's) Hill, whenever the British attacked in force.

But all these "rules" started looking dubious to Washington. The British learned quickly enough to avoid frontal assaults against American entrenchments by simply going around them, and America's amateur farmboy-soldiers were proving to be no match for hardened British and Hessian regulars in open battle, particularly when the Americans were outnumbered, which they almost always were. (In the early victory at Concord, Americans had outnumbered the British five to one, and knew it.) Now just a few months into the war, Washington faced a rapidly deteriorating situation. The British army had landed the largest expeditionary force in history in New York, which had promptly driven his army out of Manhattan, and chased it from one end of New Jersey to the other.

For Washington to hazard an all-out battle against the British at this point would have been suicide. In any case Washington's knowledge of standard military doctrine was weak; he himself had little training in the subject. But that still left Washington with the question, What do we do? British forces were now stationed on the Delaware River within an easy march of Philadelphia, the American capital. Meanwhile the enlistments for Washington's tattered and still-inexperienced army were about to expire.

. . . Satisfy the Purpose

Washington proceeded to throw out the book on warfare with its rules and truisms. He focused instead on what unique purposes he and his army needed to serve in the particular circumstances they faced. Here was food for thought. Their immediate purpose was not to defeat the British army per se—an impossible task at this stage of the war in any case—but rather to secure American independence. And that had already been established: American-run governments were up and running in each state, and a national government was operating in Philadelphia. The Americans therefore didn't need to destroy the British army right away because they didn't need to win independence; it was up to the British to take it away!

Thinking in this way, Washington saw further that time was on the Americans' side. Maintaining a huge expeditionary force three thousand miles away was a constant drain on Britain's treasury, still reeling from a world war fought just over a decade earlier. As for protecting large cities, Washington decided that in the future he would offer only token resistance. America wasn't Europe, where money and power were concentrated in a few great population centers. American patriots were scattered on farms and villages throughout the countryside, not in cities. Indeed the cities tended to be filled with loyalists, so why defend them? As for Congress or the state governments, they could always pack up and move down the road when British troops threatened, which they indeed did with little disruption to their operations.

Thus while others panicked and began urging desperate measures, Washington stayed cool. He could take the time he needed to build up a more battle-worthy army, as well as wait for potential allies like the French to enter the war. He saw only one immediate danger from the British occupation of New Jersey—not the threat to Philadelphia, but the threat to patriot sentiment where it was strongest, in the countryside. Hundreds of New Jerseyites were going over to the British side daily; meanwhile calls by Washington for New Jersey's sixteen-thousand-man militia resulted in a turnout of only a thousand or so.

By thus concentrating his attention on the particular situation at hand, Washington was able to narrow his focus to a manageable issue—in the process, he uncovered a superb opportunity. Occupying the New Jersey countryside required the British to scatter their forces and stretch their supply lines thin. Sown throughout the same countryside were thousands of patriot farmers with squirrel guns who needed just a little show of spirit to energize them. Washington decided to give it to them, knowing it was the last thing the British expected.

On Christmas Day, he led his army across the freezing Delaware and marched it on through a blizzard to the British outpost at Trenton, which it took from surprised and drunken Hessian soldiers without a fight. When the aggressive Lord Cornwallis heard of the attack and came on the fly from New York, Washington sneaked around his flank and thrust deeper into enemy territory. The British were aghast; the idiot was placing his inferior force behind a stronger one and cutting his supply lines, something a professional army would never be foolish enough to do! But Washington had thrown the book out again. He had seen for himself that citizen soldiers fighting for freedom didn't need to tie themselves down to a secure base. Unburdened by heavy equipment and able to think for themselves, they could move much faster than the British. Washington led them up the road and bagged a second British post at Princeton.

Confirming Washington's insight, the hopes of New Jersey patriots soared, and they poured out to take pot shots at the British. Suddenly it was Cornwallis who found himself in enemy territory, his supply lines stretched thin and vulnerable to emboldened militia. Now he was the hunted, Washington the hunter who chased the suddenly desperate British back to their main camp at New Brunswick. Cornwallis won that race against Washington's exhausted army (otherwise the Revolution might well have ended right there). But Washington's attack completely changed the war, making it unwinnable for the British. Never again would their army try to occupy large portions of American territory; in the future they always stuck close to deep water and the protection of their navy. By throwing out the book and asking what purpose they were trying to achieve in the unique circumstances at hand, Washington had made the American interior—and thus the American Revolution—safe from British threat. It was now only a matter of time before Britain would be thrown off the American continent for good.

How a Junior Staffer Out-thought the Expert

Washington's pragmatic approach is not just for leaders. It's open to anyone. It was used, for example, by one junior staffer in a national consumer products company to keep the firm from wasting millions of dollars—and to save millions instead.

Several years ago, the company had uncovered a variety of problems at one of its distribution warehouses: delivery delays, excessive overtime, damaged goods, misshipments, and so forth. A company vice president decided to hire a consultant (in this case an efficiency expert) to recommend a solution.

Immediately the consultant plunged ahead with gathering facts and compiling statistics—studying warehouse operations, product perishability, frequency of shipping delays, labor overtime, and other aspects of distribution costs. Her approach, like that of many experts, was to solve the problem using her arsenal of analytical tools. After much time and expense she concluded that the damage was occurring at the warehouse loading dock. Her recommendation: Spend $60,000 to automate it, which she pointed out would be earned back in eight months—an excellent return on investment. Indeed it would be a good idea to automate all twenty-four of the company's warehouses at a cost of $1.44 million.

Then, merely to be thorough, the vice president asked a junior staff engineer to review the consultant's calculations. Imagine his surprise when the young man came back with his recommendation not only that the VP decline her request, but that the company get rid of all but a few of the warehouses rather than fix them up.

Not content with just punching his calculator, the young engineer had wondered about all those warehouses in the first place. What were they doing there? Rather than focus on the problems they'd encountered, he wondered what *purposes* they served. The warehouses were placed around the country and used as intermediate shipping points, receiving the company's products from its plants and then shipping them on to customers. Most people would have accepted that state of affairs as a given, and gone on. But the young man wanted to know why the company distributed that way. He continued to ask, "Why? What's the purpose?"

Years earlier, it turned out, the company had done all its shipping by railroad directly from plant to customers. But after a ruinous railroad strike had nearly crippled the company, they decided to build regional warehouses to store inventory that could be shipped by truck, freeing the company from dependence on the railroads. But all that was fifty years ago! There are now, to say the least, a lot more distribution options available. The staffer began researching them.

With some additional figuring, he concluded it would be much cheaper to ship directly to dealers using various forms of transportation. The vice president, recovering from his initial astonishment, agreed. Instead of spending over a million dollars automating the warehouses, the company sold twenty of the twenty-four, retaining just four distribution centers at the main assembly plants and shipping goods directly to dealers, thus saving far more in overhead as well as direct costs. All because a junior staffer had thought beyond the immediate problem to be solved to the broader purpose to be served.[4]

THE LEARN-BY-DOING ORGANIZATION

At the core of such pragmatic thinking is the outlook of the experimental scientist: Pragmatists rely less on abstract theories to understand the world, and more on observation and testing. They believe people dealing with the real world can act most effectively not by fitting situations into some external theory, reasoning deductively from that, and then taking action. Rather they reason inductively, from the facts uncovered in the situation at hand, to create their *own* theory. Learning and action thus aren't separated, but *combined* in an ongoing interaction with one constantly informing the other. This is key to mastering the uniqueness and complexity inherent in real world situations.

The pragmatist is particularly wary of any knowledge that comes between him and the uniqueness of the situation at hand. For example, one common mistake made by highly educated Americans is to rely too heavily on data and quantitative methods, believing this is what it means to be objective and scientific. But such an outlook can remove one from reality as surely as excessive reliance on a theory. David Halberstam paints a vivid picture of that quantitative analyst extraordinaire–Secretary of Defense Robert McNamara during the Vietnam War and one of corporate America's most renowned executives–poring over reams of data whether he was at his desk, on a plane, or in Saigon, studying all the statistics that proved we were winning the war when the evidence that we were losing was all around him. "He scurried around Vietnam," wrote Halberstam, "looking for what he wanted to see; and he never saw nor smelled nor felt what was really there, right in front of him."[5]

A pragmatist would show at least as much interest in seeing, smelling, and feeling tangible evidence as she would in analyzing the data, and would rely much more on "what works" than on sophisticated quantitative methods.

This approach makes understanding the world far more accessible, and thus far more appropriate, as John Dewey liked to point out, to a democratic society. Few people can master all the theories or methods that pertain to their field of endeavor, but almost anyone can learn to observe and experiment.

Instilling Pragmatism on the Front Lines at PECO

Several years ago, the Eddystone Generating Station of Philadelphia Electric (now PECO) found itself suddenly in deep trouble. Deregulation had introduced aggressive new competition to a once sleepy, protected industry. In addition the plant's thermal efficiency, the amount of electricity it could generate from each ton of coal burned, had seriously declined over the years. Now the plant's survival was at stake; it had to cut costs dramatically.[6]

To achieve this, staffers and the station's engineers tried installing state-of-the-art solutions: the latest computer system for monitoring furnace efficiency, upgraded plant equipment and materials, elaborate written procedures. But these didn't work because they weren't built into the day-to-day operations of the plant; thermal efficiency, for instance, began to decline as soon as the engineers turned their attention elsewhere.

The superintendent of operations then decided to try a less artificial and more experimental approach that involved more people. He and his managers set a specific, incremental goal that would increase thermal efficiency about $500,000 worth per year, identified a few obvious improvements they could make in the next few months, and then assigned employee teams–which included people who would have to live with the results, not just engineers–to pursue them. This infused energy into the effort.

For instance, one team composed of operators and maintenance employees focused on heat escaping through openings in plant furnaces. Their first project: Make sure all ninety-six inspection doors on the furnace walls function properly and close when they're not in use. Another tackled steam loss from hundreds of valves around the plant. They began by eliminating all the leaks in one area of the plant, then moved on to the next, then the next.

With confidence growing from concrete successes, these teams invented several highly creative processes that no training program could have taught. The second team invented, for example, improvements in valve-packing practices and devised new methods for reporting leaks. And when they did take training–for instance, in analytic techniques and team building–it was done only as needed to help achieve specific goals like better performance measures or faster progress.

After the initial improvements were achieved, a steering committee consulted with team supervisors and employees on lessons learned and insights gained to establish the next series of goals. By the end of the first year, the PECO teams had doubled the original savings goal by achieving one million dollars in improved efficiency with no additional plant investment. More important, their approach to change–of combining learning and action, and doing so at the level of those who'd have to live with the results–sparked a new dynamism at the plant.

Employees who participated in the project grew more self-reliant, and their teams assumed greater autonomy. A number were asked by the steering committee to pursue their own efficiency improvement projects. Eventually the steering committee was disbanded, so that anyone pursuing an improvement project would report directly to senior management. Further, the new experimental spirit helped loosen up a once hide-bound, bureaucratic organization, making it more flexible and open to change. Setting and achieving ambitious short-term goals has entered the company's culture, causing managers to push decisions further down in the organization.

An Organization of Experimenters

Why not instill such an experimental outlook throughout an organization? Why not pursue John Dewey's dynamic vision of a society that educates all its citizens, not by instilling facts and generalized knowledge into their minds, but by giving them the tools to learn their own facts and create their own knowledge in any situation they encounter? Why not teach people throughout the organization, in other words, the methods of experimental science and have them practice these every day?[7]

You might react to that idea, and to projects like the PECO process improvement effort, by saying that while they are certainly worthwhile they are rather modest undertakings, hardly earth-shaking. Particularly for a company that needs drastic change and quantum advances that require much more dramatic measures, such as bold and sweeping new strategies, for example, or breakthrough new management concepts.

But an intensive, ongoing study by a group of twenty-seven industry executives and academics, called the Manufacturing Vision Group, has shown otherwise. It is just such humble-looking projects as the PECO effort—which take a pragmatic, incremental, and widely participative approach—that are key to making bold advances in competitive world markets. More specifically, projects that:

- have clear goals with a tangible impact on strategy or the bottom line, as opposed to broad-based management programs;
- are pursued using an experimental approach; and,
- are well integrated from the start, removing artificial conceptual barriers—particularly those between learning and action, between specialists who design and employees who must live with the results.[8]

Why are projects such as these so powerful? Because however modest they may appear, they have been central to the dramatic resurgence of American manufacturing in industries like computers, semiconductors, automobiles, and steel in the 1990s. When used to develop new products or create new production processes, they've led to dramatic breakthroughs in ways that broad-based management theories and sweeping new strategies could never achieve—such as Hewlett-Packard's foray into broad consumer markets with its DeskJet printer, or the entry by highly regarded "minimill" Chaparral Steel into higher-margin markets with a radically new casting process. They achieve such breakthroughs because they tap Americans' superb capacity for experimentation *throughout* their organizations. And this is proving more than a match for the most difficult competitive challenges,[9] as it has throughout our history.

When Chaparral Steel decided, for example, to try and develop a horizontal casting process, executives faced a major difficulty. The company's existing vertical casting process—used by all minimills at the time—was not capable of producing high grade steel. But previous efforts in the industry to create the necessary horizontal casters had failed.

Nevertheless, Chaparral executives did not hand the problem over to specialists. Instead they put together a team that included line operators, the people who would actually operate any new caster the company developed. Refusing to be limited by previous failures in the steel industry, they sent the team to study successful horizontal casting processes at copper and aluminum manufacturers throughout the world. And the Chaparral team went with a decidedly open and experimental outlook. There was no scoffing that such metals are easier to cast than steel and therefore there was nothing to learn. To the contrary, these visits prompted a rich flow of ideas that the team developed into a design it thought just might work.

At one point, executives considered hiring an engineering company to build a prototype of the new caster offsite. But they decided instead to install it on Chaparral's own shop floor where production operators could start experimenting with it right away. Eventually the caster began producing billets successfully and the company built a primitive production line, which employees continued to refine. And before launching full-scale production, the Chaparral team once again visited all the aluminum and copper casting sites and came up with additional ideas to improve their design. The result was a genuinely innovative process that eventually produced 300,000 tons of steel per year of even higher quality than executives had hoped for, a superb technical accomplishment for a minimill with fewer than a thousand employees.

THE PRAGMATIC COMPETITOR

The importance of such projects to companies like Chaparral Steel and Hewlett-Packard goes well beyond the specific processes or products they create, superb as these might be. Like PECO, the Manufacturing Vision Group found they can have a substantial impact for the better on the organization's ability to compete. In particular, they result in:

- *Better use of core competencies*
  An emphasis on such projects helps exercise a company's core capabilities and put them to work in new ways. The challenges

employees take on often result in profitable *new* capabilities. When General Electric was unable to get suitable plastics for its electrical products, for instance, it began making its own. In the process the company developed special competencies in engineered plastics, which eventually provided the basis for a major business—GE Plastics.

• *Development of better leaders*
What better way to develop future executives than by having them work "in the trenches" on new projects with clear goals that stretch people? Further, such leaders learn how to evaluate efforts whose outcome is uncertain; rather than gauge performance using previously set (and often arbitrary) goals, they learn to evaluate how well people did given all the circumstances actually encountered. This sends an important message: Management realizes that unpleasant outcomes are part of the experimental process, and it's more interested in learning from them than blaming people.

• *Better organizational learning*
Better learning is another prime benefit to an organization that emphasizes projects, because they involve a broad spectrum of employees who learn by doing something significant rather than engaging in abstract exercises.

But even these, as important as they are, don't quite capture the most beneficial impact such projects can have on an organization's competitiveness.

When they are well-focused and well-integrated, they provide perhaps the best way to overcome artificial distinctions between parts of a business—and instead emphasize their relatedness, their *interconnectedness*, a decidedly pragmatic value that fits a democratic and federal organization.[10] Nothing prompts such thinking as much as an actual project that must work and make money in the real world.

When Hewlett-Packard, for example, prepared to enter broader consumer markets with high-volume, low-cost products like personal computers and ink-jet printers, executives realized that the status of marketing and of manufacturing would have to change dramatically. No longer could high-status design engineers thumb their noses at them. The project that developed its famous DeskJet printer provided ways for executives to ensure this change.

They made sure, for example, that marketing and manufacturing were well represented in the effort, and that the designers paid attention to their concerns. Early in the project, when marketing's interactions with shoppers in malls resulted in twenty-four suggestions for design improvements, R&D engineers (as usual) ignored almost all of them. Project leaders and the marketers then pressured the designers to go out and visit the malls themselves. When they finally went, they wound up embracing seventeen more changes, including faster-drying ink and easier ways to feed paper. More important, the engineers began to understand the importance of marketing to the success of retail products.

The Power of the Humble Prototype

How can companies reinforce the tendency of such projects to break down barriers in an organization? This is essential in a turbulent, rapidly changing environment where the various parts of a company must continue to find new ways to organize, and new ways to relate to and reinforce each other. The key to doing so, as it turns out, is not exhortations from top management, but rather something much more modest—the humble prototype.

Companies like Chaparral Steel, Ford, and Hewlett-Packard have found that using prototypes in development projects can provide a powerful, unifying focus to the organization. Not prototypes in the traditional sense; that is, where they are built-in off-line model shops, only when design work is almost done, and only in order to check design feasibility and part fit. The new use taps the full potential of prototypes for integrating a complex project—in a way that emphasizes openness and experimentation. This happens when:

- They are built early and often; everyone works from them so that any proposed change can be evaluated by all.
- They are made as realistic as possible using mock-ups, computer simulations, and increasingly accurate models.
- They embody the entire system, not just one or two aspects.
- They are used not only for design but to integrate all project functions and support groups: everything from manufacturing feasibility to vendor compatibility to customer reactions.

From the first, project members thus avoid overly theoretical arguments about how to proceed; proposed alternatives can be tested right away.

Further, management needn't just *tell* people to work together and be more experimental; it can use prototypes to *build in* these traits into development projects. Ford learned this when executives assigned a team to improve the 1988 Continental in response to Japanese competition. Senior executives saw the need to integrate design, manufacturing, and marketing in the effort, but real integration never occurred. Their conclusion: The early use of prototypes in the project, which was nixed as too expensive, could have provided the necessary focus for the team. The money saved early on was more than lost in late changes, delays, and loss of profitability.

In contrast, the 1991 Crown Victoria/Grand Marquis development team built full-scale prototypes early, and right on the same production line that was building the existing model. Factory workers, thus involved in the process, came up with many suggested changes that improved the car's manufacturability, which designers were able to incorporate early on and in an orderly way. Further, the intensive learning by factory employees prompted by working with prototypes greatly smoothed the transition to full production when the time came.

The Manufacturing Vision Group found that while early use of prototypes is cumbersome and expensive at first, it ultimately leads to much faster, much less costly, and far more successful development projects overall. The reason? In traditional product development, when a new product finally reaches the production floor, change orders begin flying and confusion reigns because manufacturing is just then getting intimately acquainted with it. Under the new prototype-intensive system that involves manufacturing from the start, the flow of change orders is heavy only in the *early* stages of the development process—when drastic changes are *easiest* to make. By the time production starts, the flow has reduced to a trickle, and the change orders that do come are of a much different nature. Rather than frantic efforts just to make production work, changes tend to be localized and easily implemented, improving quality, appeal, or cost. Ideas for more radial changes can meanwhile be collected for the next generation of product.[11]

9

The Entrepreneurial Employee
Unleashing a Classic American Type

Companies have for some time felt increasing pressure to build entrepreneurism—the ability to uncover and exploit economic opportunity—into the very front lines of their organizations. Frontline employees are closer to customers, can better understand what they want, and can move faster to provide it. Also, downsized companies in a competitive world need to tap their knowledge workers' full range of talents—not just their technical expertise to do specified tasks, but their creativity and resourcefulness.

However, for American organizations there's a better reason. Entrepreneurism is a trait widely dispersed throughout American society. It almost seems that everyone—not just people like Rockefeller, Ford, Watson, and Gates—has the urge to venture in one form or another. Seventeen-year-old Benjamin Franklin escaped stifling Boston to seek opportunity in wide-open Philadelphia, where he immediately began looking for backers to start his own business, persisted until he found them, and wound up retiring at forty-two. George Washington had built up perhaps the biggest fortune in land in America by the time he died. Nathan Appleton, one of the creators of the American textile industry, used to keep one-third of his capital free for new projects and unforeseen opportunities. William Larimer ran a general store, a freight company, a coal company, a wholesale grocery, and got into the hotel, railroad, and banking businesses before trying and failing to found a city in Nebraska. Then, one step ahead of the gold rush, he tried and succeeded at founding Denver, Colorado. Nick Iacocca, an Italian immigrant and father of Chrysler chairman Lee, ran hotdog restaurants, started a car rental company (one of the first in America), and went into real estate until the Depression wiped him out. He then started over in restaurants, got back into real estate, and ultimately prospered.

Within a generation after the American Revolution, foreign observers thought virtually every American household was spending all its spare time spinning, weaving, tanning, tool-making—not just for itself but increasingly to sell in burgeoning markets. This longing to venture is undiminished to this day. More than 6 million American adults started a business of some sort—over 5 percent of the adult population—in one recent year alone.[1]

Very clearly this is a source of economic energy large organizations should be drawing upon; 71 percent of successful new business ideas come, according to a study of successful entrepreneurs by Harvard's Amar Bhide, from ideas encountered in previous employment.[2] Yet organizations have a very hard time tapping this energy.

Why Organizations and Entrepreneurs Don't Mix

In a word, the entrepreneurial process is antithetical to the way most companies do business. This is particularly true of corporate venturing, which creates not only new products but riskier, more uncertain new *businesses* that will at some point be managed separately from the core business.

Fast growing Intuit, the maker of Quicken, which has become the standard for household-accounting software, illustrates the problem. Intuit is exceptionally good at venturing; however the process is anything but smooth. Many of its ventures go absolutely nowhere, while many that do succeed require a second or third attempt. QuickBooks, the company's small-business accounting product, took several efforts and three years to create—plus another three on top of that to turn a profit. Of course, such efforts are worth it: Intuit grew from a single-product $50 million company to a multidivisional $500 million company in just four years.

But to most companies such a process looks like chaos. Traditional organizations deplore anything that seeks change, upsets markets, and disorganizes industries in ways that are inevitably unpredictable, but such are the necessary ingredients of true entrepreneurism's "creative destruction." Any number of administrative habits can sabotage successful venturing. An organizational bias, for example, may treat innovation as a stepchild of the main business; or an approval process for new ventures might be slow, unwieldy, and unfair. Factionalism and politicking might routinely block new ventures even when they manage to clear the formal approval process.

At one major telecommunications company, two well-regarded managers proposed a promising new venture: Provide basic, locally operated telecommunications services that would challenge inefficient local providers in a rapidly developing region. Two years later, the two quit in frustration and started their own company—to do exactly what they had proposed to their former employer. The reason: After well over a year of successfully navigating its bureaucracy, their original sponsor retired and was replaced by an executive who didn't like the idea and didn't want to lose the two from his area. Whatever the merits of the idea itself, this isn't how its fate, or that of two respected managers, should have been decided.

How can a company capitalize on the entrepreneurial impulses of people throughout its organization? As studies of venturing programs regularly show, such efforts often fail. We'll start here with a point of reference: What unleashed entrepreneurism in America itself?

WHAT UNLEASHED ENTREPRENEURISM IN AMERICA?

Surprisingly, it wasn't all that hard. It didn't require much central control, either to regulate individual ventures for the good of the whole country or to steer them toward selected industries or particular resources. It certainly didn't require elaborate administrative procedures.

Yet the spirit of enterprise released in America after the Revolution, the sheer desire of people to start their own businesses and get ahead in the world, was remarkable. America lacked both the technology and the knowledge of management to create major enterprises until after 1810 or so, and the overwhelming majority of Americans still lived in the country. But they turned their one-dimensional farms into robust economic engines. By 1810, 90 percent of American textile production came from households. A typical family would use all its spare time to make handicrafts, say, to trade in town for merchandise. Later it would sell them, when opportunity presented itself in the form of a local factory. Eventually the side venture would begin making more money than the family farm—a common occurrence throughout the country. And what spurred Americans to pursue these endeavors, contrary to the widespread expectation of American leaders, was not fear of poverty but the desire to make money, buy luxuries, and to get ahead in life—to pursue the "American dream."[3]

What policies contributed to this burst of economic energy? The very system of federal governance itself helped, less by any positive acts and more by removing impediments. The Constitution, for example, prevented the states from interfering with trade or otherwise restricting commerce between the people. The very smallness of the central government prevented it from interfering much in private enterprise.

Needed: A Facilitating Context

What federal policy makers added to the mix was a facilitating context in which such economic energy could flourish; namely, a market environment that rewarded opportunity-seeking. Alexander Hamilton, secretary of the treasury under George Washington, helped with a superbly innovative financial and banking system that provided access to capital in a cash-starved country. That is, rather than impose an interventionist industrial policy to spur wealth creation, Hamilton provided the context and infrastructure needed to facilitate a market economy.[4]

Hamilton brilliantly anticipated the "dynamic disequilibrium" of modern economics: Society shouldn't strive for economic equilibrium, an insight lost on many modern corporations, but rather should spawn new enterprises to exploit unused resources, meet unsuspected demands, create new value. He envisioned a flexible, diversified economy, with many centers of economic activity open to anyone with enough talent and pluck—that was the best way to fully exploit American resources and capabilities. And such an approach to wealth creation would best fit a federal system of governance, with its many centers of power.

A Natural Desire

But what really spurred so remarkable an outbreak of enterprise by Americans, hundreds of thousands of them, wasn't anything done by their leaders. Rather it was caused by the natural desire of an energetic people anxious to get ahead and finding themselves in an environment that gave them the opportunity to do so.

As for *major* venturing in America, what drove that? Here was the one great–and perhaps inescapable–flaw in Hamilton's system: He made the mistake of placing capital in the wrong hands–namely, speculators', confusing their daring and risk-taking with genuine entrepreneurism. Not only were they in it for the fast buck but their approach to wealth creation, using sneaky and mysterious means that conferred no tangible benefit on the community, was repugnant to an enduring moral strain in America that regards such activities as corruptive to society.[5]

As it turned out, Hamilton was a generation ahead of his time. Major entrepreneurial activity took off twenty years later when New England seafaring merchants–who proved to be the "right sort" of entrepreneurs because they had the patience and discipline to build tangible wealth over the long run–began to establish factories, as we've seen, in response to Jefferson's embargo and the War of 1812. Entrepreneurs like Francis Cabot Lowell and the Boston Associates not only built thriving businesses, but received much greater support from the community. Men like Lowell, in particular, had a clear concern for the welfare of workers and society at large. Such virtues were vital not only to the success of their ventures, but also to the *acceptance* of such activity by a society with distinctly Puritan roots.

The key to unleashing American entrepreneurism was this: a free society with a central authority that created a context–in particular, free markets and access to capital–appropriate to a federal system of governance. Beyond that, policy makers didn't have to do much; people's natural desire to get ahead spurred their entrepreneurism when they were exposed to the opportunities and risks of the marketplace. And those entrepreneurs among them who took a long-term view, and combined that with a concern for the welfare of society, were more likely to gain the acceptance and support of the community.

In other words, the tools and structures already described in this book–including employee citizenship, community based on values, and above all a federal framework for governing–will themselves help spur entrepreneurism in an organization. Build on them!

EXPLOITING A FEDERAL FRAMEWORK

A federal framework of governance–with many centers of power, the capacity to push power to the lowest possible point, and the tendency to use communication at all levels rather than control at the top to induce concerted action–by itself spurs innovation.

When Intuit's senior management team, once the facilitator of innovation, became the "bottleneck" as its new CEO put it, he broke the organization apart into eight separate, geographically dispersed business units. Each unit is about the size Intuit had been in its earlier, more entrepreneurial days; each has its own general manager and mission, and each focuses on one core product or market. Further, the center's authority was greatly pared back to such areas as information systems, compensation programs, and manufacturing. Although it once approved most product-related decisions—even details about software features and advertising plans—now all those decisions are left to the business units, which in turn usually leave them to the individual product team.

Such a federal framework is superbly equipped to keep entrepreneurism alive even in the largest organization, such as 3M or Johnson & Johnson, which may have hundreds of business units, each with its own balance sheet and profit and loss statement.

When one particularly superb global competitor bought a power-transmission business from Westinghouse several years ago, the business was lethargic. It had aging product lines, a weak global presence, mediocre profits, and little opportunity for growth the way it was currently run. But in just three years the unit radically restructured its operations and doubled its operating profits while expanding export sales from 12 to 20 percent of revenues. And innovation came to life as the unit acquired significant new knowledge of microprocessor-based relays technology, a solid basis for future expansion.

What happened? Did the new parent move in and take over? To the contrary, it left the same general manager, a thirty-year veteran of Westinghouse, in place. But whereas he'd had to contend with five layers of management between himself and the CEO at Westinghouse, he found only two at the new parent. Westinghouse had three thousand people in its corporate headquarters who inevitably meddled in his business; the new parent had only about a hundred—one-thirtieth as many. The manager found himself taking more initiative because he had to; his new headquarters wasn't able to control what he did, as Westinghouse had done. His unit was now a separate company, which was expected to meet the rigorous demands—not of a bureaucracy—but of the market. A manager with ideas suddenly found himself in a context that forced him to rely on them.

Who was the new parent? It would be nice to say it was an enlightened American company with a better understanding of power and entrepreneurism in a free society. However, it was the European firm Asea Brown Boveri.

The Center's Role: Break Down Barriers

This isn't to say the center has only a passive role to play in creating a more entrepreneurial environment; to the contrary, a primary reason corporate venturing programs fail is lack of involvement by senior management.[6] But not to *control* the effort; overcontrol is also a major cause of venture program failure. Rather, senior management's most important role is removing barriers that separate front-line employees from the realities of the marketplace.

Corporate infrastructure, for example, should include access to funding, plus a speedy, fair venturing process that relies on the judgment of the market rather than on the opinion of senior staffers. Why should anyone who spends 10 percent of his time on the business impose his judgment about strategy or pricing on the unit manager who spends 100 percent of her time on the business? Why should senior managers expect to find "synergies" between business units and force them into cooperative efforts that aggressive unit managers themselves don't recognize? For that matter, why should anyone force unit managers to use the functions and services provided by the center if they're available at a better price outside the firm?

Senior management should instead focus on breaking down barriers between managers and the market, many of which are embedded in the organization itself. A rule of thumb at ABB holds that removing 90 percent of the center of any organization that it acquires will, by itself, not only save costs but usually improve performance. Former CEO Percy Barnevik did this not only with ABB itself when Asea and Brown Boveri merged; he also did it with acquisitions like Combustion Engineering in the United States and Strömberg in Finland. Barnevik liked to remove 30 percent of the center entirely, place another 30 percent under the direct control of the individual businesses, and set up another 30 percent as a separate cost center forced to compete with outside suppliers.

Perhaps the most obvious disconnect between employees and the marketplace is compensation; employees have little sense from their paychecks of the actual value of their work in the market, and little incentive to tap their entrepreneurial impulses. Here's how one company works to remove that barrier.

An Entrepreneur's Reward at Thermo Electron

In the early 1980s Thermo Electron had a standard incentive program that included stock options for superior performance. But CEO

George Hatsopoulos noticed an obvious contradiction: The company's stock price was only loosely connected to the performance of any particular employee's unit, the entity on which he or she had the most impact. Therefore the company's incentives actually had little real linkage to employee performance.

Hatsopoulos decided to make that linkage much clearer and to give entrepreneurial employees a real shot at an entrepreneur's reward without having to leave the organization. The company now has a separate equity structure for its different businesses, called spin-outs, which are distinct, publicly traded divisions. But unlike spin-*offs*, which are divested by the parent, spin-outs are at least 50 percent owned by Thermo Electron.

Now employees with promising ideas have the potential to build, not just a division of the business, but their own publicly traded corporation. And they participate in its prosperity with stock options that reflect the performance not of the company as a whole, but of the spin-out they devote all their time to. Further, spin-out stock options are liberally spread among managers and employees of the spin-outs, thus giving them more direct feedback–from the marketplace and the investment community–on how well they are really doing, plus a real incentive to do better. An added plus: The spin-outs give investors the opportunity to invest in a promising new technology, without investing in the whole company.

This isn't to say the program is perfect; few social tools are. The company naturally has trouble maintaining a sense of coherence as its product lines, which range from artificial hearts to laser hair-removers to power plants, proliferate. Further, it could do a better job of fully developing and filling out its product lines to achieve a "deeper market focus" as one executive put it. However, these are less than daunting; after all, 3M has had the same problems for decades. And there is no denying that Hatsopoulos's spin-outs have unleashed tremendous entrepreneurial energy: The company grew from $200 million in revenues to $2.9 billion in the fifteen years after it altered its equity structure, with a compound annual return to shareholders of 28 percent.

WHAT ENTREPRENEURS DO

Building on a federal system that removes barriers between employees and the marketplace in such ways, an organization can give them the freedom as well as the context they need to venture. But what then? What, exactly, do entrepreneurs *do*? Such knowledge can improve the business judgment of any employee—particularly one with a talent for venturing.

We can start by dispensing with two misconceptions. Successful entrepreneurs are not daring risk takers who plunge boldly ahead and commit large resources to "go for it" all at once. To the contrary they are risk *managers* who proceed in well-considered stages. The best ones get very good at understanding and defining the risks they must take, and minimizing them as much as possible. "As for myself," said one very successful entrepreneur, "if I had wanted to be a risk taker, I would have gone into real estate or commodity trading, or I would have become the professional painter my mother wanted me to be."[7] In one sense, entrepreneurs are risk *averse*: the best ones are simply aware that standing pat with the status quo can be the biggest risk of all (a risk many organizations take much too often).

Neither is coming up with winning business concepts the mysterious process it might seem; Bhide's study found not only that 71 percent of such concepts came from ideas encountered during previous employment, but that another 20 percent were serendipitous. The entrepreneur built a business out of a temporary or casual job, or perhaps created a product he'd wanted as a customer. Successful entrepreneurs, in other words, start close to home with what they already know or have been exposed to.

Making Sense of Uncertainty

The essence of how entrepreneurs *do* operate flows from understanding this reality: The ingredients for ultimate success can't be anticipated. They will bear little resemblance to the original conception, that is, if there *is* ultimate success (nineteen in twenty new businesses fail, according to one estimate). Here's a partial list of business ideas tried and discarded by Bill Hewlett and Dave Packard when they started out in 1937: a clock drive for a telescope; a "shock machine" to help people lose weight; a bowling foul-line indicator; a sensing device to make urinals flush automatically. Such false starts are the rule, not the exception, in long-term successful businesses. But note: "False" need not mean "futile," because valuable learning often occurs. Everything entrepreneurs do follows from this realization.

What is remarkable about successful entrepreneurs is their ability to bring some kind of order and system to such a wildly unpredictable process. This is a true skill, and one that large organizations need to learn. Here's how it works.

When entrepreneurs come up with an idea worth investigating, they do *not* go off and prepare an elaborate, expensive business plan. Neither do they go out and "get all the facts." Such tendencies to collect too much data and do too much analysis, typical of would-be entrepreneurs who fail, is based on two misconceptions: that getting all the facts can help eliminate uncertainty, and that in any case doing so can't hurt.

To the contrary, successful entrepreneurs–recognizing that most ideas for a business, however "great" they sound at first, won't work–reverse those assumptions. Uncertainty in new business ventures is unavoidable, and excessive fact-gathering is a huge and potentially crippling waste of valuable time. Particularly for genuinely new ideas, such research tools as focus groups, surveys, and the like are not useful predictors. According to market research, copiers, computer mouses, and answering machines were all losers. Their success could ultimately be determined in only one place: the market.

Weeding Through Ideas–Fast

Entrepreneurs are highly adept at weeding through ideas fast. Many of the nineteen in twenty businesses that fail are based on "great" ideas that "everyone wants"–but turn out to have too little worth to customers to generate a profit, or appeal to a customer base too diffuse to reach economically. Successful entrepreneurs can uncover such fundamentally unsound business ideas quickly, by asking themselves such questions as: How much will it cost to make it? How much will people pay? How many can we expect to sell? and so forth. Often a simple, up front, back-of-the-envelope analysis will kill great sounding ideas on the spot.

As they proceed, entrepreneurs continue working to minimize research and increase real-world observation and experiment. They *combine* learning and action, moving constantly back and forth between analysis and testing, one reinforcing the other. They are quintessential pragmatists, realizing that each venture is unique, accepting that there will be considerable uncertainty as they proceed to develop it, and preferring to learn from direct evidence gathered in the marketplace or on the production floor, rather than abstract analysis. And they find ways to do so quickly, cheaply, and as cleverly as possible so they don't get bogged down in lengthy, and pointless, information gathering. Here are some tricks of the trade.

1. *Perform analysis in stages.*
   Entrepreneurs perform analyses in stages–only as needed–rather than all at once. If the new product will need patent pro-

tection, for instance, that gets put off until rough estimates of market demand are obtained. Only when it passes that hurdle are the trouble and expense of obtaining patents incurred.

2. *Avoid research you can't act on.*

For instance, a start-up niche strategy probably doesn't require the entrepreneur to understand broad industry trends, so she won't bother to learn them. Instead she might limit her inquiry to analyzing how her specific customers might buy and use her product or service. Fred Smith understood, when he started out, that most customers would probably leave it up to their mail-room managers to buy Federal Express's service. It was therefore worthwhile for him, early on, to figure out how he could get the decision moved up to a more appropriate level.

3. *Limit information-gathering at each stage to resolving a few big issues.*

Namely: figuring out what must go right for the business to work, and anticipating what can destroy it. Successful entrepreneurs ask, How big is the concept? What will it take to operate the business? What will it take to compete in this industry? If, for example, the concept is "big," if it involves a new market or industry–Apple Computers, Federal Express, and Home Depot, for instance–the new business will require boldness, genuine creativity, and lots of money. In other words, it will be hard to exploit. A niche product or service, on the other hand, requires less originality and investment.

4. *Think through what the business will require.*

If it needs expensive assets or R&D, as in capital equipment or technical software, the going will be tough. It will need a truly creative product, strategy or technology. But if the business requires only speed and pluck, like a consulting business, that will lower the need for a breakthrough idea. Also, entrepreneurs consider the industry they'll be competing in. If it's mature, that can create hard-going: The new business will have to change the established habits of customers. In newer, more shifting industries–characteristic of many foreign markets–the going might be easier. The competition likely won't be very skilled, and customers will tend to be more forgiving.

These are the sorts of issues the entrepreneur identifies and thinks through up front–the large, "Go/No-go" assumptions that can make or break a prospective business. Only after thinking through and testing these do they work their way down to the details.

An Ongoing Experiment

Above all, as we see repeatedly from the examples of great companies like 3M, Hewlett-Packard, Marriott, IBM, and Motorola, all of which were once start-ups themselves, successful entrepreneurs regard the new venture not as a vision to be fulfilled but as an ongoing experiment whose assumptions must constantly be ferreted out and tested. When unexpected problems (which are often disguised opportunity) arise, they don't despair that they were wrong; they revise their strategy.

Take one highly successful, fast-growing entrepreneurial company: Silton-Bookman. Cofounder Philip Bookman's original plan was to sell general-purpose PC-based software to small companies to use in human resource development. Unfortunately, established makers of such software for mainframes were starting to develop it for PCs. In other words, Bookman would find itself competing with giants like IBM, and as the saying goes, Bookman was no Microsoft. But rather than quit, Bookman changed to a niche strategy—developing a training registration product. Its first customer: someone from IBM who saw its ad in a computer magazine.

Thus Bookman, who originally conceived a general-purpose software product for small companies, has since gone on to great success by selling specialty software mostly to large companies. "The world gives you lots and lots of feedback," says Bookman. "The challenge is to take advantage of the feedback you get."[8]

INSTILLING ENTREPRENEURISM INTO AN ORGANIZATION

If one thing is clear about entrepreneurism from the above discussion, it's this: The whole process is foreign, and upsetting, to the way most established businesses operate. The most important fact senior management can instill about any venture it undertakes is that it is *not* an ordinary business operation that will follow clear procedures. Rather, it's an *experiment* based on *assumptions,* many of them hidden, and many inevitably wrong—that must be tested. The best way to do that is, first, *not* to administer the venture program in the same way as the company's established business, using detailed up-front planning and strict timetables.

Administering the Unexpected

Rather, companies with successful venture programs run them as experiments explicitly intended to flush out assumptions, test them, and adapt and change–or they drop the venture altogether, as fast and cheaply as possible.[9] And one of the first assumptions to go must be "the project we're doing now is just like the one we did before," particularly if the one you did before was a big success! Even great companies with clearly valuable ideas unconsciously make that error.

As Columbia University's Rita Gunther McGrath and the Wharton School's Ian MacMillan have shown, that's the mistake Disney made in Europe after the tremendous success it enjoyed with its theme parks in America and Japan. Planners simply assumed they now had the formula for Disney theme parks, and proceeded to apply it to EuroDisney (now Disneyland Paris). They figured that half of all revenues would come from admissions, and the other half from hotels, food, and merchandise, as in Disney's other theme parks. This in turn was based on further assumptions about the price Europeans would pay for admission tickets and the time they would stay in park hotels ($40 and four days, the same as visitors to other Disney parks).[10]

As it turned out, the average stay in EuroDisney hotels wasn't four days, but two. And Europeans weren't willing to pay anything near $40 for admission tickets, although they *were* willing to pay for individual attractions within the park, unlike visitors in America and Japan (a fact Disney planners missed). Neither did the Europeans buy the expected mix of merchandise, shying away from high-margin items like T-shirts and hats. This isn't to fault Disney for making such up-front assumptions; any venture requires planners to do so. The mistake is to proceed as if the assumptions are true rather than by *testing* them to find out whether or not they are true–and doing so before serious damage occurs. Disney eventually adjusted to the European market, but belatedly, in a crisis atmosphere, and too late to prevent major losses and harm to its reputation.

Had Disney instead organized EuroDisney planning to tease out assumptions and question them, it could very likely have adjusted much earlier and more cheaply. The unexpected merchandise mix EuroDisney visitors bought was in fact similar to patterns already known–to Disney's own European retail stores. The pricing model eventually forced on EuroDisney was already well established at other European theme parks. Had Disney studied them, it would have found a curious phenomenon: Unlike American and Japanese visitors who like to "graze all day," the French like to eat at noon. When they couldn't find adequate service at EuroDisney, they became outraged and left, and bad-mouthed the park to their friends and families not only for its ridiculously high admission prices but for its poor food service. By the time EuroDisney managers adjusted, it was too late to prevent damage to its word-of-mouth reputation, which is especially important to marketing recreational attractions in Europe—as Club Med could have told them.

How to Envision a $100 Million Business

Rather than treat a venture as an administrator would—like a predictable process with known factors you just roll out—corporate venturing specialist Zenas Block suggests treating it as an experimental scientist would. Create an initial *model* of the proposed business, identify its assumptions (and figure on uncovering more as you proceed), and systematically test and refine them until they are replaced by facts. Such a model does *not* start with a detailed, time-sensitive schedule of events that someone claims to know will all occur, and then becomes the "bible" used to measure everyone's efforts. Rather it starts with a more "back-of-the-envelope" projection of the new enterprise, which everyone realizes will change. People should expect the model to deepen and *eventually* develop great detail—of solid *facts* pertinent to the unique venture at hand—that replaces the initial assumptions.

For example, suppose a soap and cosmetics company has been selling "surfactants" to floppy disc makers, and wants to consider manufacturing floppy discs itself.[11] Creating an initial model for doing so would be quite straightforward. The company might decide that the risk involved requires a profit of, say, $10 million. Assuming a 10 percent sales margin, this means $100 million in revenue and thus total costs of $90 million. At fifty cents a disc, projected sales would need to be 200 million units, equal to, say, 15 percent of the projected global market. Allowable costs per unit would be forty-five cents.

That's all planners need to adequately envision a starting model for the new business. From there they can create, quite easily, an initial pro forma spec describing all key activities needed to run the business and, more important, the assumptions that underlay them.

For conventional parts of the business, they can use industry standards easily available from investment analysts or commercial lenders. For more novel features, where a new technology is being built into a product, planners can talk to a few engineers and manufacturing people to get a good idea of how it might be produced.

The initial spec would describe the sales operation needed to sell 200 million floppy discs a year at fifty cents each—including average order size, number of sales calls required to sell each order, number of sales people needed to make the calls, their salaries, and so forth.

It would also describe the manufacturing operation needed to pro-
duce 200 million units at forty-five cents each, including number of
production lines, materials costs, number of workers needed and
wages they'd have to be paid, and so forth. Similar descriptions
can be created for marketing, distribution, and capital costs. And of
course, in those areas where the venture has an advantage, in disc
quality owing to the company's knowledge of surfactants, for example—the reason it's considering the venture in the first place—planners
can make aggressive assumptions like "50 percent fewer flaws than
industry average" in the manufacturing spec.

Don't Follow the Plan, Run the Experiment

Thus venture planners can very quickly set up and begin running
their venture experiment. Such a spec immediately points out obvious and important assumptions: Can we really build this product for
that cost? Can we really sell that many? People will naturally expect
such a model to change and grow as more facts are learned to replace
the assumptions. Perhaps more important, it will encourage people to
look for *hidden* assumptions—often the most dangerous kind—and test
them before they do much damage. Here are some common ones:

- This business will work just the same way previous ones have.
- We know who our customers will be.
- They will like this product as much as we do.
- Competitors will react rationally when we introduce it.
- We can protect this product from competition.
- The rest of the organization will support this venture if it proves
  itself in the marketplace.
- We can't market this product until we can make it state-of-the-
  art.

Hewlett-Packard's Deskjet printer illustrates the concept. Even
though engineers were finally persuaded to use features requested by
potential customers, the Deskjet still started out as a disappointment.
Its surprisingly poor revenues were too low to cover the high costs of
research and factories. But rather than just try harder, engineers and
managers got together for an intensive two-day meeting to reconsider
their approach altogether.

In particular, a key marketing assumption on which the business
had been built surfaced during the discussions. They'd positioned the
Deskjet as a low-cost alternative to HP's fancier laser printers, but it
was now clear they needed to go after a much bigger market than that.
This prompted them to consider a substantial departure in marketing

strategy—why not go after the large dot-matrix market at the lower end, then dominated by the Japanese? That question provided the breakthrough. Dot matrix printers had clear problems—poor quality and poor color, two areas where the Deskjet shined. Further, it turned out that the leading dot matrix player, Epsom, was particularly vulnerable. It had no ink jet printer of its own, and was distracted by a faltering effort to sell its personal computer. HP eventually decided to make an assault on the low-end printer market and scored a smashing success, easily surpassing the needed levels of revenue.

This is how successful ventures develop in practice: not by getting all the facts and data and rolling out the business, but by *integrating* action and analysis as embodied in an ever-changing business model. The whole point is to uncover assumptions, test them, and adjust as soon and as cheaply as possible. In the process, you may uncover and correct hidden assumptions that underlay the core business itself and that could be holding it back.

Hewlett-Packard engineers had long believed, for example, that every improvement in a technology required creating a whole new platform before it could be taken to the marketplace—a hidden assumption. When the company was developing its color printer, HP engineers naturally figured on developing an entirely novel, full-featured technical wonder. But marketers at HP, aware that the company was venturing into a new, lower-end market, challenged that approach early on. Epsom, for example, had always gotten a lot of mileage out of creating a whole line of products with slight, and low-cost, variations from the basic model. Further, discussions with HP customers indicated they'd be perfectly happy with a simpler, somewhat clumsier color printer than the elaborate one the engineers were planning.

That suggestion prompted outrage from the engineers until a product manager forced *them* to poll customers, who said they were eager for a product the engineers regarded with contempt. HP wound up sticking with the existing platform and getting a jump on the booming color printer market.

THE ENTERPRISE AS EXPERIMENT

Treating projects, new products, and new ventures as experiments is one thing. But shouldn't the enterprise itself, the core business, also be treated in just the same way? Shouldn't the fundamental assumptions on which it is built be uprooted and challenged regularly, even the most fundamental ones that "made us what we are"?

These include assumptions about how the world in which the business operates works; about the fundamental purpose of the enterprise or "why we exist"; and about the strengths the enterprise must develop to carry out that purpose.

Yet even the most forward-thinking companies have great difficulty with this. Silicon Graphics, justly admired for its ability to improve and transform its products, has proven less adept in the mid 1990s at changing *itself*. SGI has long had this requirement for its products: They must generate high gross margins (about 50 percent) in order to support the company's high R&D budget. The company refuses to make any product that doesn't meet that requirement. "That's sort of an unbreakable dogma for us," as one senior executive put it. The reason is perfectly plausible: SGI fervently wants to avoid becoming a PC "commodity maker." Perhaps more fundamentally, SGI considers this requirement an essential part of its identity.

But dogmatism in any aspect of an American enterprise is suspect. As one CEO of a nimble, fast-growing company said, "We look for our competitor's 'religious behavior,' those things it does that it can't, or won't, change. And we look for ways to exploit it. Meanwhile we work like the devil to keep religious behavior out of our company." While SGI has held to its high-margin model, low-margin/high-volume competitors have been making inroads. Microsoft, for instance, has been hiring some of the best 3D software engineers in the world to challenge SGI on the lower ends of its markets. Intel has been making chips that, while still slower than SGI's in graphics applications, can match their speed in business applications.

The issue that organizations like SGI face is, What is it about us that shouldn't change? What is our core identity? How can we maintain the coherence of a group of people in a rapidly changing and competitive world? For those enterprises trying to come to grips with this issue, and to do so in a way that best reflects American traits and sensibilities—we'll conclude this chapter by considering the establishment of one long-running enterprise, the United States.

America Is an Experiment

At the Federal Convention in Philadelphia in 1787, the proposal was made to include within the new Constitution the power to *amend* the Constitution in the future. As Virginia's long-experienced George Mason put it, the system they were creating would "certainly" contain flaws that only time and experience could reveal. But a group led by young Charles Pickney of South Carolina challenged the thought of letting anyone tamper with the product of such brilliant minds that had spent so long reflecting on such hard-won experience. He feared that others coming along later would undo all their work. Fortunately, Mason's view prevailed. Changes "will be necessary," he said, "better to provide for them in an easy, regular and Constitutional way than to trust to chance and violence."

More-experienced men like Mason (Pickney was less than thirty years old) undoubtedly remembered why Britain had lost a third of its empire in the American Revolution. The reason could be boiled down to a single sentence: British officials had been unwilling to challenge the theory of their empire. The split with America did not have to occur: Americans wanted to stay in the fold. But the British would have had to drastically alter the basic economic and political assumptions on which their Empire was based, and this they refused to consider because these assumptions had served the Empire so well. That was a mistake leaders like Mason didn't want America to repeat.

Think of how little meddling the founders did in Philadelphia that summer; they devised no "strategic vision" for the nation, they made no effort then and only half-hearted—and unsuccessful—efforts later to direct enterprising Americans toward this industry or that resource. They created only a system of governance, yet even that was left open to change and experimentation. To be sure, changes could not be made frivolously: Proposals to amend would require a two-thirds majority in Congress or two-thirds of the state legislatures, and ratification would then require approval by three-fourths of the state legislatures. Nevertheless, the tools and structures the founders devised were left open to question, to change, and even to being thrown out. The very nation itself would be, above all, an experiment.

What Then Is America's Identity?

That given, what *is* our core identity as a people? What does hold Americans together and provide some kind of touchstone as we try to make sense of a world that is constantly, incessantly changing? If even the Constitution is up for grabs, what's constant?

The answer was provided best by Abraham Lincoln at Gettysburg, as historian Garry Wills has shown. What holds us together, ultimately, is certainly not a strategic vision or cultural traditions. Not even the theory of our nation, as embodied in the Constitution, can serve that purpose. All of these can, and must, change. Mason had been right; the Constitution had certainly been flawed. For one thing, it had accepted that most fatal of assumptions, the legitimacy of slavery.

What holds Americans together and gives us our identity, what provides our society with the closest thing to unchanging principles, has no legal force whatsoever: the Declaration of Independence. Instead, the Declaration provides something much more powerful: our shared *moral* values, including the one that most concerned Lincoln: "that all men are created equal."

And note, these values are not some musty ideas we faithfully adhere to because we venerate the people who articulated them. To the contrary, they have continued to prove their ability to bond Americans, and their meaning has continued to deepen—in the movements to abolish slavery, for example, to establish woman suffrage, and to establish racial and gender equality.

Here is a recurring American theme of great strength. Get clear on your moral values and continue to affirm and deepen them. *These* are what we depend on to establish our identity and hold us together; these are "sacred." But these are the *only* things that are sacred. Apart from them, place no restrictions or limits on your enterprise. Everything else, even the most fundamental assumptions on which the whole enterprise rests, and which "made us what we are," can and must change. Operating from a strong moral base, we can do anything, change anything, adapt to anything, accept any challenge the world throws at us with confidence and strength.

10

Only Americans?

This book has been written for managers who want to more fully tap the resourcefulness of *American* workforces. It urges them to align their organizations more closely with America's social, political, and intellectual heritage. But for American firms with increasingly multinational workforces—particularly those aggressively expanding overseas—this creates a clear issue: What about their French, Mexican, Japanese, or Indian employees? Can an American firm, *should* it, impose American values and ways of viewing the world on them? Or is it necessary somehow to dilute these, moderate them, temper them—or even do away with them altogether—to accommodate a more international workforce?

It would seem a high price to pay if an American firm's Japanese or French office should act like a Japanese or French company. As a former Procter & Gamble executive put it, "When I meet with P&G people anywhere in the world—I feel I am talking to the same kind of people. People I know. People I trust. Procter & Gamble people."

Japanese employees might be more change-averse than their American peers, more inclined to defer to authority, and less willing to express explicit disagreement with others.[1] But that makes little sense in a freewheeling company like GE's aggressive Medical Systems business, which expects employees to speak up and challenge managers in sometimes rowdy town-hall meetings. GEMS hasn't tried to temper such assertiveness as it brings in foreign employees (over half of its workforce is now outside the United States); rather it looks for ways to encourage outspokenness on the part of these new employees–and finds that they start to like it. As we saw earlier, even normally deferential Japanese employees learn to speak out, put real issues on the table, and challenge their superiors in an American environment.

A global company's need for a set of shared values and behaviors is well described by Yoshiaki Fujimori, general manager for GEMS global CAT-scanning business. GEMS' policy, he points out, is to hire local nationals to run offices or plants in other countries such as Korea, Taiwan, or Germany. After all, they understand the local ropes. But they must also understand *GEMS.* "We like to move fast when we decide to start a new joint venture or open a new facility," says Fujimori. "If a prospective employee has a great track record of results, that's not enough. But if he or she also has the GE values and does things the GE way–no matter what country or background they're from–we'll have a high chance of success. That's how we move fast."

Values with Transnational Appeal

More important, we've seen that values and an outlook that include individual freedom and self-determination, equality, community, a philosophy of the unexpected, and a preference for observation and experiment over theory are not only widely shared among Americans, but are also essential to American ingenuity and entrepreneurism. What firm that has managed to tap these would want to dilute such a dynamic "core competence"?

Aren't there good reasons to think a company doesn't need to? The values and habits described here are based not on racial or ethnic traditions, but on *ideas:* the dignity and worth of the individual, the desire to make the most of oneself and get ahead, the benefits of freedom, the value of living according to ideals. Their genesis lay in our Puritan heritage: to build a "city on a hill," that provides a beacon and a refuge for anyone in the world looking for a new and better way of life.

And the appeal of these values is a remarkable story in world history, as proven since by the tens of millions of immigrants who came here and generated a sustained explosion of entrepreneurial energy and creativity themselves, attracted by the prospect of liberty and the chance to get ahead.

Equally important, history strongly suggests that these principles provide a solid foundation not only for attracting, but also integrating diverse peoples and getting them to work together. In what other country but the United States could a widely despised minority, using lawful means, establish itself in that country's greatest commercial center and eventually take over its government—as the Irish-Americans did in New York City?

An Exploding World Middle Class Is Embracing American Values

And the appeal of such principles is only going to get stronger. The rise of market economies around the world is spawning a huge population of middle-class strivers—the pool for foreign national employees. Before the Berlin Wall fell, one billion people lived under market-friendly economies. Today over four billion do. About 100 million people in China, India, and Indochina are now "middle class," having incomes over $13,000 per year. By 2010, 700 million will, roughly equal to the combined populations of North America, Europe, and Japan.[2]

And these new, middle-class strivers are eager to acquire wealth. Working couples in Mexico City are investing in mutual funds for their children's education. Workers in China's boomtowns are taking out mortgages to buy their own condos. And of course, it's getting increasingly easy for American firms to tap this vast new source of middle-class ambition: Engineers in Taipei hooked up to the Internet, for instance, are helping U.S. software writers design state-of-the-art digital phone systems.

These people are far from the isolated, indoctrinated unfortunates of a generation ago. "They've grown up with U.S. television, MTV, and American culture," observes a Sieman's executive about young people in China, "and they're slowly coming into management." One enlightened Indian executive senses the aspirations of this growing world middle class. "We see our managerial work as nation building," he says of himself and his peers. "As we learn to manage complex enterprises, we empower people with the confidence they need to become responsible, innovative, and self-reliant."[3] That, of course, is precisely what *American* firms should be offering foreign national employees.

Contrast that with this observation by a Chinese manager describing the arrogance of some of his American counterparts: "North Americans feel that because they give us jobs, we can't argue," he says. (What an attitude for descendants of Jefferson and Lincoln to take!) "But the Chinese people don't need their jobs. We can replace them with another foreign company, we can import from another place."[4]

In the rest of the chapter, we'll take a fresh look at the power of the ideas described in this book. For those American managers who fear they're not appropriate in certain foreign operations, we'll see in particular how they fared in an environment that might seem to be the last place they'd work.

JEFFERSON IN BRAZIL

Semco S/A is a relatively small Brazilian capital-goods manufacturer–several hundred employees making marine equipment and food-processing machines–that has managed to survive and even thrive in a very stormy economy. During the 1980s, inflation swung wildly in Brazil between zero and 1,600 percent a year. Then the economy utterly collapsed in 1990: Gross industrial product fell 34 percent in three years–a depression by any standard. Signs of disaster were everywhere. More than one-fourth of Brazil's capital goods producers went bankrupt. Capital goods output fell at one point to 1977 levels.

Under majority-owner Ricardo Semler since 1980, Semco had become a plausible candidate for the world's most resilient company. The once-stagnant company's productivity rose sevenfold and sales ninefold during the decade, despite the turmoil. Semco ranked number one or two in every one of its markets, often outperforming divisions of much larger multinationals.

Then when Brazil's economy completely collapsed, Semco's overall profits somehow remained intact through several months of near-zero sales (not sales growth, but *sales*) in some businesses. Despite the extreme stress, loyalty among employees remained high and quality excellent, and profits eventually began growing again. Labor unions and the press regularly tout Semco as the best Brazilian company to work for. The company was featured in *Harvard Business Review* twice. Polls of Brazilian executives have named Semler business leader of the year twice since 1990.

What explains Semco's resilience? Some commentators attribute it to Semler's iconoclastic genius–certainly he *is* different. He stopped wearing a watch years ago, believing "time should be measured in years and decades, not minutes and hours." He takes month-long vacations to remote places where he can't be reached, to build the company's self-reliance.

But Semco's success is no aberration that other companies can't learn from, particularly American firms with large numbers of foreign employees. Under extreme duress, Semco completed the management cycle many companies are still groping with. It long ago abandoned top-down control as inefficient and dispiriting to employees. It tried and rejected a parade of management fads that didn't deliver. Then Semler, who reads widely, including the classics and history, began to focus on governance issues; that's where he sensed the real problem with morale lay. He finally succeeded in freeing up the ambition and ingenuity of Semco's employees by instilling democratic values into Semco's organization.

What is particularly remarkable is that they worked in a highly authoritarian society, where people are used to showing deference to superiors and have little sense of individual identity.[5] Nevertheless, the worse things got, the more Semler relied on democratic values; each time they delivered. Here's his remarkable story.

A Corporate Diagnosis

When Semler first became president of Semco, he and his executives tried to increase efficiency with tight controls and disciplined leadership. One executive took personal charge of the underperforming Hobart Brazil division, which makes industrial dishwashers. He fired a number of people, imposed twelve- to fourteen-hour days, overhauled products, changed prices, and redesigned operations. His performance struck Semler as hardnosed and businesslike, except for one thing: The plant's deliveries were still late. Further, a general malaise infected plant workers, who were clearly disengaged from their jobs. They were being pushed by management; Semler began wishing they were "self-propelled."[6]

When a management rift opened between autocrats and a newly assertive "touchy-feely crowd" at Semco, Semler began seriously rethinking the company's management style. The anti-autocrats thought that if employees could be motivated by a sense of involvement, they would rise to the company's challenges. Eventually Semler sided with them. Here's how he proceeded.

Eschewing any rote method or program for instilling democratic principles, Semler started pragmatically, with a diagnosis of Semco's particular social and political makeup. He focused on:

- What are Semco's actual values? Which behaviors did management really encourage (perhaps inadvertently)? Which behaviors did he *want* to encourage? Apart from company rhetoric, the prevailing ethic in Semco's factories was: Work hard, do what you're told, obey the rules, and you won't get fired. In

Semco's offices it was: Keep your head down, respect boundaries, and protect your turf. Semler wanted to flush out the artificial behavior, as well as a noticeable tendency by people to speak "managementese," in favor of a much simpler, more natural culture based on trust and cooperation. He wanted bosses to treat employees with scrupulous fairness, without which management could never win their trust, much less their enthusiasm.

- What really motivates people? It struck Semler that fear and docility were the order of the day. Why should employees consider management the "enemy" when both groups clearly had a strong mutual interest, namely, maintaining a thriving business? Semler asked how employees' interests could be aligned with those of the company.
- Finally, who decides what? Increasingly, decisions at Semco were all in the hands of a few top executives, aided by the management controls they'd installed. If Semler could instill the right values and motivation at Semco, he would feel comfortable having people down in the ranks and close to the problem or opportunity, making decisions.

Semler didn't underestimate then, and doesn't understate now, the difficulty of achieving such ambitious social goals. It required deep, far-reaching changes in company policies, changes that most companies who dabble in participation or employee empowerment would never consider.

A Democratic Cure

Semler started out by changing his own workaholic style, by setting a time when he would leave his office at the end of the day "no matter what," resolving to delegate "furiously," and deciding to trust his intuition more and the experts less.[7] He then worked on humanizing the company. He came to regard manuals, rules, and regulations in general as "poppycock" that rarely solve real problems, and abolished them. In their place he instituted a new "rule of common sense" that put employees in the unaccustomed position of having to use their judgment.

Semco's exhaustive statistical controls were eliminated, replaced with a few important numbers that concisely measure company performance. Some four hundred accounting cost centers were pared down to fifty; hundreds of classifications and dozens of accounting lines were done away with. "Finally," Semler observed, "we can see the company through the haze."[8]

Semco factories eventually got rid of dress codes and time clocks, along with security checks and ID badges as well. Semler knew this would tempt the 2 or 3 percent of employees inclined to steal. But what sense does it make for a company to base its relationship with employees on the dishonest few? Why not establish a relationship of trust with the 97 percent who are honest?

What replaced the controls? Semler strived for an ambitious new order in which employees would feel as much of a stake in Semco's welfare as he did, and then find ways, on their own, to advance it. To achieve this, Semler built Semco's new governance on three precepts, in an effort to convert Semco's employees from passive subordinates to more engaged citizens.

1. Employee participation
2. Profit sharing
3. Open information systems

Semler intended first to give people control of what they did, second to give them a tangible reason to do it better, and third to give them an essential tool for succeeding at it. And these were more than just platitudes for company newsletters; Semler instilled the new concepts into the culture with a genuine feel for the dignity of his employees as well as a certain flair for boldness.

First he recognized the legitimacy of unions, including their right to strike. Significantly, strikes have become rare at Semco—but when they do occur, strikers can still receive meals and hold meetings at Semco's cafeteria.

Also, Semco instituted a vigorous program of employee involvement. Workers are urged to join factory committees that have a broad mandate from management: "Look after the workers' interests." To encourage strong participation, no employee can be fired while he serves on a factory committee or for one year thereafter. The committees have taken an increasingly active role in decisions once thought to be the exclusive province of management. For instance, they participate in product and process design, evaluation of peers and bosses, and even oversight of spending on executive retreats.[9]

Semler wanted still more employee concern and involvement: Why think employees will care about the company if they don't have a stake in its welfare? Semco now has an attention-grabbing profit-sharing plan; fully 23 percent of profits made by each autonomous unit go to employees, who then distribute each share among themselves by vote. At first the money was just shelled out, but that failed to take advantage of the plan's potential. Semler wanted to use it to make workers better informed, in particular to help them understand the impact their work has on the bottom line.

Company books are now opened to employees monthly, giving them access to all costs, overhead, sales, profits, payroll, and taxes. And employees are given classes on how to read and understand them, taught by members of one of their unions, so they can see more clearly the connection between their work and the bottom line.

How does Semco hire people? That too is subject to a democratic process. No single person can decide a new job will be opened up; an executive can suggest that a business unit needs a new manager, but the unit must agree. Preference for new hires is given to Semco employees, former Semco employees, and friends and acquaintances (but *not* relatives) of existing employees, under the theory that no one would dare suggest a friend who wasn't up to the company's standards of performance. New hires are interviewed by their peers, and must be acceptable to them. This naturally selects out people who are comfortable with an unstructured, participative environment.

In addition, before new bosses are hired, the people who will work with them must ratify the selection. Does this result in hiring popular bosses who won't be effective and tough when needed? Semco's experience suggests the answer is no—when employees' interests have been closely aligned with the company's.

On one occasion, for example, the company needed a new treasurer. Several employees in the finance department favored a well-liked former employee, who was less qualified than the outsider preferred by senior executives. Given the importance of the position, some executives considered overriding Semco's democratic process this one time, but were restrained by Semler. They needn't have worried. In a close vote, employees picked the outsider.

A "Self-Propelled" Workforce

Semco's new governance was not without problems. Some authoritarian executives who were fired were nonetheless getting results. People complained that decisions, more of which were now made by consensus, were sometimes too slow in coming. But the profound change in employees has been worth the trouble. "Workers who had for years—even decades—reported to the plant and promptly turned their minds off became full-fledged industrial citizens," says Semler.[10] Here was a portrait of an emerging corporate republic in Brazil.

The autocratic manager in the Hobart plant was removed. Its workers, increasingly convinced of their new autonomy, gradually assumed new responsibilities starting with their work environment. The plant's women began prodding the men to clean up their locker rooms. The men in turn built a recreation room for use during lunch and after work. Houseplants began appearing around machinery here and there. A group of assembly workers decided to paint the factory; colors for each column were picked by the five or six people who worked closest to it. A committee was formed to oversee the cafeteria food, which went from atrocious to good. Spontaneously, employees were building a community.

Gradually they gained enough confidence to make decisions about their work. On their own, workers put up scoreboards around the factory to track production against monthly goals, which they set themselves. Teams were formed, some with no direction from management, to improve product design. One changed the casing on meat grinders from steel to fiberglass, improving their performance, cost, and looks. Another figured out how to preweld the base on Semco's industrial scales, saving twenty-seven dollars per unit. Another redesigned a slicer to make it more attractive and hygienic. When it turned out to be too expensive, one of the team members (on his own initiative and after hours) figured out how to cut its costs substantially. Sales of the slicer jumped from a few dozen a month to several hundred.

Other teams looked for "reengineering" type improvements and efficiencies. One group changed an assembly line from a sequential to a batch process, where teams of workers perform many different functions rather than one repetitive task. The new system puts parts in open racks on the factory floor, giving workers control over inventory. Before, if no bolts were available on the assembly line, work just stopped. Now workers themselves watch inventory levels and order parts when they see the need.

Dealing with Disaster

How did the new sense of employee control at Semco work when Brazil's economy crashed and factory closings loomed? At one point, sales of industrial dishwashers fell from forty a month to five and inventory was piling up. Joao Soares, a factory committee leader, who dreaded the prospect of working at a non-Semco plant, persuaded his committee and then management to agree to an extraordinary plan to save the factory.

The workers would take a drastic 30 percent pay cut, and perform all the plant maintenance chores normally done by contractors, such as meal preparation, guard duty, and so forth, even cleaning bathrooms. In return they asked (rather optimistically) for a greater share of the profits, and for extraordinary power to make all business decisions jointly with management, even signing checks. Such comanagement is too radical over the long run, even for Semler, but he agreed to the arrangement on a short-term basis.

The results were phenomenal. Costs were cut so much that they even made a small profit on dishwashers in the first month. When sales of washers rose and stabilized at (a still paltry) twelve a month, and with increased sales of spare parts to strapped customers holding on to their old dishwashers, workers soon began drawing enough from profit sharing to restore their salaries.

Indeed, throughout Semco, the factory committees became a dynamic force when hard times hit. They took the initiative to lower salaries or increase hours as needed, and participate in the painful decisions of whom to lay off, which helped convince workers the process was fair. Some employees knowingly worked themselves out of a job when market conditions required it, the result of being kept fully informed and having acquired a less paternalistic view of management.

Management in turn reciprocated. In a down economy, companies often will cut permanent employees and contract more work to outsiders, which may be necessary financially. But that can destroy employee morale and results in loss of a considerable base of knowledge and talent. Even in the midst of a depression, Semco managed to balance these needs with great creativity. It encouraged most former employees to set up their *own* "satellite" businesses, and offered to lease them Semco office space and equipment (with payments deferred for two years). To ease the transition, Semco farmed out a specific amount of work to these "satellite employees," who then could develop other customers over time. Thus, unlike other downsizing companies, Semco farmed out all the work it could to former employees rather than strangers. Of 500 Semco employees at the time of the crash, some 450 were still associated with the company two years later as full employees, satellite employees, and a few who worked part-time in both capacities.

Semco's management would strike many as iconoclastic, even astonishing. But in fact its success in the harshest conditions rests on sound political principles Thomas Jefferson valued: Self-determination rather than paternalism and control, educated employee-citizens rather than passive subordinates, and community based on values such as trust and the dignity and worth of all members. And Semco's experience provides an important lesson in today's global economy: These principles work in a culture much different from our own, suggesting their universal appeal. In a very tough environment, Semco's continued reliance on these principles continued to pay off.

11

The Myth of the Transformational Leader

Clearly leadership is important to great enterprises. But what kind? In particular, what kind best fits Americans–who are notoriously skeptical of authority? As it turns out, not the kind we've been led to think.

The Myth

Great enterprises require great or "transformational" leaders, according to a widely held belief and numberless books on leadership. A superb company like General Electric, Motorola, or Hewlett-Packard, or for that matter a prominent university, or church, or even a great nation such as our own must have been *planned* by someone–an exceptional leader or group of leaders–who foresaw the result and made it happen. Such extraordinary people take charge of the enterprise. They conceive a bold and inspiring vision that cuts through factional bickering, devise a clear strategy for making it a reality, and use compelling charisma to "transform" followers from self-interested individuals into a cohesive whole that "buys-in" to the leader's concept of the future.[1]

That outlook has become deeply entrenched in American management. One sign of this: When companies perform exceptionally well, or recover from a slump and turn themselves around, who reaps the reward? Very often the CEO and a few senior executives do so, lavishly—while rank-and-file employees get modest bonuses, if that. The message is clear: If the company does well, the credit goes not to people throughout the organization, but to a few people at the top, presumably practicing the skills of transformational leadership.

Much of this view of leadership is based on anecdote rather than empirical studies, as well as the somewhat romantic notion that leaders who run businesses should pattern themselves after the towering figures and great events in history. If that strikes you as somewhat puffed up and dubious, read on. There is powerful evidence it is—with important implications both for leaders and their organizations.

Did the Founding Fathers Believe in Transformational Leadership?

Certainly our own heritage, even the experiences of our greatest leaders, suggests that a different model of leadership works better in America. The Founding Fathers stand among the greatest leaders of all time; they organized millions of quarrelsome, independent-minded Americans into a unified whole (what leadership challenge was ever tougher?)—while laying foundations that would make America the richest, most powerful nation in history. Nevertheless, as Michael Keeley points out, in leading America the founders flatly rejected anything approaching the transformational or hero-leader model.[2]

This was not for lack of a superb candidate: George Washington, after all, was hero of the Revolution—the warrior who inspired frightened American farm boys to cross the Delaware River, the leader whose character, bravery, and judgment earned the veneration of his countrymen and the confidence of his peers. Had the founders thought the key to America's success lay in installing a great leader in power, they could have saved themselves the trouble of a long hot summer in Philadelphia in 1787, hammering out the Constitution. Instead they might simply have angled to put Washington in charge in the midst of the crisis then facing the country, together with themselves close by, and worked to place supreme power in his hands while systematically destroying all other contending sources. They would then have been free to practice the art of the transformational leader.

But they did nothing of the sort. They were all, including Washington—and more important, so was most of the rest of the country—too skeptical of the supposed wisdom of unaccountable leaders, too fearful of the damage autocracy (the dark side of transformational leadership) can inflict, and too committed to establishing a society whose dynamism would come not from hero leaders but from free, initiative-taking citizens.

The founders therefore took a much different path. America's success would not be based on what any one leader or group of leaders did—the treaties they might sign, the economic policies they might pursue, even the wars they might win. Rather the founders focused on establishing a system of governance—institutions, processes, mechanisms—to ensure good decisions would be made and outstanding leaders picked, long after they were gone. The great insight of the founders, including George Washington, was to think less of being great individual leaders and more about building a great and enduring nation.

DO GREAT ORGANIZATIONS
REQUIRE HERO LEADERS?

And this, according to persuasive evidence in two respected studies of organizational success, is the right approach to take today in building successful organizations. One study, by the University of Maryland's Robert Birnbaum, examined successful leadership in colleges and universities—institutions that can be quite difficult to change.[3] The other we've already encountered, Stanford's James Collins and Jerry Porras' report on long-term business success.[4] Both were longitudinal studies, both emphasized empirical findings over anecdotes, and both arrived at very similar conclusions: Outstanding leadership is important to organizations, but *not* the "transformational leader" kind.

Must Successful Leaders Be Visionary?

Take the notion that successful leaders must be visionary. Aren't great companies established by such founders, who envision a brilliant future and guide people toward it? As it turns out, only three of the eighteen great companies studied by Collins and Porras (Johnson & Johnson, GE, and Ford) started out that way. And of the three, GE's original great idea (Edison's, of pursuing DC current) was inferior to that of its "also-ran" competitor Westinghouse (pursue AC). Meanwhile Henry Ford's great idea (the Model T) was not conceived until *after* he had started his car company (which was one of more than five hundred founded in the early 1900s) and after he'd built five previous models (the A, B, C, F, and K)!

Far more typical for great companies is this sort of story: Sam Walton was relatively late getting into the discount retailing business, and tended to copy competitors like Kmart. J. W. Marriott started business as an A&W root beer franchisee, the only idea he could think of. Nordstrom started as a shoe store; Merck as an importer of chemicals from Germany; Motorola as a battery-eliminator repair business for Sears radios; Philip Morris as a retail tobacco shop in London! The list of great companies with decidedly *un*visionary foundings goes on and on. Hewlett and Packard started their company in 1937, as we've seen, with no idea what they wanted to make, and tried everything from bowling foul-line indicators to an automatic flusher for urinals before getting a contract from Walt Disney for eight audio oscilloscopes. HP continued its scattered ways until a bevy of war contracts finally focused it on technical instruments.

Even more interesting: *More* of the also-ran comparison companies in the Collins and Porras study (*eleven* out of eighteen) started out right away in the line of business in which they would ultimately prosper–their leaders were, in that sense, more visionary. Yet each time, they were overtaken by their originally unfocused competitor.

But what about the "Mt. Rushmore" image of our greatest leaders: that of far-seeing visionaries whose uncanny ability to divine the future still guides us even today? That also is pure fantasy. Although George Washington, Abraham Lincoln, and Thomas Jefferson all had superb judgment, none of these men had a crystal ball. Washington, for instance, continued believing that America would settle its quarrel with England even after Congress made him commander in chief of the Continental Army. Indeed he continued toasting the king nightly at his officers' mess, several months *after* George III himself had given up and declared the colonies in revolt! Thomas Jefferson, for his part, was convinced that America's destiny lay with its yeoman farmers. He wanted to discourage the growth of cities, factories, and banks in America because of their corrupting influence–and he was horrified when they began to flourish. Lincoln thought civil war could be avoided when he took office. When it couldn't, he was convinced it would be short and that Southern moderates would end it by rising up and removing the radicals from power. Far from the visionary of legend who expertly guided America to a future he'd somehow foreseen, Lincoln admitted as the war raged on, "I claim not to have controlled events, but confess plainly that events have controlled me."[5]

Then how *do* effective leaders set a goal and direction for the future? Successful university leaders in the Birnbaum study did *not* create their own personal vision and then work to get buy-in from constituents. The Birnbaum researchers asked one college president who'd successfully changed the direction of her campus how she'd conceived her vision. The answer: *she* hadn't. "When I arrived the media wanted to know what my plans were for the college, what changes I would be making," she recalled. "But I never thought of the presidency in those terms. What I spent a lot of time on was letting people know that I would not be imposing my version of the truth. Together we shaped a vision of the college."[6]

Presidents who successfully lead a university—through a merger, say, or a dramatic shift in emphasis from research to teaching, or through an aggressive expansion from single- to multipurpose programming—do so in a way that makes sense in a democratic society. They state goals that show they've sought out the views of constituents and been influenced by them. They find that compelling goals are *already* there, *within* the organization, awaiting discovery and elaboration. One successful president described his approach to mobilizing a complex organization—not by taking charge and issuing orders but by doing "a lot of listening," as he put it. "And when you do that, solicit the dreams and hopes from the people. Tell the people the good things you are finding. And in three to six months, take these things and report them as the things you would like to see happen."[7] This doesn't mean successful presidents agree with everything they hear—to the contrary. But when they *do* buck the wishes of constituents, they let people know that their opposing concerns were understood, considered, and are still regarded as important.

Must Successful Leaders Be Charismatic?

What about charisma—the ability that transformational leaders have to create a deep emotional bond with followers that unites them behind a transcendent cause? Isn't this essential to organizational success? Collins and Porras cast serious doubt on that too. They found that some of the most important leaders in their visionary companies were distinctly *not* of the high profile, charismatic variety. Indeed, many were rather shy and a bit boring—such as 3M's low-key, virtually unknown William McKnight (described by company history as "unobtrusive and soft spoken," "modest," "quiet, thoughtful, and serious," "slightly stooped"); George Merck ("the embodiment of Merck restraint"); both Proctor and Gamble (who struck Collins and Porras as "stiff, prim, proper, and reserved—even deadpan").[8]

The Birnbaum study of successful university presidents goes further. While charisma in a leader can indeed attract and excite people, and make an immediate impact on their willingness to support her goals, somewhat like love at first sight, there is a distinct downside. Charismatic leaders also demonstrate narcissism, a grandiose certainty, disdain for subordinates, intolerance of dissent, and a sense that the normal rules don't apply to them—as the Founding Fathers knew very well when they designed elaborate checks and balances for the nation's government. When studied over an extended period in a number of universities, the Birnbaum study concluded that "charismatic leaders have created more problems than solutions."[9]

One campus, for example, had a president described as very charismatic by a faculty leader, but the institution was in trouble because the president believed it was important to be "totally independent of people," as she put it. "You must have enough confidence in yourself to sift through what people say; the hidden agendas are many, and you have to make your own decisions." Such distancing enhanced her charisma—but ultimately thwarted her efforts to make change. The faculty, for example, were angered at the unilateral way she made decisions.

WHAT SETS SUCCESSFUL LEADERS APART?

None of this denies the value of great leaders like Jack Welch, Herb Kelleher, or Andy Grove—any more than one would deny the importance of a Washington, Lincoln, or Woodrow Wilson to the United States. Collins and Porras found, for example, that the outstanding companies in their study produced many outstanding executives such as George Merck, J. W. Marriott, Bill Hewlett, David Packard, William Procter, R. W. Johnson, Sam Walton, and Paul Galvin. These leaders displayed high levels of persistence, overcame significant obstacles, attracted dedicated people, influenced groups of people toward organizational goals, and played key roles in guiding their organizations through periods of crisis.

But—and this is the significant point—so did the counterpart, less-successful companies in the study. In a remarkable finding, Collins and Porras reported that the also-ran competitors like Pfizer, Howard Johnson, Texas Instruments, Colgate, Bristol-Myers Squibb, Ames, and Zenith were *just as likely* to have solid leadership during the crucial, formative years—namely, Charles Pfizer, Howard Johnson, Pat Haggarty, William Colgate, William Bristol, the Gilman brothers (Ames), and Commander Eugene F. McDonald—as the visionary companies. These leaders displayed high levels of persistence, overcame significant obstacles, attracted dedicated people, influenced groups of people toward organizational goals, and played key roles in guiding their organizations through periods of crisis.

But there was a crucial *difference* between the leaders of the great companies and those of the less-successful competitors.

The notable leaders of the most successful organizations concentrated less on being a great individual leader, and much more on designing and building a great, enduring institution.

Leaders in the exemplar companies worked not to convert people to their vision of "what we should do and how we should do it"–a dubious task in a diverse society–but rather, to establish organizational processes and dynamics that would ensure continued success long after they were gone. They were "clock builders," as Collins and Porras put it, as opposed to "time tellers." To these leaders, quite similarly to the American founders, the *organization and its governance*–not product mixes, strategies, or markets–were the most important things.

Leadership in a Democratic Society

What *kind* of processes and dynamics do leaders of great enterprises instill? The Founding Fathers created a Constitution that accomplished three things: It limited the power of officials; it expanded the liberty of individuals; and its processes struck Americans as fair, and still do after 200-plus years. The great classic work on American governance isn't *The Prince*, telling leaders at the top how to gain, manipulate, and hold on to power, but *The Federalist*, proposing a system that places power in the hands of the people, who exercise it through representatives.

On the subject of what kind of organization great companies create, Collins and Porras don't have as much to say–that's been the focus of this book. But what they did observe is consistent with the American founders' approach. Executives in the great companies they studied appear to have instilled democratic values into their organizations: respect for individual freedom and autonomy, meaningful participation by people in decisions that affect them, open access to information, encouragement of individual initiative, experimentation, and entrepreneurism.

Sam Walton, for instance, who valued change, experimentation, and constant improvement, didn't just order these. He instituted concrete organizational mechanisms–such as profit sharing, stock ownership, cash awards, and contests, plus regular forums that focused on these aspirations–all of which tended to reinforce democratic values. His competitive counterparts meanwhile, the Ames leaders, dictated all changes in company procedures from the top, in elaborate policy and procedure books that left no room for individual initiative, and that people expected would be rewritten by senior management when circumstances changed.

Founder Paul Galvin encouraged free-flowing debate and dissent of company policy at Motorola, and worked to develop an organization that gave individuals plenty of latitude to show what they could do on their own. He stimulated change and improvement not by issuing detailed policies, but by issuing challenges and letting people figure out for themselves how to meet them, while accepting that failure and mistakes were part of the process.

Commander Eugene F. McDonald, by contrast, founder of Motorola's also-ran competitor Zenith, more clearly fit the transformational leader mold. He was charismatic, self-assured, forceful (he expected all but intimates to address him as "Commander"), and a visionary who could anticipate changes in public tastes with remarkable acuity. And Zenith *did* soar under McDonald's leadership. But—and here's the point—it languished over the years after he died. Meanwhile, Motorola continued flourishing long after Galvin's death (within eighteen months of McDonald's), going into technologies and industries even the visionary McDonald could never have anticipated.

Birnbaum's study found a similar pattern in universities. One dynamic president, whose faculty went from a sense of malaise and lost opportunity to one of "excitement" and belief that they were on their way to becoming one of the premier colleges in the United States, embodied democratic values. He was "highly sensitive to the limits of his authority." He spent a great deal of time learning and then strengthening the organization's dynamics and structures. He studied its budget process closely, developed a rational planning process, and reviewed management procedures. And he sought in particular to increase faculty participation in governance. He spent time with the deans and actively sought the consultation of faculty members. Even once-disillusioned senior faculty members became more involved, and influential, in college affairs. Compared with the way things were under a previous administration, "there's a lot more talking—plain talking—between committees and senior administrators," said one. "We all know what's going on."[10]

As a result, the president was able to move decisively in planning and devising programs. The faculty embraced his master plan not because he conceived a vision and got their buy-in, but because it incorporated their goals and aspirations and they knew it.

For those who prefer a more tangible model of superb American leadership, we'll close this chapter with one. This leader faced challenges the likes of which very few people in history have ever faced, and did so with remarkable aplomb and success. He is arguably the greatest leader ever—yet curiously, within the pantheon of history's great leaders for use as a management role model today, he gets very short shrift.

LEADERSHIP SECRETS OF GEORGE WASHINGTON

Ask people to name the greatest role models for leaders and chances are they'll mention Napoleon, Alexander the Great, Mao Zedong, Caesar, Churchill. In the late 1980s Attila the Hun enjoyed a revival on business bookshelves. These were strong individuals who took control and dominated situations with the force of their personalities. George Washington, on the other hand, rarely gets mentioned, dismissed because he seems rather bland and plodding, even a figurehead. Other more-gifted men working behind the scenes actually built the nation, or so many people think.

What a misconception! Washington was a leader of extraordinary achievement. As commander in chief during the American Revolution, he was handed an amateur army of farm boys outnumbered two to one in the field by hardened British professionals, yet still managed to defeat the mightiest empire since Rome and secure American independence. Washington then discreetly pushed for a forum to allow some of the best minds in the country, including James Madison, to devise a governance formula entirely new in history: A republic strong enough to provide national focus while allowing the states as well as individuals plenty of freedom to develop on their own. Washington also served as the nation's first chief executive, established the institutions of that office that endure to this day, and assembled brilliant leaders like Alexander Hamilton and Thomas Jefferson to lay the economic and foreign policy foundations for a richly successful nation. And all this, of course, he did to the great chagrin of Europe's autocrats who thought that nations could be consciously formed only by force.

Douglas MacArthur exaggerated when he said that Washington, his great role model along with Lincoln, "founded the United States."[11] But among the superb leaders that effort brought forth, Washington was first in importance, the "indispensable man" in James Flexner's phrase.[12] His role in America was like that of business giants Thomas Watson of IBM or Alfred P. Sloan of General Motors, whose character, strength, and skill established enduring business enterprises. But of course Washington laid the foundation for an enduring nation—the greatest leadership challenge of them all.

The reason we miss his greatness might be because Washington doesn't fit the stereotype. Though a superb athlete and horseman, he was devoid of flamboyant charisma or "star power." He was quite modest in company, which one visiting Frenchman found "astonishing. He speaks of the American [Revolution] as if he had not been its leader." He was an indifferent speaker and writer who rarely uttered a quotable line. He wasn't from the cream of American aristocracy, and never went to college. At the same time he was too stiff to ever be considered a man of the people. Even his military prowess had its shortcomings; at the start of the Revolution, he almost blundered into a war-ending defeat in the Battle of Long Island, and actually achieved few clear-cut victories in the field.

But the best way to understand his remarkable effectiveness is to look not at his charisma or vision, but at his understanding of power in American society. As historians such as Edmund S. Morgan and Garry Wills have noted, this is the real source—and the real lesson—of his remarkable leadership genius.[13]

A Light Touch with Power

George Washington's uncanny feel for how leadership works in America is best shown in his reaction when he reached the pinnacle of power. In late 1783, American negotiators in Paris signed a peace treaty with Great Britain ending the American Revolution. Washington was vaulted at that moment to the very height of world prestige: He was commander in chief of the army that had defeated the mighty British Empire and secured a new nation, the most celebrated figure of the age.

Meanwhile contempt for Congress was almost as widespread in America, particularly throughout the army, as was veneration of Washington. If Americans were ever ready to accept a king, Washington was the man and this was the moment. Yet he gathered his officers for a final farewell, traveled alone to Congress to return his military commission, and continued on to his home at Mount Vernon and back to private life.

That was an extraordinary moment in history, and the defining moment in establishing the United States. Here was a victorious general giving up his arms. Other great "men on horseback" like Caesar or Cromwell, and later Napoleon or Simon Bolívar (the so-called George Washington of Latin America) always expected to get political power commensurate with their victories. But when Washington arrived at the apex of power, he relinquished it.

Unlike most leaders, Washington never regarded power as something he was innately entitled to because of birth, class, talents, or genius, or even accomplishments. He understood and strictly adhered to the principle that power comes from an external source, a principle often breached by strong leaders in every era including our own. The resignation of his military commission and refusal to become king was simply the most famous example of his unvarying practice.

But note: Washington's resignation was not abandonment of his ambition but an integral part of it. Because it was sincere, it awed the world. The London painter John Trumbull tried to describe the astonishment Washington's conduct caused throughout Europe. It seemed "so novel," he wrote, "so inconceivable" to English political leaders who, far from giving up powers they have, "are willing to convulse the empire to acquire more."[14] But in America, Washington's stunning retirement was in fact the first step in his ultimate rise to the presidency, because it confirmed Americans' belief that he could be trusted with power.

Washington's Unvarying Principle

Don't think it was any easier for Washington to accept limits to his authority than it is today for any other strong executive. Indeed, no group of directors or shareholders ever gave a CEO more reason to turn autocrat than Congress gave Washington during the Revolution. Congress was grossly ineffective in raising taxes and funding the army, and notoriously inefficient in general. Washington had to deal with endless committee meetings just to feed, clothe, and pay his troops. Incredibly, Congress refused to draft a professional army until a full year into the war, forcing Washington to start with amateurs who headed back to their farms just as soon as they were trained. Only slowly and painfully was he able to build a professional fighting force that could "look the enemy in the face."

Then came this moment. Late in the war Congress began welshing on the considerable back pay (going back as much as six years!) it owed to American soldiers. At that Washington's officers finally went ballistic. On top of everything else, now that the war was almost won Congress was turning its back on those who'd borne the burden of the war, and their widows and orphans. In a righteous rage these veterans prepared to march on that body and take over the country.

But Washington stood squarely, and quite alone, against his

own enraged men in a dramatic meeting at Newburgh, New York. He stood ultimately on the principle that they must not arrogate power unto themselves. Here was a severe test of his leadership; battle-hardened men who'd been wronged were in no mood to hear about high-flown principle. Yet they were slowly reduced to tears at the sight of their aging commander, fumbling with reading glasses they'd never seen him wear before, urging them to display the same devotion to duty that they knew he always had. The Newburgh mutiny—the greatest threat to the United States in its history—dissolved at that moment. Washington moved his men not with his personal vision, but by reminding them of the very principle they'd been risking their lives for all along.

How many strong leaders are baffled and even exasperated at Washington's deference to Congress? Why didn't he march on that rabble of congressmen at the head of his angry officers, as Alexander Hamilton and a powerful coalition of business and military leaders urged, instead of standing in their way? But Washington saw the big picture and the longer term better than they.

The Ultimate Goal

Rather than take charge of the country and make sure things worked right on his watch, he wanted to establish a country that would work right far into the future. That meant accepting even serious incompetence by Congress for a time rather than set a precedent that a future would-be dictator could use to grab all the power. Here was Washington's great insight into leadership and power that eludes so many strong leaders: More important than the success of the particular things he did was the long-term success of the enterprise he established. And most important to long-term success, in American society, was to build strong institutions that spread power around rather than concentrating it in a single person or group.

It was easy to blame Congress for the country's ills, and justifiable. Congress was not merely incompetent; it needed basic institutional reform. But better to reform the institution using legitimate means than trample on a principle so essential to the nation's future. Only after he resigned his military commission did Washington energize the effort to draft a new Constitution. In that light, isn't it less of a wonder that his countrymen voted—unanimously—to entrust him with the newly created executive branch despite their deep suspicion of such power?

As the Collins and Porras and the Birnbaum studies suggest, successful executives still rediscover the lessons Washington knew: All-powerful leaders don't make the best decisions. The best decisions are made when leaders are accountable and power is wisely dispersed. Smart CEOs not only don't mind this, at least one has encouraged it in the last several years, even in a turnaround situation. CEO David Johnson didn't ask his board for all the power to turn around troubled Campbell Soup. To the contrary, he asked the board to take a stronger and more independent role in corporate governance, including stringent oversight of his own performance. Under Johnson's tenure from 1990 to 1997, Campbell's previously lackluster profits soared, as did its share price.

Notes

CHAPTER 1

1. See, for example, Robert H. Waterman, Jr., *What America Does Right,* New York, Norton, 1994, 293–296, showing that American workers, even at the height of the Japanese and German "invasions" of American markets, were still the most productive of the three countries, by far.

2. See Chapter 5 for more on these studies, and their citations.

3. *Inc.,* "The State of Small Business 1996," 74.

4. For organizations today, see James C. Collins and Jerry I. Porras, *Built to Last: Successful Habits of Visionary Companies,* New York, HarperBusiness, 1994, especially Chapter 2. See also Robert Birnbaum, *How Academic Leadership Works: Understanding Success and Failure in the College Presidency,* San Francisco, Jossey-Bass, 1992. For the early American Puritans, see Bernard Bailyn, *The New England Merchants in the Seventeenth Century,* Cambridge, Harvard University Press, 1982, 3d printing, Chapters III and IV; and Daniel Boorstin's short, incisive discussion in *The Americans: The Colonial Experience,* New York, Vintage Books, 1958, 29–31. For the United States itself, see Gordon Wood, *The Radicalism of the American Revolution,* New York, Vintage Books, 1993, and compare Chapter 1, "Hierarchy" with Chapter 18, "The Celebration of Commerce."

5. Collins and Porras, 28–31.

6. Daniel Bell, *The Cultural Contradictions of Capitalism,* New York, Basic-Books, 1978, 83.

7. Alfred P. Sloan, Jr., *My Years With General Motors,* Doubleday Currency, 1990, vii.

8. For an overview of the new scholarship on America's formative experiences, see Joyce Appleby, "A Different Kind of Independence: The Postwar Restructuring of the Historical Study of Early America," *The William and Mary Quarterly,* 3d Ser., Vol. L, No. 2, April 1993, 245.

CHAPTER 2

1. Stephen Innes, *Creating the Commonwealth: The Economic Culture of Puritan New England,* New York, Norton, 1995.

2. Alexis de Tocqueville, *Democracy in America,* New York, Vintage Classics, 1990, Vol. 1, 31.

3. Bell, *The Cultural Contradictions of Capitalism,* 56, 83. See also Max Weber, *The Protestant Ethic and the Spirit of Capitalism,* New York, Scribner's, 1958. See Robert Bellah et al., *Habits of the Heart: Individualism and Commitment in American life,* New York, Perennial, 1985, 27–31, for a concise summary of Puritan influence on American society.

4. The Waccamaw River slaves in South Carolina, for example, formed a large community to protect each other from the whims of their existence. If (more accurately, "when") their families were split up by death, bankruptcy, or other change in a master's fortune, the Waccamaw community would provide help for the orphaned child or the remaining spouse. To deal with the white menace to their lives, the most resilient American Indians likewise formed communities. Indeed, the Cherokees established their own territorial republic in Georgia, complete with its own constitution, and its own written language and requirements for citizenship—while adapting American laws and Christian theology as they found them useful. The cohesion and self-government they learned were essential to their survival after Andrew Jackson drove them into Indian Territory over the "Trail of Tears." Edward Countryman, *Americans: A Collision of Histories,* New York, Hill and Wang, 1996, 131–132, 136–139.

5. "GE Plastics (A)," Case 9-991-008, Boston, Harvard Business School, 1991, 4; "GE Plastics (B)," Case 9-991-009, 1.

6. "GE Plastics (C)," Case 9-991-010, Boston, Harvard Business School, 1991, 3.

7. Ibid., 5.

8. Ibid., 6–7.

9. Ibid., 7.

10. *New York Times Magazine,* September 13, 1970.

11. Or any other purpose for that matter. Colonel Harry G. Summers, Jr., *On Strategy: A Critical Analysis of the Vietnam War,* New York, Dell, 1984, Chapter 9. The "torch of idealism" quote is from Thomas A. Bailey, *The American Pageant: A History of the Republic,* 3d edition, Boston, Heath, 1966, 727.

12. "Jack Stack (A)," Case 9-993-009, Boston, Harvard Business School, 1993, 4–5.

13. Collins and Porras, *Built to Last*, Chapter 3.

14. Ibid., 52–54.

15. Incidently, where did Ford's ideals come from? His decision to double workers' wages came in part from the great interpreter of American culture and keeper of the Puritan flame, Ralph Waldo Emerson, in particular his essay, "Compensation." As Collins and Porras point out, Ford also realized that his company's highly attractive wages and low prices would make and sell a lot of cars. "Pragmatism? Idealism? Yes!" Collins and Porras, *Built to Last*, 53.

16. John P. Kotter and James L. Heskett, *Corporate Culture and Performance*, New York, The Free Press, Macmillan, 1992.

17. Ibid., 53. The authors "found considerably more evidence at the higher performers of a value system that really cared about all key constituencies. Which constituencies were stressed the most varied. . . . But no group was ignored, and fairness to everyone was a standard feature–a commitment often described as an emphasis on 'integrity' or 'doing the right thing.'" Ibid., 52.

18. *Democracy in America*, New York, Vintage Classics, 1990, Volume 1, 43–44.

19. Collins and Porras, *Built to Last*, 68–70.

20. *Democracy in America*, Volume 2, 121.

21. *Democracy in America*, Volume 2, 122.

22. *Built to Last*, 47.

23. Noel M. Tichy and Stratford Sherman, *Control Your Destiny or Someone Else Will*, New York, Currency Doubleday, 1993, 142–146.

24. Ibid., 137.

CHAPTER 3

1. Innes, *Creating the Commonwealth*.

2. Bailyn, *The New England Merchants in the Seventeenth Century*, Chapters III and IV.

3. Ibid., Chapter III (52ff in particular).

4. Francis J. Bremer, *The Puritan Experiment: New England Society from Bradford to Edwards*, Hanover, NH, and London, University Press of New England, 1995, 120.

5. "Motorola: Institutionalizing Corporate Initiatives," Case 9-494-139 rev., Boston, Harvard Business School, 1994, 6.

6. Richard Bruner, "Tungsram's Leading Light," *International Management*, December 1992, 42. Subsequent quotes are from this article.

7. Bruner, ibid.

8. Tichy and Sherman, *Control Your Destiny*, 204.

9. Robert Slater, *The New GE: How Jack Welch Revived an American Institution*, Homewood, IL, Business One Irwin, 1993, 217.

10. *Control Your Destiny*, 102 (quoting Jim Paynter, a GE employee-relations manager).

11. *The New GE,* 228.

12. Ibid., 219–220.

13. Jeffrey Pfeffer, *The Human Equation: Building Profits by Putting People First,* Boston, Harvard Business School Press, 1998, 166–167.

14. Daniel Boorstin, *The Americans: The National Experience,* Vintage Books, 1965, 68.

15. *The Prairie Traveler: A Handbook for Overland Expeditions,* 1859, issued under auspices of the U.S. War Department and reissued several times, Williamstown, MA, Corner House Publishers, 1968, 23–24.

16. Robert H. Waterman, Jr., Judy A. Waterman and Betsy A. Collard "Toward A Career-Resilient Workforce," *Harvard Business Review,* July–August 1994, 87.

17. Pfeffer, *The Human Equation,* 163.

CHAPTER 4

1. Lenin's one-line order, which was faithfully carried out when he was asked what to do about 8,000 Russian priests thought to be disruptive to the Russian revolution.

2. Countryman, *Americans: A Collision of Histories,* 49–50, quoting Gouverneur Morris.

3. Jefferson later wrote that he hadn't aimed for "originality of principle or sentiment," when he drafted the Declaration. Rather, it was "intended to be an expression of the American mind and to give to that expression the proper tone and spirit called for by the occasion." Thomas Fleming, *The Man from Monticello,* New York, Morrow, 1969, 53.

4. For a full description of the development of the committees and why they were effective, see Pauline Maier, *From Resistance to Revolution: Colonial Radicals and the Development of American Opposition to Britain, 1765–1776,* New York, Knopf, 1972.

5. "Remember Us," *The Economist,* February 1, 1992, 71. Based on research performed by Great Britain's National Institute of Economic and Social Research and supported by a 1992 report from Britain's National Economic Development Council.

6. "Jack Stack (A)," Case 9-993-009, Boston, Harvard Business School, 1993, 4.

7. Jack Stack, *The Great Game of Business,* New York, Currency Doubleday, 1992, 111.

CHAPTER 5

1. Mark A. Huselid, "The Impact of Human Resource Management Practices on Turnover, Productivity, and Corporate Financial Performance," *Academy of Management Journal,* June 1995, Vol. 38, No. 3, 635; Brian E. Becker, Mark A. Huselid, Peter S. Pickus, and Michael F. Spratt, "HR As a

Source of Shareholder Value," *Human Resources Management,* Spring 1997, Vol. 36, No. 1, 39.

2. "The Straining of Quality," *The Economist,* January 14, 1995, 55.

3. These studies are summarized in Pfeffer, *The Human Equation,* Chapter 2. Automobile factories, for example, that combine lean manufacturing methods with employee participation achieve huge gains in quality and productivity—47 and 43 percent respectively—over companies that stick with conventional manufacturing and employment practices. Textile factories that combine a new "modular" system of production with employee participation achieve large gains in sales growth, gross margins, and finished inventory turns—49, 22, and 21 percent respectively—over companies that continue to use the old "bundle" manufacturing system and conventional employment practices.

4. Between the last two editions of the book by that title, they've developed:

- much more employee participation and ownership, as well as education and training;
- much more management responsiveness to employee input;
- cultures based increasingly on freedom and trust and much less on control.

Robert Levering and Milton Moskowitz, *The 100 Best Companies to Work For in America,* Revised Edition, New York, Plume, 1994, xiv-xv.

5. See Commission on the Future of Worker-Management Relations, John Dunlop, Chairman, *Fact Finding Report,* Washington, DC, U.S. Department of Labor and Department of Commerce, 1994, Chapter II.

6. Michael Quarrey and Corey Rosen, *Employee Ownership and Corporate Performance,* Oakland, CA, The National Center for Employee Ownership, 1996.

7. Stephen L. Nesbitt, *The "CalPERS Effect" on Targeted Company Share Prices,* Santa Monica, CA, Wilshire Associates Inc., September 9, 1996. Note that Nesbitt's paper considered the possibility that the rebound in stock performance after CalPERS' intervention was caused more by depressed stock prices than by anything done by CalPERS. A control group of low-priced stocks unaffiliated with CalPERS was also studied, and showed none of the gains enjoyed by the CalPERS stocks.

8. Robert F. Felton, Jennifer van Heeckeren, and Alec Hudnut, "Putting a Value on Board Governance," *The McKinsey Quarterly,* 1996, Number 4.

9. Margaret Blair, *Ownership and Control: Rethinking Corporate Governance for the Twenty-First Century,* Washington, DC, The Brookings Institute, 1995.

10. Neither is it clear that the federal government itself is the leviathan of inefficiency pundits like to portray, given that it must govern hundreds of millions of people who have much less in common than, say, employees of a corporation. The spectacular stories of federal waste and abuse are anec-

dotal; there are more careful studies that have shown that bureaucracies like the Social Security Administration have served clients with fairness and efficiency relative to resources. See Michael Keely, "The Trouble with Transformational Leadership: Toward a Federalist Ethic for Organizations," *Business Ethics Quarterly,* Volume 5, Issue, 1, 1995, citing James Q. Wilson, *Bureaucracy: What Government Agencies Do and Why They Do It,* New York, Basic Books, 1989; Charles T. Goodsell, *The Case for Bureaucracy: A Public Administration Polemic,* Chatham, NJ, Chatham House, 1983; and Jerry L. Mashaw, *Bureaucratic Justice: Managing Social Security Disability Claims,* New Haven, CT, Yale University Press, 1983.

11. Levering and Moskowitz, *The 100 Best Companies to Work For in America,* 123.

12. Ibid., 124.

13. This is based on Waterman, *What America Does Right,* 95–96, and the author's conversations with Ms. Henson.

CHAPTER 6

1. See Thomas H. Davenport, *Information Ecology: Mastering the Information and Knowledge Environment,* New York, Oxford University Press, 1997, 68–72, citing Paul Strassman, *The Politics of Information Management,* New Canaan, CT, Information Economics Press, 1995, 43–49. See also Charles Handy, "Balancing Corporate Power: A New Federalist Paper," *Harvard Business Review,* November-December 1992, 59; and James O'Toole and Warren Bennis, "Our Federalist Future," *California Management Review,* Summer, 1992, 73–90.

2. Davenport, *Information Ecology,* 70.

3. Ibid., 70.

4. Tichy and Sherman, *Control Your Own Destiny,* 164–166.

5. "Changing the Role of Top Management: Beyond Strategy to Purpose," *Harvard Business Review,* November-December, 1994, 79; "Changing the Role of Top Management: Beyond Structure to Process," *Harvard Business Review,* January-February, 1995, 86; "Changing the Role of Top Management: Beyond Systems to People," *Harvard Business Review,* May-June, 1995, 132. Their new book is *The Individualized Corporation: A New Doctrine for Managing People,* New York, HarperBusiness, 1997. Also see their *Transnational Management: Text, Cases and Readings in Cross-Border Management,* 2d Edition, Chicago, Irwin, 1995.

6. Bartlett and Ghoshal, *Transnational Management: Text, Cases and Readings,* 790ff.

7. Ibid., 796ff.

8. "The Trouble With Teams," *The Economist,* January 14, 1995, 61.

9. Guillermo J. Grenier, *Inhuman Relations: Quality Circles and Anti-Unionism in American Industry,* Philadelphia, Temple University Press, 1988.

10. Wood, *The Radicalism of the American Revolution,* 363.

11. Ibid., 256–259.

CHAPTER 7

1. Eileen C. Shapiro, *Fad Surfing in the Boardroom*, Reading, MA, Addison Wesley, 1995, 186–188.

2. In the early 1990s, a flurry of studies appeared showing that total quality efforts fail two-thirds of the time. Re-engineering programs fared at least as poorly when they were studied. These are surveyed in Shapiro, *Fad Surfing in the Boardroom*, Chapters 14 and 15. One of the hottest fads of the 1980s was Japanese management methods such as quality circles, just-in-time manufacturing, and Japanese-style automation. These were installed by American companies at a cost of nearly one *trillion* dollars in capital investment and training–equal to the combined profit of the entire Fortune 500 for the whole decade! A study of their effectiveness in five hundred manufacturing companies by A. D. Little found "paltry gains" in performance in relation to the massive amount of money spent. Companies had become, as one A. D. Little partner put it, "too obsessed with one fad idea or another at the cost of overall focus." Amal Kumar Naj, "Some Manufacturers Drop Efforts to Adopt Japanese Techniques," *Wall Street Journal*, May 7, 1993, A1. See also Frederick G. Hilmer and Lex Donaldson, *Management Redeemed: Debunking the Fads That Undermine Corporate Performance*, New York, Free Press, 1996; and Robert G. Eccles and Nitin Nohria, *Beyond the Hype: Rediscovering the Essence of Management*, Boston, Harvard Business School Press, 1992. One of the more vivid descriptions of management fadism is in Robert H. Schaffer and Harvey A. Thompson, "Successful Change Programs Begin with Results," *Harvard Business Review*, January-February, 1992, 80.

3. The parallel between the outlook infecting many organizations now and the one that prevailed in seventeenth- and eighteenth-century Europe is striking. Compare this description of European society by a renowned historian with the ones below of modern business cultures.

"By the early 17th century, Europe had accumulated a rich but cumbersome cultural baggage. Systems of thought, established institutions, professional traditions, dogmatically defined bodies of knowledge regarded as all that was worth knowing–these cluttered the landscape of England and of Europe. The bare earth was almost nowhere visible. . . . In most past societies–certainly in the aristocratic societies of western Europe–rulers and priests had been the 'explaining' classes. They were the acknowledged possessors of the ways of knowing, the secret keys to the ancestral treasurehouse of mystery and knowledge. . . . The common people could show their good sense only by acting according to ways approved by their betters." Boorstin, *The Americans: The Colonial Experience*, 149–150.

Boorstin's point, of course, is that such an outlook was completely foreign to the way thought and action developed in America–which "quickly proved uncongenial to any special class of 'knowers.'" Nevertheless, compare this description of American business over the last decade or so:

"The 1980s witnessed the spectacular rise of management schools, consultants, media and gurus who fed on the insecurities of American managers. . . . Mistrustful of their own judgment, many managers latched on to these self-appointed pundits, readily adopting their latest panaceas. . . . Adopting 'new' ideas became a way for companies to signal to the world that they were progressive. . . ." Nitin Nohria and James D. Berkley, "Whatever Happened to the Take-Charge Manager," *Harvard Business Review*, January-February, 1994, 128.

And note this description by two seasoned consultants horrified by the burst of fadism in companies they work with:

"Management takes action steps because they are "correct" and fit the program's philosophy. . . . Staff experts and consultants indoctrinate everyone into the mystique and vocabulary of the program. . . . Staff experts and consultants urge managers and employees to have faith in the approach and to support it." Schaffer and Thompson, "Successful Change Programs Begin with Results," 83.

4. Madison, for example, in *The Federalist,* drew heavily on David Hume's reasoning that large republics could be made to work, but he dismissed out of hand the philosopher's suggestions for how to do so–later remarking that "Hume was among those bungling lawgivers." William Lee Miller, *The Business of May Next: James Madison and the Founding,* Charlottesville, VA, University Press of Virginia, 1992, 58.

The crusty John Adams was himself often contemptuous of the pretensions of the great philosophers, particularly the notion held by sophisticated Europeans that mankind should place itself in their hands: "What a pity," Adams wrote of one, "that this man of genius can not be king and priest of the whole human race." He agreed with a protégé of his that American circumstances defy such "system mongers"–referring to Europe's theoreticians, in particular to Montesquieu, who was "too fond of hypothesis . . . too mechanical." Bernard Bailyn, *The Ideological Origins of the American Revolution,* Cambridge, The Belknap Press of Harvard University Press, 1992, 372.

While Jefferson was effusive in his praise of philosophers like Francis Bacon and John Locke, his greatest achievements reveal a pragmatist's ability to put aside high-flown principle in the interest of getting results. See Bernard Bailyn, *Faces of Revolution,* New York, Vintage Books, 1992, Chapter 2, and John Patrick Diggins, *The Promise of Pragmatism,* Chicago, University of Chicago Press, 1994, 74ff. This was true even when he drafted the seminal statement of American political ideology, the Declaration of Independence. His letters to close associates, and theirs to him for that matter, show little interest in political theory down to the date of the American Revolution. Daniel Boorstin, "Revolution Without Dogma," reprinted in *Hidden History: Exploring Our Secret Past,* New York, Vintage Books, 1989, 102. And when he sat down to draft the Declaration, he consulted "neither book nor pamphlet" as he later put it, wanting only to explain "the common sense of the subject" using "terms so plain and firm" as to "command" mankind's assent. The principle of liberty announced in a few short lines by the Declaration–that all men are created equal and endowed with certain inalienable rights–was already widely held by Americans.

5. This isn't to say Americans brought a completely blank mind to a situation–an impossible thing to do. Philosopher Thomas Kuhn argued that every observer's perceptions depend not only on what he is looking at, but also on his own previous experience and training–plus, for the scientist, the prevailing theory or "paradigm" in his field. But some observers are more unfettered by their training and experience, like card readers in the experiment who can more readily "see" the black four of hearts, because they are more receptive to novelty. In science these tend to be younger professionals, or those new to the field who don't have as much invested in the existing paradigm, and bring different and varied experiences to the situation at hand. *The Structure of Scientific Revolutions,* 2d edition enlarged, Chicago, University of Chicago Press, 1970.

6. Peter Drucker, *Innovation and Entrepreneurship: Practices and Principles,* New York, Perennial Library, 1986. This is a thorough and incisive treatment of business innovation, with Drucker's usual flair for historical perspective.

7. Boorstin, *The Americans: The National Experience,* 3.

8. Drucker, *Innovation and Entrepreneurship,* 43–44.

9. Collins and Porras, *Built to Last,* 151–152.

10. Paul Carroll, "The Day Bill Gates Overthrew IBM," *Wall Street Journal,* August 16, 1993, B3, excerpted from the book, *Big Blues: The Unmaking of IBM,* New York, Crown, 1994.

11. This was increasingly suggested by a steady stream of anecdotal evidence that MITI and the Ministry of Finance backed losers in industries like airlines and computers, and tried to squelch winners like Honda and Sony. A comprehensive (and little reported) study by the University of Alberta's Richard Beason and Harvard's David Weinstein settled the issue. Beason and Weinstein analyzed Japanese government support from 1955 to 1990 throughout thirteen broad industrial sectors such as electrical machinery, transport equipment, and chemicals. They found that, far from exerting a positive impact on its economy, Japan's bureaucrats chalked up a *negative* statistical correlation between government support and economic growth in each sector. For example, the ministries gave the most tax relief, cheap loans, and net transfers to mining companies–Japan's second-*slowest* growing industry. In other words, the study confirms that Japanese ministries in general picked losers not winners; Japan's economic recovery happened *despite* them, not because of them. Richard Beason and David Weinstein, *Growth, Economies of Scale, and Targeting in Japan (1955–1990),* Harvard Institute of Economic Research, Discussion Paper 1644.

12. Bailey, *The American Pageant: A History of the Republic,* 197.

13. DeTocqueville, *Democracy in America,* Volume 1, 35.

CHAPTER 8

1. Pauline Maier, *American Scripture: Making the Declaration of Independence*, New York, Knopf, 1997, 136.

2. I. Bernard Cohen, *Benjamin Franklin's Science*, Cambridge, Harvard University Press, 1990, Chapter 2.

3. For a fuller discussion of the pragmatist's approach to learning, see Diggins, *The Promise of Pragmatism*, Chapter 5.

4. This story is from Gerald Nadler and Shozo Hibino, *Breakthrough Thinking: Why We Must Change the Way We Solve Problems, And the Seven Principles to Achieve This*, Rocklin, CA, Prima Publishing, 1990, 111–113.

5. David Halberstam, *The Best and the Brightest*, New York, Penguin, 1983, 304.

6. Schaffer and Thompson, "Successful Change Programs Begin with Results," 87ff.

7. Here's a quick course on how to experiment:

There is no universally applicable scientific method for all situations (a most *un*-pragmatic notion). However, there is a familiar, recurring pattern. And the best way to learn it is not in the abstract, but by applying it to real world situations, as the PECO teams did earlier–to improve processes, or to develop new products, or even create new ventures.

1. *Be curious–and opportunistic.*
   Recognize a problem or potential opportunity; that is, a situation that deserves further inquiry and possibly action. Regard unexpected events in particular as prime sources of opportunity–not problems to be shunted aside.

2. *State a purpose.*
   Once a problem or opportunity is identified, articulate a specific goal to strive for. Then locate and define the difficulties and barriers to reaching it.

3. *Develop hypotheses.*
   Brainstorm ideas and suggestions on how to proceed to overcome the barriers and achieve the purpose. For complex situations such as developing a new product or corporate venturing, this amounts to developing hypotheses.

4. *Anticipate what will happen.*
   Use common sense and your reasoning ability to envision consequences of the various suggested approaches. Previous experience and theories can help inform this but should never be regarded as definitive. "It hasn't worked before," for example, is not the last word on whether it should be tried now.

5. *Test and learn.*
   Don't make the common mistake of stopping with step 4–*test* the most promising idea or hypothesis. Verify and confirm it, or discard and reformulate it based on lessons learned. Keep performing all these

steps again and again. No knowledge is final—particularly in business these days, as ever-shortening product life cycles show.

A few comments should be added. First, this is not a method of decision-making, it's a program of *action*. The experimental process is not something done "off to the side" preparatory to acting, it shows *how* to act. Pragmatism disdains the view that thinking and doing should be separated—that you "Plan your work then work your plan"—an outlook that, strictly followed, can inhibit learning once the action begins. Rather the two should be *combined* so that one continues to inform the other; learning shouldn't stop just because decisions have been made.

Thus, the above steps are not clearly separated like a flight of stairs. They tend more to merge into each other like steps in a dance; one should move freely back and forth among them. For example, articulating a purpose and identifying difficulties to overcome (step 2) can by itself suggest approaches to doing so (step 3). If you continue thinking about the second step even after you've started on the third, you might continue to uncover valuable options, as the junior staffer did in figuring out that his company should get rid of its warehouses.

Neither is this mere trial and error; it's a systematic way of learning from and deepening experience. How? Because, and this is the greatest value of this approach to learning, the experimental method flushes out and identifies assumptions everyone is making, and forces their testing. It helps uncover in particular the most deadly kind of assumptions: those that people make without knowing it.

And as John Dewey observed, the cultural changes that such an approach to thinking and action can generate are truly exciting. People who learn to experiment and practice it routinely—whether they are members of the PECO teams or a Benjamin Franklin—develop greater awareness that all knowledge is based on assumptions whose validity can change for any number of reasons, known and unknown. Such people are not likely to become rigid and dogmatic in their thinking. Around them can be built a truly dynamic "learning organization."

8. H. Kent Bowen, et al., editors, *The Perpetual Enterprise Machine*, New York, Oxford University Press, 1994. Participants in the study included executives from Hewlett-Packard, Ford, Chaparral Steel, Kodak, and Digital Electronics, plus academics from Harvard, MIT, Stanford, and Purdue University. Their goal was to understand how American industry must change to meet the competitive challenges of increasingly global competition.

9. Marco Iansiti and Jonathan West, "Technology Integration: Turning Great Research into Great Products," *Harvard Business Review*, May-June, 1997, 69; Bowen et al., *The Perpetual Enterprise Machine*.

10. John Dewey in particular pointed out the tendency of all institutions to make fixed schemes out of instruments that once served dynamic purposes, but now stifle progress and growth. Leaders, he thought, could combat this by emphasizing and reinforcing the interconnectedness, the

relatedness, of parts to the whole. For institutions to retain their effectiveness in a dynamic, unpredictable environment, they must find ways for the parts to create new patterns, and support each other in new ways. For a fuller discussion of this, see Elizabeth Flower and Murray G. Murphey, *A History of Philosophy in America*, New York, Capricorn Books and Putnam, 1977, Volume 2, 877–882.

11. Bowen et al., *The Perpetual Enterprise Machine*, Chapter 7. For a more thorough description of how to use prototypes to dramatically improve new product development, see Marco Iansiti, "Shooting the Rapids: Managing Product Development in Turbulent Environments," *California Management Review*, Fall 1995.

CHAPTER 9

1. William J. Dennis, Jr., "More Than You Think: An Inclusive Estimate of Business Entries," *Journal of Business Venturing*, May 1997, 175–196.

2. Amar Bhide, "How Entrepreneurs Craft Strategies That Work," *Harvard Business Review*, March-April 1994, 151.

3. Wood, *The Radicalism of the American Revolution*, 315.

4. Hamilton's views on industrial policy have been something of a political football down to the present day. Those who advocate (or increasingly, "once advocated") a strong, Japanese-style industrial policy for America argue, with some force, that Hamilton himself favored such an approach. But my emphasis here is less on what any leader envisioned for America—even one as brilliant and open to new possibilities as Hamilton—and more on how things actually worked out.

For example, the Society for Establishing Useful Manufactures Hamilton set up in New Jersey was indeed an ambitious effort to kick-start manufacturing in America—he planned an entire town on the Passaic River, together with machinery and skilled artisans producing a host of consumer and industrial goods. But the effort fell flat on its face: While Hamilton dreamed of a quasi-government project that would lead America's economy into the next century, the stockholders he'd recruited to fund it began unloading their shares for a quick profit almost immediately.

As for Hamilton's superb *Report on Manufactures*, it did arguably contain some elements of an industrial policy: It called for protecting infant industries, facilitating inventions, encouraging immigration of skilled artisans, and employment of women and children. But alone among his state papers this one languished in Congress due to Southerners' suspicion of federal power—even when federal policies were meant to benefit them.

Hamilton himself, who was not always politically astute, was nevertheless well aware of this emerging temper in the new United States. The first draft of the *Report* (which was prepared by an assistant) *would* have created a full-blown MITI-style industrial policy: It had extensive proposals for government loans to manufacturers, land grants to industry, monopoly privileges to certain types of business, duty-free imports on raw materials for American exporters, prohibitions on rival imports, protective tariffs, and so forth.

But Hamilton realized that such proposals were clearly impossible in America—why bother to revolt from Great Britain if we're going to do the same thing to ourselves? He eliminated most of them from the final draft, and those that remained were either concessions to American mercantilists or simply a realistic acknowledgment that rival nations still practiced mercantilism themselves. Hamilton's primary emphasis in the *Report* was on raising revenues and shoring up the credit of the financially precarious United States. Donald F. Swanson and Andrew P. Trout, "Alexander Hamilton's Invisible Hand," *Policy Review*, Winter 1992, 86. For a concise discussion of Hamilton's policies for encouraging industrial ventures, see Forrest McDonald, *Alexander Hamilton: A Biography*, New York, Norton, 1982, 232ff. To see how Hamilton's policies fit into and were accepted by emerging American society, see Stanley Elkins and Eric McKitrick, *The Age of Federalism*, New York, Oxford University Press, 1993, 258ff.

5. Elkins and McKitrick, *The Age of Federalism*, 281–282.

6. Zenas Block and Ian C. MacMillan, *Corporate Venturing: Creating New Businesses within the Firm*, Boston, Harvard Business School Press, 1995, 34.

7. Drucker, *Innovation and Entrepreneurship*, 139.

8. Bhide, "How Entrepreneurs Craft Strategies That Work," *Harvard Business Review*, 161.

9. Block and MacMillan, *Corporate Venturing*, Chapter 7.

10. Rita Gunther McGrath and Ian C. MacMillan, "Discovery-Driven Planning," *Harvard Business Review*, July-August, 1995, 45–46.

11. This example is based loosely on Kao's experience doing exactly that in the 1980s, and comes from the McGrath and MacMillan article. All numbers are gross approximations to keep the example simple.

CHAPTER 10

1. See "National Culture and Management," Case 9-394-177, Boston, Harvard Business School, 1994, for an overview of the literature on the role of national culture in business management.

2. Estimates by the Office of Economic Cooperation and Development, assuming the GDPs of these countries grow at 6 percent per year (the average in China over the last decade has been 8 to 9 percent), and their income distributions remain unchanged. See "War of the Worlds: A Survey of the Global Economy," *The Economist*, October 1, 1994.

3. Gurcharan Das, "Local Memoirs of a Global Manager," *Harvard Business Review*, March-April 1993, 47.

4. Rosabeth Moss Kanter, "Collaborative Advantage: The Art of Alliances," *Harvard Business Review*, July-August 1994, 105.

5. P. Christopher Earley and Miriam Erez, *The Transplanted Executive*, New York, Oxford University Press, 1997, 21, 26–27.

6. Ricardo Semler, *Maverick: The Success Story Behind the World's Most Unusual Workplace*, New York, Warner Books, 1993, 52.

7. Ibid., Chapter 9.

8. Ricardo Semler, "Managing Without Managers," *Harvard Business Review*, September-October, 1989, 84.

9. "A hell of a waste," complained one worker when told of the five-figure cost for an upcoming executive retreat. He asked why the executives had to meet in such a high-priced hotel, why their spouses had to come, and what, for that matter, did they plan to *do* there? "Now," reflects Semler, "we have much cheaper conventions, with fewer managers, and much less fun." *Maverick*, 78.

10. Ibid., 84.

CHAPTER 11

1. There is an extensive management literature on the subject, flowing from James MacGregor Burns's study of leaders in history, *Leadership*, New York, Harper Torchbooks, 1978.

2. Michael Keeley, "The Trouble with Transformational Leadership: Toward a Federalist Ethic for Organizations," *Business Ethics Quarterly*, Volume 5, Issue 1, 1995, 68. Of course, the term "transformational leader" did not exist then–but there was the "man on horseback."

3. Robert Birnbaum, *How Academic Leadership Works*, San Francisco, Jossey-Bass, 1992.

4. Collins and Porras, *Built to Last: Successful Practices of Visionary Companies*, Chapter 2. Note that Collins and Porras didn't set out to study American companies per se, but that seventeen of the eighteen pairs of companies they compared were American (the exception was the exemplar company Sony and its "also ran" competitor Kenwood.)

5. Indeed, this is respected Lincoln historian David Herbert Donald's central thesis in *Lincoln*, New York, Simon & Schuster, 1995.

6. Birnbaum, *How Academic Leadership Works*, 27.

7. Ibid., 26.

8. Collins and Porras, *Built to Last*, 33.

9. Birnbaum, *How Academic Leadership Works*, 31–34.

10. Ibid., 134–36.

11. William Manchester, *American Caesar: Douglas MacArthur 1880–1964*, New York, Dell, 1979, 562.

12. James T. Flexner, *Washington: The Indispensable Man*, New York, Signet, 1984.

13. Edmund S. Morgan, *The Genius of George Washington*, New York, Norton, 1980; Garry Wills, *Cincinnatus: George Washington and the Enlightenment*, Garden City, NY, Doubleday, 1984.

14. Wills, *Cincinnatus*, 13.

Selected Readings

How do you transform and energize an organization, and unleash the wealth-creating potential of its employees–particularly an organization of American employees? That's the main challenge addressed by this book. I've taken the position that, for today's executive social architect, the most essential knowledge and insight for doing so comes from a clear understanding of how our own society was transformed.

For those who'd like more on this, a good place to start is with Thomas Fleming's vivid *Liberty: The American Revolution*, New York, Viking, 1997, the companion book to the recent, wonderful PBS series. Fleming is both a respected American historian and a superb novelist who knows how to tell a good story. He has a great feel, both for the relevant and the interesting.

Daniel J. Boorstin's classic and well honored *The Americans*, 3 Volumes, New York, Vintage Books, 1958, is a highly readable survey of America's social and cultural history. Boorstin's focus is on society, not hero leaders. He looks for patterns and continuing themes in how ordinary Americans think and act, and his insights are still remarkably fresh and valuable.

For those who'd like to plumb deeper waters, here's an outline for a master class in American social transformation. All these works are distinguished by their readability and elegant prose, which makes them seem less lengthy than they unfortunately are. (Remember: You can always skip around, and you don't have to read the whole thing.)

Bernard Bailyn's *The Ideological Origins of the American Revolution*, Cambridge, The Belknap Press of the Harvard University Press, 1992, is the definitive account of how Americans thought about the sort of society they wanted to live in during that remarkable time in history when the power to transform it was in their hands. It won both the Pulitzer Prize and the Bancroft Prize for history when it was first published in 1967.

Bailyn clarifies the development in America of concepts like liberty, power, rights, social status, and the relation of leaders to the led–issues with which every organization must deal. While he traces their roots to Enlightenment rationalism and other sources, he focuses on something much more important: what these concepts came to mean to ordinary Americans, which he explains with great precision. The first step in transforming a society is to develop a *language* of social transformation: one that resonates with people, gives a meaningful framework to what must be done, and–what's too often missing–provides clear and well-defined terms so that different people won't mean different things when they use them. For that, this book is simply indispensable.

The second step is to turn such concepts into action. Leaders must devise practical tools for transforming society that fit the ideology–that fit people's sensibilities and expectations. For superb insights into creating such tools, turn to Gordon Wood's sweeping *The Creation of the American Republic, 1776-1787*, New York, Norton, 1993 (winner of the Bancroft Prize in 1969). Here is an exhaustive (the biggest of these books at over 600 pages) but fascinating account of how the Founding Fathers devised governance that harnessed the forces of democracy when they were set loose in America and nearly tore it apart. The founders' achievement was, as I've tried to indicate in this book, brilliant, monumentally successful, and highly relevant to leaders seeking to free up American employees today. Wood is a pleasure to read: brilliant (he is setting the agenda among historians of this period), an elegant writer, free of political correctness, and clearly awed by what he beholds. (And remember, you don't have to read the whole thing!)

Finally, how does it all turn out? Once you understand the ideology of social transformation, and then once you implement the tools to achieve it– what should you expect? Not, as it turns out, what you might think! Wood tells us in his more recent (and much shorter) *The Radicalism of the American Revolution*, New York, Vintage, 1993.

He describes, with subtlety and precision, the three phases of social transformation in America: America as a hierarchical society (under British rule); America as a republican society envisioned by the Founding Fathers just after the Revolution; and finally, the America we recognize today. The America that ultimately emerged–and it was not at all what the Founders expected or hoped for–was a fluid, radically egalitarian, rambunctious, and entrepreneurial society. For anyone who wants to understand the dynamics of transforming a hierarchical society, *The Radicalism of the American Revolution* is also indispensable.

Still, the first word on American society in its earliest, most vibrant stages after the transition to democracy was complete is Alexis de Tocqueville's *Democracy in America*, 2 Volumes, New York, Vintage Classics, 1990. Here is a superb portrait by a brilliant and sympathetic foreigner, revealing the vast potential of our democratic society. Any executive/social architect today can read this and recognize immediately—yes, these *are* our values and we should affirm them, these are our strengths and we should be exploiting them, and these are the pitfalls we're prone to and had better guard against.

Here are some other suggested books:

HISTORY AND BIOGRAPHY

Edward Countryman, *Americans: A Clash of Histories*, New York, Hill and Wang, 1996. Countryman is working to determine what it means for the broad spectrum of our people, including blacks and natives, to "be American," an important subject as corporations wrestle with diversity.

Stanley Elkins and Eric McKitrick, *The Age of Federalism*, New York, Oxford University Press, 1993. Whatever happened to the Founders' vision of America—with a virtuous citizenry, or at least virtuous leaders, who would wisely steer the ship of state while dispassionately balancing the interests of the people? This massive but elegant book shows us. Its portraits of the Founding Fathers are fascinating.

Gerald Gunderson, *The Wealth Creators: An Entrepreneurial History of the United States*, New York, Plume, 1990.

James Thomas Flexner, *Washington: The Indispensable Man*, New York, Signet/New American Library, 1984.

Benjamin Franklin, *Writings* (includes his *Autobiography*), New York, Library of America, 1987.

James Madison, *Notes of the Debates in the Federal Convention of 1787*, New York, Norton, 1966.

James Madison, Alexander Hamilton, and John Jay, *The Federalist Papers*, Chicago, William Benton, 1952.

BUSINESS AND CONTEMPORARY

Russell Ackoff, *The Democratic Corporation*, New York, Oxford University Press, 1994.

Daniel Bell, *The Cultural Contradictions of Capitalism*, New York, Basic Books, 1978.

Robert Bellah et al., *Habits of the Heart: Individualism and Commitment in American Life*, New York, Perennial, 1985.

James C. Collins, and Jerry I. Porras, *Built to Last: Successful Habits of Visionary Companies*, New York, HarperBusiness, 1994.

Peter Drucker, *Innovation and Entrepreneurship*, New York, Perennial, 1985.

Kevin Freiberg and Jackie Freiberg, *Nuts: Southwest Airlines' Crazy Recipe for Business and Personal Success*, Austin, TX, Bard Press, 1996.

Andy Grove, *Only the Paranoid Survive*, New York, Currency Doubleday, 1997.

John P. Kotter and James B. Heskett, *Corporate Culture and Performance*, New York, Free Press, 1992.

Robert Levering and Milton Moskowitz, *The 100 Best Companies to Work For in America*, Revised Edition, New York, Plume, 1994.

Jeffrey Pfeffer, *The Human Equation: Building Profits by Putting People First*, Boston, Harvard Business School Press, 1998.

Ricardo Semler, *Maverick: The Success Story Behind the World's Most Unusual Workplace*, New York, Warner Books, 1993.

Jack Stack, *The Great Game of Business*, New York, Currency Doubleday, 1992.

Robert Waterman, *What America Does Right*, New York, Norton, 1994.

Index

Adams, Samuel, 52–53
Albertson's, 27
American Revolution, 6, 23
  changes to Americans fostered
    by, 11–13, 111, 130–131
  differences from other types of
    revolution, 50–51
  grassroots energy of, 52–53
Ames Stores, 163, 164
Andersen Consulting, 85
Apple Computers, 47, 138
Appleton, Nathan, 128
Aragona, Frank, 46
Archer Daniels Midland, 27
Asea Brown Boveri (ABB), 85,
  133
federal organization of, 78, 79–80,
  134
Astor, John Jacob, 100

Bankers Trust, 27
Barnevik, Percy, 134
Bartlett, Christopher, 85–86
Bell, Daniel, 9–10, 17
Bhide, Amar, 129, 136
Bill of Rights, 10, 11, 68–69
Birnbaum, Robert, 160, 161–163,
  165, 169
Blair, Margaret, 66
Block, Zenas, 141
Boeing, 24, 25, 28
Bolivar, Simon, 167–168
Bookman, Philip, 139
Boone, Daniel, 18
Boorstin, Daniel, 98, 99
Bossidy, Larry, 30
Boston Associates, 132
Bristol-Meyers Squibb, 24, 163
Bristol, William, 163

British Petroleum, 78, 79
Built to Last (Collins and Porras),
    24–28, 160–165

Caesar, Julius, 166, 167–168
California Public Employees
    Retirement System
    (CalPERS), 65–66
Cambridge Platform, 29, 35
Campbell's Soup, 170
Chaparral Steel, 124
Chrysler, 54
Cin-Made Corporation, 93–95
Citizen. *See also* Twin citizenship
    as the basis for transforming soci-
        ety, 65–69
    definition of, 65, 67
    employee as, 10, 13, 43, 65–67,
        70–71, 73, 81
    importance of educating, 36
City on a Hill, 16
Civil War, 23, 85
Coca-Cola, 78
Colgate, William, 163
Colgate, 163
Collard, Betsy, 46
Collins, James, 24–28, 160–165
Community,
    ability of to bond Americans,
        16–19
    characteristics of, 19
    economic dynamism of, 31–32
    governance and leadership
        appropriate to, 33–34
    importance of higher purpose
        to, 22
    importance of virtue to, 27–28,
        30
    temporary or "traveling" com-
        munities, 44–45

Compaq, 62
ConAgra, 27
Constitution, U.S. 10
Cook, Scott, 106
Cornwallis, Lord, 118–119
Costco Wholesale Corporation
    (Price/Costco, Inc.), 114–115
Countryman, Edward, 18
Cromwell, Oliver, 167–168

Dell, Michael, 106–107
Democracy,
    difficulty of establishing in
        America, 65, 67, 77–78, 90–91,
        102–103
    tools for controlling the forces of,
        67–68, 91–92
    creating strong leadership in a,
        68–69
    wealth-creating potential of, 92,
        129, 130–132
Dewey, John, 116, 121, 122–123
Disneyland Paris. *See* EuroDisney
Donnelly Corporation
    representative governance at,
        70–71
Drucker, Peter, 10
DuPont, 100

Eaton, Robert, 54
Employability, 46–48
Employee participation,
    impact on organizational perfor-
        mance, 59–61
    difficulties of installing, 61–63
Entrepreneurism, in organizations,
    128–130, 139–146
Entrepreneurs,
    what they do, 135–139
Ethicon. *See* Johnson & Johnson

EuroDisney, 140–141
Experimentation
  method of, 123n.7
  in organizations, 122–127

Federal Express (FedEx), 10, 138
  accountability of leaders at, 74
  employee bill of rights at
    (Guaranteed Fair Treatment),
    72–73
Federalism,
  characteristics of, 78–80
  as a model for energizing large
    enterprises, 79–95
  as a spur to entrepreneurism,
    132–135
The Federalist, 164
Findley, William, 91
Ford Motor Company, 25–26, 28,
    160
  Taurus, 56
  Edsel, 103
  use of prototypes at, 126–127
Ford, Henry, 26, 160
Founding Fathers, 8
  how "empowerment" in America
    was established by, 63–65,
    77–80
  how excessive democracy was
    controlled by, 67–69
  lack of vision of, 51, 90, 91
  leadership style of, 11–12, 164;
    distinguished from "transfor-
    mational leaders," 9, 91–93,
    145, 159–160
  outlook of, distinguished from
    ours, 97–98, 102, 111
Franklin, Benjamin, 36, 51, 128
  discoveries in electricity,
    111–112

Junto, 18
  on power in America, 65
Frey, Robert, 93–95
Fujimori, Yoshiaki, 142

Galvin, Paul, Sr., 163, 165
Gamble, James, 162
Gates, Bill, 101–102
General Electric, 24, 28, 29, 78,
    160
  Corporate Executive Council
    (CEC), 82–83
  360 degree review at, 73–74
  twin citizenship at, 81–84
  Tungsram plant, community
    building at, 38–39
  Work Out, 10, 40–43
General Electric Medical Systems
    (GEMS)
  American values of, 147–148
  Group Operating Council
    (GOC), 83–84
General Electric Plastics
  Community building at, 19–22
Gerstner, Louis, 80
Ghoshal, Sumantra, 85–86
Green and Jersey Company, 18, 44
Grove, Andy, 66

Haggarty, Pat, 163
Halberstam, David, 121
Hamilton, Alexander,
  encouragement of entrepre-
    neurism in America by,
    131–132
  urges Washington to disband
    Congress, 169
Hatsopoulos, George, 134–135
Henry, Patrick, 53
Henson, Cyndi , 74–76

Hewlett-Packard, 9, 24, 25, 139,
    161
    development of DeskJet printer
        by, 125–126, 142–143
    strategy-creation at, 55
Hewlett, Bill, 9, 136, 163
Home Depot, 138
Honda, 71, 103–104
Huselid, Mark,
    on financial impact of "high-
        performance" organizations,
        59
Hutt, Joel, 19–22

Iacocca, Nick, 129
IBM, 80, 100, 101–102, 139
Intel, 66, 85, 144
Intuit Inc., 106,
    entrepreneurism at, 129,
        132–133
Irish-Americans, 149

James, William, 116
Jefferson, Thomas, 156
    and the Declaration of
        Independence, 51n.3, 111
    on determining truth in a democ-
        racy, 90–91
    during the American Revolution,
        53
    embargo imposed by, 107, 113,
        132
    on liberty, 12
    on New England town meetings,
        10
Johnson, R.W., Jr., 103, 163
Johnson, David, 170
Johnson, Howard, 163

Johnson & Johnson, 24, 28, 84, 133,
    160
    Baby Powder, 103
    Ethicon, "rat system at,"
        88–90
Junior staffer, 119–120

Kao, 85
    federal organization of, 87
Kelleher, Herb, 105
King, Roland, 105
Kmart, 160

Larimer, William, 129
Leadership
    in a democratic society, 34–35,
        92–93
    myth of transformational leader,
        7, 158–166
    "SOB executive," 7
Levering, Robert, 70, 72, 73
Levi's, 24
Lewis, John, 108–109
Lincoln Electric, 85
Lincoln, Abraham
    and the strength of twin citizen-
        ship, 85
    on what holds Americans togeth-
        er, 145–146
Lowell, Francis Cabot, 114, 132

MacArthur, Douglas, 166
MacMillan, Ian, 140
Madison, James, 67
    political innovations devised by,
        102, 105, 166
Manufacturing Vision Group,
    123–126

Marcy, Randolph,
  on bonding people in temporary
    communities, 45, 47
Marriott, 28, 139, 160–161
Mason, George, 144–145
Massachusetts Bay Colony, 5, 15,
  30
  covenant as basis for governance
    of, 33–34
  emergence of democracy in,
    32–35
  emphasis on education, 35–36
  prosperity of, 31–32, 99.
  sense of mission, 16–18, 22
Mather, Cotton. 17
McDonald, Eugene F., 163, 165
McDonnell Douglas, 24
McGrath, Rita Gunther , 140
McKinsey & Company, 66
Mcknight, William, 101, 162
McNamara, Robert, 121
Melville, 24
Merck, George, 162, 163
Merck, 24, 25, 28–29, 161
Ministry of International Trade and
  Industry (MITI), 103–104
Ministry of Finance, Japan,
  103–104
Morgan, J.P., 100
Morison, Samuel Eliot, 30
Morris, Robert, 91
Moskowitz, Milton, 70, 72, 73
Motorola, 24, 28, 139, 161
  emphasis on education by, 36–37
  Penang facility, community
    building at, 37–38;
Moulton, Paul, 114–115
Muse, Lamar, 105

National Center for Employee
  Ownership (NCEO), 63
New England factory builders,
  107–108, 113–114
Nissan, British,
  involvement of supervisors in
    strategy-creation at, 56
Nokia Group, 54–55
  strategy-creation at, 54
Nollet, Abbe, 112
  rivalry with Benjamin Franklin
Nordstrom, 24, 161
Norton, 24
Nylon, discovery of, 100

Ohio Associates, 18, 44
Okie, Francis G., 100–101
*100 Best Companies to Work For In
  America,* 70, 72
Onetto, Marc, 83–84
Owens-Corning, 80

PacBell, 108–109
Packard, David, 9, 136
Paine, Thomas, 111
Participative management (see
  Employee participation)
Pfeffer, Jeffrey, 47
Pfizer, 24, 163
Pfizer, Charles, 163
Philadelphia Electric (PECO),
  121–122
Philip Morris, 27, 161
Philosophy of the unexpected,
  98–99
Pickney, Charles, 144–145
Pierce, Charles, 116
Pike, Zebulon, 18

Pilgrims, 15

Porras, Jerry, 24–28, 160–165

Pragmatism, 115–116, 120–121,
    125
  instilling in organizations,
    121–127

Price/Costco, Inc. *See* Costco
    Wholesale Corporation

The Prince, 164

Procter & Gamble, 28, 147
  regards self-managed teams as
    competitive advantage, 60

Procter, William, 162, 163

Protestant work ethic, 16

Prototypes, new use of, 126–127

Puritans, 5, 15, 32, 99
  influence on Founding Fathers,
    17
  reputation as spoilsports, 30

Quicken. *See* Intuit Inc.

Raychem, 46

Revolution,
  types of, 49–50

Rothschilds, 100

Rowe, Brian, 83

Royal Dutch Shell, 78

Schipke, Roger, 82–83

Schultz, Howard, 105–106

Semco S/A, 150–157

Semler, Ricardo, 150–157

Silicon Valley,
  establishing a sense of "commu-
    nity" in, 45–48

Silton-Bookman, 139

Sloan, Alfred P., 10, 166

Smith, Fred, 10, 138

Smucker, J.M.
  strategy-creation at, 54

Solectron, 62–63

Southwest Airlines, 24, 105

Springfield Remanufacturing
    Company (SRC), 58

Stack, Jack,
  communicates the threat to front-
    line people, 56–58
  conveys sense of meaning to
    employees, 23–24

Starbucks, 105–106

Sun Microsystems, 47–48

Teams
  GE Work Out distinguished
    from, 41
  in participative organizations, 4,
    60
  problem with, 88–90

Texas Instruments, 24, 163

Thermo Electron,
  "spin-outs" at, 134–135

3M Company 24, 28
  entrepreneurial culture of, 79, 85,
    100–101, 133

Tocqueville, Alexis de, 24, 108
  on the influence of New England
    Puritanism on America, 17;
  on self-interest and virtue, 28;
  on the synergy between seeking
    moral satisfaction and pursu-
    ing wealth, 27

Trani, John, 43, 83

Trumbull, John, 168

Turner, Ted, 101

Twin citizenship, 81–82

United Airlines, 8
  employee ownership at, 63
Univac, 100

Vagelos, P. Roy, 28–29
Varga, George, 38–39

Wal-Mart, 11, 101, 160
Walton, Sam, 105, 160, 163,
  164–165
Washington, George, 51, 52
  on human nature, 64
  leadership of, 159, 166–170
  as strategist, 116–119
  wealth of, 128
Waterman, Judith, 46
Waterman, Robert, 46

Watson, Thomas, Sr., 100, 166
Welch, Jack,
  models Work Out after New
    England town meeting, 40–41,
    43
  use of democratic reforms at
    General Electric, 29–30,
    73–74, 79, 81–83
Westinghouse, 24, 133
Wills, Garry, 145
Wilson, Woodrow, 23
Winn-Dixie, 27
Winthrop, John, 16, 32
Wood, Gordon S., 90, 91
Wright, Bob, 83

Zenith, 24, 163